THE TRAIL TO TRANQUILITY

Your Personal Guide to
Attaining Genuine Inner Peace

By Lazer Brody

Author of:
The Worry Worm
Chassidic Pearls
Lazer Beams

Composer of:
Calming Waters

Translator of:
The Garden of Emuna
The Garden of Peace
The Garden of Yearning
The Garden of Riches
In Forest Fields
Women's Wisdom
Little Nachman

Seventh Edition

ISBN: 978-0-9829740-0-1

Printed in USA

Inspiring Ink Press
12555 Biscayne Boulevard, Suite 400
Miami, FL 33181

www.inspiringink.com

THE TRAIL TO TRANQUILITY

Acknowledgments – Seventh Edition

First and foremost, I wish to express my deepest gratitude to my beloved rabbi, teacher and spiritual guide **Rabbi Shalom Arush**, whose holiness, wisdom, guidance and encouragement illuminate my path. May The Almighty grant him and his family long and joyous days.

I wish to thank my readers from around the world who visit me daily at the **Lazer Beams** weblog – www.lazerbrody.net – your fabulous input, comments, and encouragement helped me tremendously in the preparation of this book.

The "Rocket Team" – David Reckles, Michael Sigel, and Cynthia Nelson – has now made my books and CDs readily available everywhere. May The Almighty bless them and their families with all their hearts' wishes for the very best.

A special thanks to Shelli Karzen for her contribution to this edition. May she see joy and success in everything she does.

My cherished wife Yehudit, my unequivocal best friend and lifelong partner, has forever been a woman of valor standing faithfully at my side. She deserves the credit not only for this project, but for every other blessing in my life. To her happiness and good health, I dedicate this book.

May The Almighty bless all the wonderful people who helped produce this new edition of TTTT with the very best in material and spiritual abundance, long lives, good health, joy from their loved ones, happiness, and peace of mind.

Finally, I extend my inexpressible gratitude to my beloved Father in Heaven, who has protected and sustained me always and accorded me the privilege of writing this book and helping to make people's lives a little bit happier.

Lazer Brody

Table of Contents

If you believe that it's possible
to ruin a life

Then believe that it's possible
to rectify a life.

Rebbe Nachman of Breslev (1772 – 1810)

Introduction

A man went to a cobbler to have his shoes repaired. As the cobbler began to work, they started a lively conversation, discussing the state of the world in general and their own lives in particular.

When they eventually touched on the subject of spirituality, the cobbler said: "I don't believe in all that nonsense about spirituality, a soul, or an omniscient creator."

"Why do you say that?" asked the customer.

"Well, go out in the street and see for yourself; no rosy world of spirituality could possibly exist. Tell me, if humans have a soul that comes from a perfect creator, and the creator purportedly is good and kind, then why do people kill each other? Why's there so much crime? Why's there so much anger in the world? If a divine creator really existed, would there be so many sick people? Would there be abandoned children? No! There would be neither suffering nor pain. I can't imagine how a divine creator would permit all of these things."

The customer thought for a moment, but didn't respond. Arguing the point wouldn't be conducive to a good repair job.

The cobbler finished resoling the customer's shoes. The customer paid and then left the shop. Just in front of him on the sidewalk was a down-and-outer with long dirty hair, an unkempt beard, patched and ragged clothes, and torn shoes.

The customer made an immediate about-face and reentered the cobbler shop: "You know what," he exclaimed, "cobblers do not exist."

"How can you say that?" asked the astonished cobbler. "I am here, and I am a cobbler. And I just repaired your soles!"

"No!" the customer declared adamantly. "Cobblers don't exist because if they did, there would be no people with torn shoes like that man right outside your door."

"Wrong! Cobblers *do* exist! People have torn soles because they don't come to me!"

"That's exactly the point," affirmed the customer. The Creator too, *does* exist! Humans *do* have a divine soul that's a perfect tiny part of The Creator himself. All the anger, crime, violence, sickness and trouble in the world come from torn souls. Their souls get torn when they don't come to Him, either."

* * *

Few of us are aware of our souls. Spiritually, we don't know ourselves at all. That's problematic, because emotions stem from the soul. The turbulent emotions of frustration, anxiety, and especially anger come from torn and damaged souls. We owe ourselves the freedom from the chains of these turbulent emotions, but do we dare dream about a life of inner peace? Is an anger-free life really within an average person's reach? Is it possible to mend a blemished soul? Most people would say no. I say yes.

This book is a guide to attaining inner peace and an anger-free life. In the coming pages, we'll see how to develop our spiritual potential and to maintain a healthy soul. Since the soul thrives on spirituality, spiritual development is a requisite for a healthy soul. A healthy soul is the only dependable immunization against anger and frustration. As such, spiritual enhancement leads to peace of mind *and* health of body, and serves as the world's most effective tool in helping us achieve our coveted goal of inner peace.

* * *

I am neither a psychologist nor do I accept much of psychological theory. I am a rabbi who specializes in family and emotional counseling in one of the world's highest-stress, most problematic environments. Unlike psychological theory, my knowledge bank doesn't change from year to year. As opposed to the time-limited, once fashionable schools of Freud, Jung, and

Skinner, the wisdom of the Torah[1] has a virtually endless shelf life, as freshly vibrant today as it ever was. The teachings of Talmud[2] and Kabbala[3] are just as relevant to modern living as they were to ancient lifestyles. Moses, Rabbi Shimon bar Yochai[4], Maimonides[5], Nachmanides[6], Rabbi Isaac Luria Ashkenazi[7], and Rabbi Israel Baal Shem Tov[8] never go out of style. The soul-healing techniques of Rebbe Nachman of Breslev[9] are as clinically successful today as there were over two hundred years ago, when he helped thousands of oppressed peasants cope with the physical, mental and emotional ordeals of Czarist Russia.

The methods of this book aren't fad methods – they've been time-tested for over 3,300 years. My source material is the Torah – both written and oral – which has been passed down from scholar to understudy by way of an unbroken chain that links directly to Moses on Mount Sinai.

---

[1] Written Jewish law, which includes Pentateuch, Prophets, and Scriptures.

[2] Oral Jewish law, which includes Mishna and Gemorra.

[3] Jewish esoteric tradition.

[4] Author of The Zohar, Israel, end of 1st Century CE

[5] 12th Century CE scholar in Egypt, whose condensation of the Talmud serves as one of the principle foundations for Jewish religious law; Maimonides was also a noted astronomer, as well as the personal physician of Saladin, ruler of Egypt

[6] 13th Century CE Kabbalist and Talmudic scholar in Spain, a master of religious law and ethics, and a healer of the soul

[7] Israel, 16th Century CE father of Kabbala, whose teachings were recorded by his prime understudy, Rabbi Chaim Vital

[8] Ukraine, 18th Century CE founder of the Chassidic movement and school of thought, designed to elevate the spiritual level of the masses.

[9] 1772-1810, a classic master of the inner workings of the soul; great grandson of the Baal Shem Tov.

The average person – especially the English speaker – doesn't have access to much of the traditional Jewish source material that deals specifically with spiritual health. Even the Hebrew-speaking layman has difficulty understanding the jargon of Talmud and Kabbala. This book, the product of a decade's efforts, gives the reader access to an immense amount of classical Jewish knowledge, which I've presented in an easily-read, enjoyable, frequently allegorical and digestible format for the benefit of all people.

As a clergyman and emotional counselor who is also a combat veteran of Israel's Special Forces, I've synthesized my ultra-high stress experience with centuries-old methods of spiritual training to develop a practical way of neutralizing anger and achieving genuine inner peace.

During my first clerical counseling post as chaplain and spiritual rehabilitation director of a major prison, I had the unique opportunity to test my methods on the most turbulent members of our society – convicted criminals. The same methods used to help hardened inmates attain lives of tranquility are now presented for the first time to the general public, in this book.

By developing your spiritual potential, you will reap an abundance of practical benefits. **The Trail to Tranquility** will show you how your life can become vastly more successful, in every measure, simply by overcoming anger and achieving greater peace of mind. From years of direct experience with my clients, I can point to a number of significant improvements in the quality of their lives:

Happiness. The pursuit of happiness is a basic human right. But, how many people do you know who are truly content and at peace with themselves? Anger is the enemy of happiness, because you can't be angry and happy at the same time. Anger impairs the pursuit of happiness, enslaves us, and thereby limits our freedom. Once you start to develop your spiritual potential, you will reduce the anger in your life and make room for real happiness.

Improved appearance. True inner peace is radiant: no makeup in the world can give you the serene, luminous aura that a tranquil mind bestows.

Improved physical health. Research conclusively shows that the more we eradicate anger from our lives, the less we suffer from a great range of common health problems. For example, anger-prone individuals suffer 300% more heart attacks than people with low levels of anger[10], and they have a 75% higher incidence of coronary artery disease[11]. The risk of stroke in angry people is also 50% higher[12].

Better mental health. By ridding ourselves of anger, we remove the anxiety and frustration that cause depression. Anger-prone people are nervous, jumpy, and rarely relax. Excessive wear and tear on the nervous system cripples both personal performance and quality of life. Once we free ourselves of anger, we feel calmer, happier, and more successful.

Improved clarity of thought, judgment, and decision-making. Anger causes a contraction of blood flow to the brain, as well as a surge of hormones; both phenomena hamper clear thinking and encourage instinctive reactions that are detrimental to rational decision-making.

Greater personal effectiveness. When your thinking, judgment, and powers of decision-making are enhanced, you become more efficient, and enjoy a higher level of success in everything you do.

Higher utilization of potential. The more effective we are, the more opportunity we have to express and to utilize our potential. The more we free ourselves from anger, the more we are at liberty to tap our vast mental reserves.

---

[10] 1996 study published in *Circulation* magazine.

[11] 1998 study published in the *Journal of Epidemiology and Community Health*.

[12] Psychosomatic Medicine Journal, 1998.

Increased popularity. People naturally gravitate to anger-free people, and seek their company.

Better relationships. Anger is public enemy number one to interpersonal relationships, since it destroys communication. Good relationships are built on effective communication. Nothing improves communication like an anger-free relationship.

Better income. When you're competing with a co-worker for a promotion – and your skills are equal – the better personality will land the better position. Often, well-liked tranquil people do better than angry colleagues with superior professional skills.

Heightened spiritual sensitivity. The human spirit is housed in the brain. Anger's inhibition of basic mental functions completely neutralizes one's potential for spiritual cognizance. Spiritual cognizance is the quality that makes humans superior to other creatures.

Better overall performance. Only an anger-free existence can assure optimal cooperation and functioning of the body, the mind, and the spirit. The more we mobilize all three, the better our overall performance in whatever we do.

At this point, you may be asking yourself, "Can my life *really* improve for the better?" The answer is a simple yes. Emotions come from the soul. The soul is part of the human mind, and thrives on spirituality. Spiritual development is therefore a requisite for peace of mind. This book is a basic, comprehensible four-segment plan of spiritual development to help you achieve the goal that everyone dreams of – inner peace.

Segment One of **The Trail to Tranquility** includes the first three chapters, and illustrates the different relative levels of anger, the causes of anger, and the damages of anger. Segment Two – chapter four – is a program to enhance our spiritual awareness. Segment Three – chapters five through eight – shows us how to make peace with G-d, with our fellow man, and with ourselves. Segment Four – the final two chapters – is our personal trail to lasting happiness and spiritual gratification.

We're about to take our first steps up **The Trail to Tranquility**. You'll see my footprints all over the trail – I've been hiking it for several decades now. As your guide, companion, and friend, just as I have been for many people before you, it's now my greatest pleasure and profound privilege to take *you* along.

LB

1

Old Isaac the Innkeeper

The first segment of our trail begins by determining our current position on the anger-tranquility continuum.

The rigors of a strenuous hike up a mountain are well worth the double reward that awaits us at the peak. First, we obtain a breathtaking view of indescribable grandeur. Second, we derive the deep satisfaction of seeing the miles that we've traversed on the way to the top.

Spiritual hikes are similar to physical hikes, but even more rewarding. Like a mountain trek, the higher we climb in spirituality, the better we see ourselves and the world around us. Also, spiritual ascent and character improvement go hand in hand. Overcoming a negative character trait is more gratifying to the human soul than any material achievement.

Material amenities can't buy character improvement *or* inner peace. The fame and fortune of Marilyn Monroe, Elvis Presley, Janis Joplin, and a long list of other rich and famous people didn't prevent their descent to the grave at an early age – often overdosed and always miserable. Investing lifelong effort in an area that won't guarantee happiness – like money or fame – simply doesn't make sense.

Overcoming anger is one of the prime benefits of spiritual gain. The more we rid ourselves of anger, the more we tap our buried treasure of potential. The more we realize our potential, the happier we are.

Anger is a prime obstacle to happiness. By moving anger aside, we enter the express lane to self-fulfillment and tranquility. Once we reach our goal of genuine inner peace, we succeed in life's critical area where many of the world's most famous personalities have failed.

To some people, spiritual growth means lofty platitudes, revelations, and exotic rituals. To me, real spirituality is quite practical and tangible, gauged by happiness and inner peace on the positive side, and by anger on the negative side. Happiness comes from the divine human spirit within, and *not* from outside stimuli. Simply speaking, the happier we are, the more spiritual we are. For that reason, authentic spirituality has the power to help us overcome anger and attain happiness.

Getting to know the real "you" is the first step toward spiritual growth. As in medicine, proper diagnosis is half the cure. This chapter discusses ten exemplary levels of the anger-tranquility continuum. By looking at examples of others, you'll learn about yourself. "Aha," you might say to yourself, "I react just like the character on level so-and-so!" You thereby can establish your current position along the continuum. As such, this chapter is diagnostic in nature, and serves as the point of origin on your journey to an anger-free life.

The Spiritual Continuum

Imagine a spiritual continuum where total anger is at one end and tranquility at the other:

What seems to be your present position on the continuum? Write your self-estimation score on a piece of paper, and put it aside in a safe place. Later, you can compare it with your renewed estimation of yourself at the end of this chapter.

Now, let's see how accurate your self-appraisal is.

Your journey up the trail to tranquility takes you from your present position on the continuum, to a higher level on the spiritual and emotional plane. The more progress you make, the less anger controls your life, and the closer you come to genuine inner peace. Spiritually speaking, the higher you progress up the continuum, the more freedom you obtain from base character traits. Spirituality is therefore synonymous to personal liberty.

The first principle of navigation is to know your point of embarkation. Without knowing your current position on the map, you don't know which path takes you to your destination.

Let me give you an example. Suppose you're looking at a road map, and you want to reach New York City. Yet, you don't know whether you're currently positioned in Philadelphia or Boston. Which way do you go, north or south? Which road do you take? You can't possibly know. Therefore, you must first determine your point of origin in order to reach your destination.

Spiritual navigation works the same way. Personal goals resemble destinations. Your current spiritual and emotional status is quite similar to a point of origin on the map. You need to know where you are in order to arrive at your spiritual destination, your goal in life.

For example, if you think that you are currently positioned on level seven, when actually you're on level three, you lose all hope of reaching tranquility, since you haven't traveled the complete spiritual route that takes you away from turbulence. As in academics, you can't skip from elementary school to a master's degree program.

People easily see faults in others, but have difficulty seeing their own shortcomings. Self-objectivity is nearly impossible for a human being. For that reason, this chapter is designed to assist you in evaluating yourself.

While establishing your present position on the anger-tranquility continuum, you'll be visiting new sites and meeting new people. Some of them are quite real, and some proverbial. They'll probably remind you of yourself and of people you know.

Ten Exemplary Levels from
Total Anger to Total Tranquility

Let's now learn more about the ten exemplary levels from total anger to total tranquility.

Level one: Overt anger and violent revenge.

When I was ten years old, I saw a memorable television broadcast of a United Nations debate. Over forty years later, the image of Soviet Premier Nikita Khrushchev – banging on the speaker's podium with his shoe – sticks vividly in my mind. The year was 1960, and he was threatening President Kennedy and the citizens of the United States: "We shall bury you," he bellowed. Imagine, a world leader, removing his shoe in the middle of a speech in front of the entire world!

Khrushchev's delirious behavior at the UN was standard level-one anger. Other infamous names that exemplify level-one tyrannical wrath include Adolph Hitler, Joseph Stalin, Idi Amin, and Saddam Hussein.

Anger completely dominates the life of a level-one individual. Both the human mind and the human body are slaves to extreme anger. Extreme anger kindles the lust for revenge – like a spiritual wildfire – and literally chars a person's soul, rendering that person a spiritual cripple. The following centuries-old rabbinical tale tells about an irate woman who took her anger to the grave:

Old Mrs. Broigges

Old Mrs. "Broigges" (*Yiddish term for extremely angry*) asked her oldest son to approach her sickbed. "Jacob, run fetch the Rabbi; don't delay!"

The Rabbi arrived immediately. "Mrs. Broigges," he whispered gently in her ear, "In order to assure your place in the World to Come, you must confess your sins and make peace with your fellow man before you leave this world."

"Yes, Rabbi," the old woman nodded. "I want to make amends. For the last forty years, I've been feuding with

Yenta Grossman. Please summon her so I can beg her forgiveness."

The Rabbi sent his understudy to summon Mrs. Grossman as fast as possible. Within fifteen minutes, she joined the others by the dying Mrs. Broigges's bedside.

Mrs. Broigges opened her glossy eyes, and focused on Yenta Grossman. She extended two frail bony hands, and said, "Yenta darling, I'm so sorry for the years of hate and anger. I want to beg your forgiveness. Come closer, dear, so I can kiss you before I leave this earth."

There wasn't a dry eye in the room. Obviously moved, Yenta Grossman leaned tenderly toward Mrs. Broigges, to kiss her on the lips. All of a sudden…

"Yahowwwwwwwwwiiiiiii". Yenta released the most blood-curdling scream you ever heard. Blood splattered all over the room. Just as she was about to kiss Mrs. Broigges, the sly old warhorse clamped her teeth around Yenta's nose with the ferocity of an irate lioness. Yenta Grossman's nose was nearly severed from her face.

"Now, I can die peacefully," sighed Mrs. Broigges, closing her eyes for the last time, with an ear-to-ear grin on her face.

Don't think that the story is far-fetched. Angry people are willing to sacrifice an eternity of bliss for one bittersweet moment of revenge.

Maybe you're thinking, "That's not me! I'm no tyrant! I would never attack another person!" Physically violence is only the *extreme* manifestation of a level one. There are other forms of level-one anger.

Psychologists would say that if you refrain from hitting a person when you're angry, you've succeeded in managing your anger. If you refrain from shouting as well, you score high on the anger management scale. Anger management techniques often succeed in taming violent deeds and speech. But do they eradicate angry thoughts?

> Three garments clothe the human spirit. The innermost garment is a person's thoughts. The middle garment is a person's speech. The outer garment is a person's deeds. – *Rabbi Isaac Luria, father of Kabbala*

Unless you uproot anger from your heart and mind, *you* become the victim. An angry person might learn to exercise superb restraint, and refrain from harming a fellow human. Yet, anybody that harbors thoughts or feelings of residual anger becomes a candidate for high blood pressure, a cardiac arrest, or a stroke. To avoid harming yourself, you must eradicate anger from your thoughts as well.

Let's examine the ramifications of anger in one's thoughts. Kabbala teaches that the thoughts are the inner garment that clothes the soul. Anger-free deeds and speech resemble a clean suit jacket and a clean shirt, while anger-ridden thoughts resemble soiled undergarments.

Have you ever been on a crowded elevator, bus, train, or subway in the middle of August? The person next to you may have been dressed in an expensive suit, but he or she smelled like they had been wearing the same smelly underwear for several days. Didn't you feel nauseous, or like you wanted to faint?

When we make spiritual gain, our souls are allowed to enter higher spiritual worlds. The higher we go, the better our cognizance and thought processes become. Kabbala teaches that each successive spiritual realm has a sweeter, more sublime aroma to it. That's where the expression "heavenly aroma" originates. The soul of a person with angry thoughts assumes a spiritual stench. That person is subsequently denied entrance to the higher spiritual realm.

Even though people refrain from hitting or shouting, as long they harbor thoughts of anger and revenge, they contaminate their divine human spirits. This notion is easy to understand. Thoughts of anger lead to hate, resentment, and jealousy. They also cause as much – if not more – damage to the individual than angry deeds and speech cause. For that reason, spiritual gain is preferable to anger management, in that the latter uproots anger from all three garments of the human spirit – deeds, speech, *and* thoughts.

Now, test yourself by answering the following questions:

1. Do you often feel like hitting someone?

2. Do you feel an urge to retaliate when someone has insulted or harmed you?

3. Do you hate a person who has dealt with you unfairly?

4. At night, while lying in bed, do you think about people who have angered you?

You may not be a full-fledged level one, but if you've answered at least one of the above questions in the affirmative, you still have level-one tendencies. Two "yes" answers indicate potential explosiveness, and three or more "yes" answers indicate that you're solidly entrenched in level one.

Knowledge of emergency first-aid procedures is vital. Potentially explosive emotional situations are frequently more dangerous than a physical trauma. Therefore, I'd like to share with you a few field-tested methods of dealing with level-one aggressors:

▪ Level-one anger is no different than a bomb. If you don't know how to defuse a bomb, move away quickly. If you don't know how to placate a level one, excuse yourself politely and make a quick getaway.

▪ You can defuse level-one anger by placating the person. Don't ever argue with a level one, even when you know you're right. Tell the irate driver that you're sorry, or concede the point to your irate spouse. Wait for a calmer opportunity to offer your opinions.

▪ All level ones suffer from a terribly low self-image. Since they feel emotionally weak and inadequate, they use anger and physical intimidation to trample other people, thus making themselves feel better. Immediately, tell the level one that he or she is better than you. For example, suppose a level one husband yells at his wife for forgetting to pay the phone bill. The wife should answer calmly, "Honey, if I were blessed with your fantastic brainpower, I wouldn't have forgotten". Such reactions deflate a level one. Again, placated level ones lose the need to assert themselves.

- Return a level one's cruelty with kindness. While a level one is yelling at you, smile, compliment him or her, or make them a cup of their favorite tea or coffee. Kindness disorients and disarms a level one individual. You're then the winner.

- When you can't avoid the hot coals of a level one, close your eyes and imagine that your suffering is cleansing your soul, and saving you a worse fate like disease or bankruptcy (*more on this subject in Chapter five*).

Level-one parents have a devastating emotional influence on their children.

Recently, I received a phone call from a superb second-grade teacher who had a good working knowledge of graphology and interpretation of children's drawings. The teacher had a reclusive child in class who was progressively falling behind the group learning pace. She asked the child to draw herself. The child drew a little girl with arms tightly clutching her chest, a forlorn expression, and lowered head. She then asked the child to draw her mother. The child drew a head with a tremendous crease in the forehead, a jagged mouth, and no body.

"Rabbi," the teacher said, "I'd like to show you the child's drawings." The drawings, all in black crayon, tore at my heartstrings.

The teacher explained, "The child's self portrait with the drawn-in arms indicates extreme fear, and the droopy head shows melancholy and introversion. She drew her mother without a body, because the mother is away from home all day long. The crease in the mother's forehead and the jagged mouth illustrate extreme continuous anger. The child is bright and sweet, but the damage to her life is irreversible."

The teacher asked me if I would be willing to help her save the little girl's life. I readily agreed. I called the mother – a "successful" and very hard-hitting businesswoman, identified myself, and the nature of my call.

"Rabbi," she said, "My time is money. Besides, I didn't ask you to butt into my life. Put your nose back in your holy books, and leave the upbringing of my children to me. Goodbye." The phone slammed in my ear. The thud of the phone made me cringe, as if I heard the lid of a coffin slamming on the little girl's emotional life.

Level two: Silent anger and emotional revenge.

Would you believe that silent anger is an effective murder weapon? I've seen people use silence as a mode of emotional revenge. Deliberately ignoring another person kills slower than a gun or a knife, but it's almost as effective. Often, the victim's life becomes unbearable, and if he/she doesn't die, he/she loses any semblance of emotional stability.

Many emotionally abused children suffer from level-two parents. One level-two father refused to talk to his son for six months, because the poor boy made an error in a little league baseball game. A level-two mother gave her sixth grade daughter the cold shoulder because the unfortunate little girl received a "B" in geography. "Any daughter of mine *has* to be a straight-A student." Such statements are common amongst level-two parents, who vent their anger and frustrations on their offspring.

Here's a classic Chassidic anecdote about the absurdity of level-two thinking, which uses silence as a means of retaliation.

Ruben the Shipwrecked Hermit

Ruben disappeared at sea. Thirty years later, voyagers found him on a deserted island. The island was bare except for a few palm trees, Ruben's modest cabin, and two exquisite mahogany synagogues. Other than a few monkeys and cockatoos, Ruben was the sole inhabitant of the island.

The visiting voyagers asked Ruben, "Who built those two magnificent synagogues?"

"I did," said Ruben proudly.

"What do you need *two* houses of worship for?" asked the voyagers.

"I got into an argument in the first synagogue, so I'm not on speaking terms with anyone there; that's why I had to build the second synagogue."

Level two people – like shipwrecked Ruben – can't even get along with themselves. Therefore, they do quite irrational things. Ruben, at least, didn't harm anyone else. Level twos on the other hand, destroy their own lives as well as the lives of others in their proximity.

Level one and two anger borders on mental illness. Unlike other mental illnesses, **anger can be cured relatively easily**, as we'll soon discover.

Test yourself by answering the following questions:

1. Do you ever willfully ignore a family member or friend?

2. Do you ever hang up the phone in the middle of a conversation?

3. Do you ever walk out of a meeting or leave the house in protest?

4. Do you interrupt others in the middle of a sentence and say, "I don't want to listen to you[13]"?

One affirmative answer indicates level two tendencies. Two "yes" answers show a strong tendency toward silent anger and emotional revenge, and three or more yes answers qualify as a full-fledged level two.

For your emotional health and happiness, you should familiarize yourself with the following emergency methods of dealing with level-two aggressors:

▪ If a level two refuses to speak to you, write him or her a conciliatory letter. Most level twos are curious enough to read

---

[13] According to Jewish law, one is allowed to tell another person, "I don't want to listen to you," if the latter is speaking slander or gossip.

your letter.

- Remember that level twos are spiritually and emotionally immature. Like pouting babies, they *want* you to run after them. Put your pride aside and appease the level two individual. In that way, you're giving the level two a chance to make a dignified descent from his or her high horse. Peacemaking is the quiet show of *your* strength.

- If a level two is refusing to speak to you, use a mutual friend as a third-party courier to convey your message. If the level two is your spouse, and you don't want to involve others in your domestic affairs, use a discreet clergyman who's well-versed in family counseling.

- As with level one, kindness disorients and disarms a level-two individual.

- When you pity a level two, rather than hating him or her, you'll create a spiritual environment that will melt the freeze.

Level three: Incessant overt anger, but no revenge.

Level threes as easy to recognize. Often, they enjoy impressing people with a good show of anger. They think that a violent display of indignation makes them important. Maybe you remember a boss, a teacher, or a relative who fits this description.

In all fairness, a level-three temper tantrum differs substantially from a level-one vocal expression of anger. Whereas a level three is either blowing off steam or trying to attract people's attention, the level one is attempting to cripple his or her victim with words.

Level three characteristics include uninhibited speech, constant aggravation, yelling, and in the case of level-three parents – frequent slapping. Family members, coworkers, neighbors, and employees of level threes often suffer from the "foxhole syndrome".

Just as a veteran combat soldier automatically ducks his head whenever he hears the whistling shriek of an incoming shell, foxhole-syndrome sufferers wince or hide behind raised arms whenever a level three opens his or her mouth, as if they are fending off an attack.

Level threes do substantial damage to their children and to their spouses. Even though they don't hold grudges, their family members become nervous wrecks from the constant yelling and slapping.

The Talmud tells a story about the extent to which a level-three parent is liable to damage a child:

A little boy from the town of Bnei Brak accidentally committed a misdeed that would surely invoke the wrath of his anger-prone father. The little boy was petrified with fear, and failed to come home from school that day. Instead, he jumped into a deep well and drowned.

Imagine, preferring suicide to another emotional torture treatment of anger! Don't think that such an episode is a fantasy. The best-case scenario for children of level-three parents is a future of no self-confidence, frayed nerves, and a low self-image.

Having a level-three individual for a spouse is a tribulation in itself. In my counseling experience, I've often seen discord, financial instability, and psychosomatic ailments in households of level threes.

Don't lose heart – if your spouse is a level three, teaching him or her to overcome anger is a lot easier than divorce. Talk to your mate about happiness, tranquility, and spirituality. Arouse his or her interest in the subjects we discuss in this book. Show him/her the benefits of an anger-free life *(see introduction)*. Take drives to the country or to the beach, and get your spouse to try the "Seven-Day Plan" *(see chapter four)*. Don't make the mistake that many people do by divorcing their current level three, only to discover that their next mate is a level three or worse.

Test yourself with the following questions:

1. Do you feel like shouting at someone almost every day?

2. Do other people frequently upset you?

3.   When you drive or travel, do you find yourself yelling at other people on the road, even under your breath?

4.   Do you throw or kick things when you're angry?

One "yes" answer shows level-three tendencies. Two "yes" answers indicate a problem with overt anger. Three or more yeses mean than you're knee-deep in level three.

> A soft answer dispels wrath.
> – *King Solomon's Proverbs*

Now, let's learn a few tips in coping with level three's:

▪ When a level three begins a raging tirade, react with a smile and a soft answer. Offer to prepare two cups of coffee, and invite the level three to sit down with you on the sofa to discuss the matter calmly. Let the level three soliloquize – be a perfect listener and don't interrupt. The level three wants your undivided attention, so let him or her have it. You've then succeeded in defusing an explosive situation.

▪ Agree with whatever the level three is saying. Make your point at a later, calmer, and more opportune time.

▪ Don't ever get pulled into a shouting match with a level three. You'll never win.

▪ Buy time, and delay confrontation! If you feel you're about to be sucked in to an argument and you can't remain calm, excuse yourself with a *good* excuse, like saying you must urgently use the toilet. After you've calmed down and collected your thoughts, refer back to the afore-mentioned tip of a cup of coffee and a sofa discussion.

▪ Soft mood music usually mollifies a level three. Level threes have difficulty yelling with Richard Clayderman playing a piano rendition of "Scarborough Fair" or "Bridge Over Troubled Waters" in the background. Once again, put a cup of herbal tea in the hand of your level three, sit him or her down on the sofa, and discuss the matter calmly.

▪ Divert the level-three individual from the path of anger by giving him/her a compliment. Be truthful and sincere though, and the level three will soon be eating out of your hand rather than biting it off.

Level four: The conventionally polite – calm in public, angry at home.

Recently, I was caught in a traffic jam. I estimated that my trip home would take another hour. A husband and wife whom I had been counseling were scheduled to be at my home in fifteen minutes.

I dialed the couple's home phone number to apologize for my delay and to reschedule our session for a later time. The wife picked up the phone; she was sure that her husband was on the other end of the line.

With no prior verbal amenities, she shrieked, "Where the blazes are you, Martin! I told you not to play golf this afternoon! Doesn't our marriage mean anything to you? For all I care, you can take a seven-iron, and ram it up your…"

I didn't want "Paula Bergstein" (*imaginary name*) to finish that sentence. "Hello, Mrs. Bergstein. This is Rabbi Lazer Brody speaking." Silence… "Are you all right, Mrs. Bergstein?"

"Oh, R-rabbi, I'm so embarrassed. Please forgive me," she said, her tone changing from daggers to milk-and-honey, "I thought it was my husband."

"Don't worry, Mrs. Bergstein, I hear things like that all the time. Anyway, I'm glad you told me to shove the seven-iron, and not Martin…"

> "If you treat your husband like a king, then you're a queen. If you treat him like a floor mop, then you're a wet rag." – *Yiddish folk expression*

* * *

Modern society literally teaches a person that level-four behavior is perfectly acceptable – be a politician away from home, and your real angry self at home.

To balance the above anecdote, I asked Martin Bergstein why he couldn't take the initiative, and address his wife in a warm, loving tone. "Rabbi," he answered, "I can't wear a mask *all* day long!"

Too bad people prefer a mask to making themselves truly beautiful. If level fours would overcome their anger, they wouldn't need the politician's mask with the plastic smile.

Many of us are emotional politicians. Ask yourself if you put your best foot forward outside the house. Think whether you use your family circle to release the pent-up pressures that you've accumulated during the day. Would you allow strangers to abuse your loved ones in such a manner?

Whereas levels one to three make no effort to overcome their anger, level four "diplomats" do exert effort, only in the wrong areas. Rather than developing their character and spiritual potential, they work on image development – on impressing other people.

Level fours remind me of silver-plated objects; they shine on the outside, but they're cheap. Real silver sometimes tarnishes, but with a little polishing, always regains its shine. Scratched silver-plated objects are worthless. Wouldn't you rather be like real silver? The human spirit, like real silver, can always be polished.

Level fours are capable of immediate spiritual gain if they put their mind to it.

Try this brief level four self-examination:

1. Do you have more patience for your peers and your superiors than you do for your spouse and/or children?

2. Do you speak more respectfully to your boss than you do to your parents?

3. Are you concerned more about strangers' opinions of you than you are about your family members' opinions of you?

4.   Do you find yourself smiling in public and grouchy at home?

The more you answer "yes" to the above questions, the more of a diplomat you are. Don't worry, though; soon, you'll be redirecting your diplomacy efforts in the direction of true spiritual gain. By saving the energy you used to waste on play-acting, you'll be more relaxed and more fulfilled. You'll feel better about yourself and much more tranquil.

If you desire a happy marriage and emotionally healthy children, and you see level-four tendencies in yourself, then try your hardest to break the chains of level four as fast as you can. Moving up to level five will cement your marriage, improve your children's future, and make you a lot happier. Climbing another single spiritual rung is tantamount to beginning a new and better life.

As a level four, you *have* the capability of being a wonderful person. You know how to work hard, invest effort, and succeed. Once you decide to move up the spiritual ladder, you'll be just as popular at home as you are at work or with your friends. Once you've tasted around-the-clock tranquility, you won't be satisfied with partial happiness.

The greatest benefit of graduating from level four upwards is shedding your variety of masks. Acting differently in different situations drains your emotional energies. It also causes you to pretend, to lie, and to exaggerate. By moving up to level five, you begin to act naturally *wherever* you go. You save emotional energy and begin to acquire inner peace, since you stop forcing yourself to play different roles. Your soul wants to be its own, shining self.

Level five: Periodically explosive, but trying to do better.

Allow me to coin a term – "angerholic". The minute angerholics decide that anger is dreadful, and they must eradicate it from their lives, they resemble an alcoholic who has joined Alcoholics Anonymous. Such a person is on the road to recovery. Once you make the decision to overcome anger, you jump to level five.

Why is anger a part our lives?

For the last two hundred years, the great Rebbes and Kabbalists have agreed that *all* the people alive today have reincarnated souls, which have returned to this world for the task of *tikkun emuna,* or the spiritual correction of lack of faith. This principle provides the spiritual explanation why anger is ingrained in literally every human soul.

A person with no anger sees no need to improve. Once a person feels angry, he or she loses happiness. Many feel that material gains will compensate for the lack of happiness, so they squander time and effort in chasing after money, prestige, short-term enjoyment, and new possessions. None of these satisfy the soul.

When people are prudent enough to seek a spiritual solution for their lack of happiness, then they not only overcome anger – they gain spiritual awareness, develop faith, attain cognizance of God, and thereby accomplish the mission that their souls were sent here to do. Once its *tikkun hashalem,* or complete spiritual correction is completed, a soul is invited to assume its rightful place in eternal bliss.

Ingrained anger is therefore a favor, showing us that our souls need correction and giving us the opportunity to prevent a future reincarnation. The Kabbalists teach that purgatory is preferable to an additional reincarnation.

Level five people are learning about spirituality. They're acquiring the tools they need to cope with high-stress situations without losing their composure. Yet, they still "fall" every once in a while. That's fine. If today's level five used to shout at his or her family every day back at level three, and now he or she only loses his/her temper once every other week, then that's a sign of tremendous progress.

Where there's a will to succeed, success is not far away.

You have the ability to grasp the reins of life in your hands at any moment. Many people feel that their lives are uncontrollable, like wild horses. Not true. With PWI (perseverance, willpower, and inner strength), you can move up the spiritual and emotional ladder.

The wonderful quality about level-five people, despite their periodic explosions, is their desire to improve. Once a person recognizes his or her problem with anger and desires to overcome it, he or she can quickly acquire the spiritual tools to do so. Any good doctor knows that proper diagnosis constitutes fifty percent of the cure.

On this level, we don't ask diagnostic questions any more. No matter how low you may have scored on the turbulence-tranquility scale, the minute you decide to grab your anger by the horns and eradicate it from your life, you can and you will. You are now an official candidate for level-five status. Believe in yourself, and believe that God will give you a helping hand.

Question: Hold on a minute, Lazer. Up until now, you've been talking common sense. Now, you slip the "God" business in the back door. I'm not interested in religion, why are you trying to sell it to me?

Answer: Not true. The Jewish religion doesn't believe in proselytizing, so I'm not a recruiter. I am offering you spirituality – your own personal relationship with God and the recognition of your own divine human spirit, which is a tiny spark of God. That's the basis for eradicating anger, or any other negative trait or habit in your life.

Question: Why do I need anybody running my life and telling me what to do?

Answer: You already have somebody telling what to do. If you're not yet firmly entrenched in level five, and well on the road to becoming a level six, then you're a slave to your anger and your base impulses.

Question: Why can't I reach level five with plain, secular anger management methods?

I'll remind you that anger management will help tone down your deeds and speech, but it won't eradicate the anger from your thoughts – only spiritual ascent can do that. Besides, just as the notion of "alcohol management" doesn't work for a problem drinker, anger management falls short in bringing the angry to an even emotional keel. You have to shoot for total eradication of the problem.

Question: Isn't alcoholism different from what you call angerholism? Who ever heard of using God and spirituality to get an alcoholic off the bottle? Alcoholics Anonymous is a wonderful organization; do they go around peddling spirituality like you do?

Answer: I agree with one thing you just said: Not only is Alcoholics Anonymous (AA) a wonderful organization, it's a gift to society. Accusing me of "peddling" spirituality is like accusing a lifeguard of peddling artificial respiration. I'm simply using centuries old, field-tested methods of helping you find genuine happiness.

Alcoholism and angerholism are similar, in that both stem from a troubled human spirit. In order to overcome them, you must treat the spirit. Only spirituality can help the spirit, as AA researchers have discovered during years of trial-and-error experience in the field. That's exactly why spirituality plays such a major role in the AA program. Let's examine several of AA's twelve underlying principles[14]:

✓ AA's point number two expresses the belief that only "**a Power greater than ourselves**" has the ability to restore a person's sanity. The "Power" they're referring to is none other than The Almighty. AA uses the term "power" in the beginning of their program, so you won't be frightened away if you're an atheist or an agnostic. As a rabbi, I speak simply and openly, and use the term "God" or "The Almighty".

✓ AA's point eleven encourages you to seek "conscious contact with **God**", by way of personal prayer and meditation. You'll learn about that in chapters four and nine of this book. AA

---

[14] AA members refer to them as "the twelve steps".

recognizes that a personal relationship with God is capable of giving you the inner strength you need to create a better life for yourself.

✓ AA's point twelve attributes the victory over alcoholism to **"spiritual awakening"**. AA's founding members reached this conclusion after long and trial-and-error methods. In their own words, "after many other approaches had failed". Do you have time to experiment on yourself? I want to shorten your path to happiness and tranquility, so I'm offering you a direct and easy spiritual solution to anger.

✓ AA's other points express the need for courageous personal assessment, good relations with yourself, with God, and with your fellow man, and personal resolutions to do better. These points, and more, are all subjects in this book.

Question: C'mon Lazer, you're pulling my leg. I expect a rabbi to be serious and honest. Didn't *you* invent those points?

Answer: I would be proud to say I did, but I can't take credit for something I didn't compose. I'll tell you what, though – if you plug in the word "anger" instead of "alcohol" in the AA's twelve points, you get a good outline of what this book will be teaching from chapters four to ten. If AA – as successful as everyone knows they are – relies so heavily on God and spiritual development as part of their program, why can't I?

Your human spirit – your divine soul – is a part of God. Without tuning in to God, you have no contact with your divine soul.

Without being in touch with your own divine soul and its needs, you're in big trouble. How would you feel alone in the Sahara Desert with no food, no water, and no guide? Panicky? Terrified? Doomed? That's how your soul feels when you ignore it, and that's the cause of *all* your emotional ills.

An airplane flies through a storm or through darkness with the help of avionics – that is, navigational instruments. Aircraft maintain radio-vector contact with successive air traffic control towers along their route. With no visibility and without a radio vector, the airplane is lost.

This world – the lowest on the spiritual scale of all the worlds – is like stormy turbulence to the soul. The soul, in order to be healthy, must maintain its spiritual direction, or purpose in life. Contact with God gives a person spiritual direction. A person's relationship with God is therefore like a plane flying safely in a storm, by virtue of its connection with the control tower.

Be candid with yourself: Is your life genuinely peaceful, or are you jumping from relationship to relationship, never really satisfied with your life, or seeing an analyst and taking pills? Do you feel anxiety and stress? Do you worry? Saying you don't want to overcome anger by hearing about God is like a diabetic saying that he doesn't want to hear about insulin.

Spiritual growth is meaningless without your establishing a personal relationship with God. You don't need to attend a house of worship, you don't need to affiliate, and you don't need to practice rituals.

By denying God, you don't give yourself a chance to achieve genuine happiness and inner peace. You also neglect your divine soul, which is a tiny spark of God. Again, a healthy soul is a prerequisite for inner peace and happiness.

At this point, you may tell me that you know plenty of religious people who are far from happy. Maybe they're angry, downright nasty, violent, or dishonest. I agree. Many "religious" people don't have a real relationship with God. If a person is angry or nasty, he's light years away from God. By the way, any human who kills, lies, or steals in the name of God is nothing other than an enemy of mankind and an anathema to The Almighty, who has infinite love for *all* of His creations.

Whenever this book mentions the word "faith", it is referring to your personal relationship with God.

Level six: The advanced spiritual trainee – no more outward manifestations of anger.

Take a level-five person at the start of his spiritual journey, and after a few short weeks of spiritual awareness training, he'll move up to level six.

A level-six person never loses his temper. His brain understands that anger and negative emotions are self-destructive and serve no purpose whatsoever, yet his newly acquired spiritual awareness has not yet filtered down to his heart.

I once overheard two people arguing about what the longest distance in the world between two points is; one said, from the North Pole to the South Pole. The other said from Hawaii to Saudi Arabia. I suggested that neither was correct: The longest distance in the world is the distance between the heart and the brain. People can travel the whole globe a lot faster that they can internalize what they learn. Therefore, spiritual trainees move quickly up the spiritual ladder the minute they decide to open their hearts and minds to *internalizing* the lessons that we'll be learning throughout this book.

A level-six life changes drastically for the better within a few short weeks. Yet, small coals of anger still burn within. That's understandable – Rome wasn't built in a day. Building a tranquil soul is much more difficult than building a metropolis, or even conquering the world. Ask Alexander the Great.

Alexander the Great Arrives in Jerusalem[15]

Alexander the Great arrived victoriously to the Land of Israel, after conquering all of Europe, the Near East, and North Africa. On the back of a stunning white horse, he led his army on a glorious parade-march from the port of Jaffa to the holy city of Jerusalem, a distance of forty-five miles.

The entire population of Jerusalem, including the sages and the priests of the Holy Temple, welcomed the new ruler of the civilized world.

---

[15] Based on Talmudic lore.

At the gates of Jerusalem, Simon the Pious, high priest of the Holy Temple dressed in his best ceremonial white, led the entourage of dignitaries who joined to honor the hero of Macedonia.

Alexander saw Simon the Pious, dismounted, and fell prostrate at the high priest's feet.

The Greek commanders were aghast. "Why is our king bowing down to the feet of an old Jew?"

Alexander rose to his feet and looked over his shoulder to his staff officers: "That is no old Jew. That's the angel who stood before my eyes each time we were victorious in battle". From that poignant moment, Alexander opened his heart to the priests and wise men of Jerusalem.

One of the elderly wise men addressed the king: "Congratulations, Your Majesty; now that you have won the little war, you're prepared to fight the big war".

The wise man's words both perplexed and astonished Alexander the Great. "Rabbi, do you call the battles of Gall, Italy, Mesopotamia, and Egypt a little war?"

The frail but intrepid sage answered, "Certainly, Your Majesty. Fighting external enemies is easier than fighting the internal enemy, one's evil inclination. Defeating anger is a greater challenge than ruling the world."

Alexander the Great conquered the world, yet remained prisoner to negative emotions. When he listened to gossip about rivals plotting against him at home in Greece, he lost his temper and lost control of his empire. He subdued entire continents, but never succeeded in subjugating his own evil inclinations and inner turbulence. Had he been a level six, maybe the Macedonian Greeks would be ruling the world to this day.

Level seven: Forgives and forgets, no more anger in his or her thoughts, but still hurts when reminded of painful experiences.

Allow me to interject a word about levels. Graduating from one level to the next higher level is far more significant than moving from the ninth grade to the tenth grade in school. Each level of progress on the scale from turbulence to tranquility represents a new lease on life.

Levels one through four describe the relative anger levels. Levels five and six are the spiritual trainee levels. Level seven is the introductory level of inner peace.

Level seven is beyond the reach of anger management. One cannot possibly eradicate anger from the mind and heart without concerted spiritual effort, as you'll learn from chapter four onward.

Level sevens are always calm. If you remind a level seven of a painful experience, he/she might wince, but won't succumb for a moment to any trace of negative feelings. Level seven people are highly attuned to the feelings of their fellow human. Here's another poignant story from the Talmud, which describes level-seven deportment to the letter:

The Young Israelite and his Ex-wife

A young Israelite at the time of the Roman occupation had a shrew for a wife. For several years after the wedding, he suffered in silence. But, once the woman began acting like the Roman occupiers, the young man divorced her.

The young Israelite became wealthy, but his ex-wife married a Roman soldier, and they became destitute. One day, he saw them dressed in rags and searching for a morsel of food in the garbage heap at the marketplace.

Despite the emotional scars she left on his heart, the young Israelite took pity on the couple, put a roof over their heads, and placed food on their table.

At level seven, you bear no malice toward a single person in the world that has harmed you. On the other hand, level seven people are lovers of humanity, and won't forgive tyrants that harm other people.

> "If a person disregards an insult, The Almighty disregards *all* that person's transgressions." – *Babylonian Talmud*

Level eight: The peacemaker

The peacemaker forgives, forgets, and doesn't feel pain in his heart when he encounters someone who hurt him in some way. Why? The peacemaker of tranquility level eight knows that everything comes from God. If God sends him pain or insult, he knows that it's for his own benefit. Therefore, level eight people never have a negative focus on their fellow man. The Talmud teaches, "If a person calls you a jackass, put a saddle on your back." In other words, concede the point rather than arguing. Tell the belligerent person that he or she is right, and you'll disarm them and preserve the peace. The Almighty especially loves peacemakers.

Let me tell you a story about a classic level-eight individual, Old Isaac's neighbor and best friend:

Jerry Miller

Isaac's friend and neighbor Jerry Miller owns the stable and the horse farm down the road from the inn.

Once, a chauffer driven cream-colored Bentley pulled up in front of the stable. Out came a couple dressed in formal English riding gear, from breeches to switch and all the trimmings.

Jerry came to greet the English couple, dressed in his blue overalls and smelling like week-old horse manure, since he'd just finished changing the bedding in the stables. The visitors winced, turned up their noses, and said in a Lancaster house-of-lords tone, "We'd like to rent a pair of thoroughbreds."

Jerry responded with his usual smile, "No problem, I have just the two horses you want." In a few minutes, Jerry returned, leading a handsome pair of saddled thoroughbreds.

The visiting nobleman reacted with an abhorred look on his face. "Are you daft? Don't you know that equestrians use English saddles? What are those western monstrosities? Haven't you the sense of a mule?"

Despite the cruel slander, Jerry only smiled. He unbuckled the western saddle from one of the horses, put it on his own back, got down on all fours, and declared happily: "Sir, not only do I have the sense of a mule, I can ride you on my back, too. If you'd prefer to rent a mule, I'm at your service. I beg your pardon, though – if you do prefer an English saddle, I'll prepare one for you right away."

Jerry completely melted the icy snobbishness of the aristocratic couple. He changed the saddles, and they had the ride of their lives. Despite their opposite backgrounds and personalities, Jerry and the English couple became the best of friends.

> Making peace means connecting two opposites. Therefore, don't be upset if your fellow man's opinions are the opposite of yours. Don't say you can't make peace with such a person. On the contrary, genuine peace is achieved by connecting two opposites. God creates humans by connecting two opposites – the body and the spirit. – *Rebbe Nachman of Breslev*

Level eight people resemble their Creator, insofar as they spread peace wherever they go. Their humility makes them beautiful people. Not only are level-eights at peace with their fellow human, they're at peace with themselves.

The inner strength of a level eight peacemaker is apparent: Insult him, and he'll acknowledge that you're right. You can't argue with such a person – you can only love him.

Level nine: Repays cruelty with kindness.

When King David said, "The meek shall inherit the earth" (Psalms 37:11), he was referring to level nines. Meek does not mean weak – it means inner strength and peace. For our purposes, meek is synonymous with modest; shying away from publicity and not seeking to harm others even when they harm us.

I'd like to share a story with you, about one of my former classmates at rabbinical seminary.

Steven Sternhartz[16]

Steven had a master's degree in finance from Harvard. For his own spiritual growth, he decided to devote a few years to the study of theology in Israel. I don't like to generalize, but oftentimes, people who deal in money and finances are very closely tied to the material world at the expense of their spiritual lives. Steven is an exception. Today, he's a successful banker. You'd be hard pressed to find a more ethical and upright banker than Steven Sternhartz.

Steven's parents lived in Boston. During winter semester break, he'd fly home to visit his parents, and spend a few days skiing in Vermont. One day, while on the ski slopes, Steven lost his wallet with all his money and his return ticket to Boston.

With no other choice, he asked the ski shop owner, Mr. Beadle, for a short-term loan. Beadle refused. Penniless and hungry, Steven hitchhiked home in a snow blizzard from Vermont to Boston.

After our graduation and ordination, I became the rabbi and spiritual counselor of a prison and Steven returned to the world of finance.

In the meanwhile, Mr. Beadle sold the lift, shop, and slope franchise, and moved to Washington, D.C. There, he opened a souvenir shop near the White House on Pennsylvania Avenue. Two years later, he ran into financial difficulties. He urgently needed a loan to beef up his inventory and to stimulate his cash flow. He phoned for an appointment with the loan officer of the First National Bank of Washington.

You guessed right – the bronze nametag on the loan officer's desk was none other that Steven Sternhartz. Mr. Beadle made no mental connection between the skier with the Harvard sweatshirt from several years ago and the loan officer in the herringbone

---

[16] Names, circumstances, and locations slightly altered to protect privacy and to prevent embarrassment.

Botany 500 suit on the opposite side of the desk. Steven on the other hand, recognized Beadle on sight.

Beadle barely met the bank's criteria for the requested loan. Steven could have easily done business by the book; he had justifiable reason to refuse Beadle's request. Instead, he went out on a limb and approved the application. Never, did Steven tell him, "Hey, I'm the guy who lost his wallet on the slopes, and whom you refused to lend the money for a ticket home." To this day, Beadle has no idea who the kind loan officer of First National was.

Level nine individuals perform good deeds with no ulterior motives, no publicizing, and no drum rolls. No matter how badly a person mistreats a level-niner, level-nine individuals wouldn't dream of reciprocating with anything other than compassion and lovingkindness. Their only wish is to emulate Divine behavior.

Sharon, Steven's wife, says that being married to him is like living in heaven. Level nines don't criticize others, no matter what. Steven thanks his wife profusely for each tiny favor, yet demands no thanks for everything he does. Steven, like all other level nines, is a giver. Level nine is already a full-fledged level of inner peace.

Level ten: Loves God and his fellow human no matter what, and is equally happy at bad times as at good times.

At this point, I'd like to introduce you to Old Isaac the innkeeper. Old Isaac is an allegorical character, but I've had the privilege learning from several saintly and scholarly individuals who resemble Old Isaac in every way.

Old Isaac the innkeeper transcends time. He looks like a combination of Rip Van Winkle, Elijah the Prophet, and Heidi's Alpine grandfather. He's as massive as a medium-sized Brahma bull, but as gentle as a lamb. He loves people.

That's him standing over there on the front porch, in his black-leather knee-high Cossack boots, sheepskin vest, and Ukrainian fur cap. Don't be shy – go say hello. You're about to receive the warmest greeting you can imagine. Old Isaac's semi-tooth smile is as warm as summer sunlight.

I'm going to tell you two stories about Isaac; the first describes a typical level ten's relationship with God, and the second describes the way level tens react toward their fellow human.

The Hailstorm

Thunder and lightning exploded in the heavens. The roof of the barn sounded like a thousand drums. Hailstones the size of apricots were falling to the ground in curtains. Before you knew it, eighteen inches ice pellets had accumulated on the ground outside.

After thirty minutes of atmospheric bombardment, the storm subsided. The clouds disappeared as fast as they arrived. The sun had the last word for the day, reappearing about four fingers above the hills in the west.

Isaac took advantage of the remaining hour of daylight, and ran to survey the damage to his apple orchards. Strong hail is capable of splitting adult trees.

That morning, the trees were overloaded with shiny, succulent, aromatic Jonathans. The harvest was to begin tomorrow morning.

Isaac's heart skipped a beat. The earth was carpeted with apples. The hail had knocked most of the crop clean off the trees. The few that remained on the branches had gaping holes in them. The entire crop was ruined.

Jerry Miller, Isaac's best friend and neighbor, came running out to the orchard. Tons of apples covered the ground. The harvest was ruined, but Isaac was laughing and dancing an Irish jig.

"Isaac," Jerry gasped, "nearly half of your income has gone down the drain! How can you laugh at a time like this?" Jerry thought that poor old Isaac had lost his mind with sorrow.

Isaac stopped dancing and smiled patiently. "First of all, my friend, The Almighty sent the hail, and everything He does is compassionate. A hailstorm is always preferable to a bodily affliction, heaven forbid. Second, The Almighty provides for me. If there won't be money from apples, there'll be something else. Third, I was laughing when I thought about the merry time my goats and your horses are going to have, eating apples and apple silage all winter long!"

That night, Isaac hired a local 4-piece klezmer band, with clarinet, fiddle, organ, and drum. He declared a festival and donned his best Sabbath garments – his fur *shtreimel* cap and black silk robe. He looked like a character from *Fiddler on the Roof*. He, his neighbors, and his guests danced all night long.

"Isaac," Jerry pulled him aside in the middle of the dancing. "I understand your faith in God and your acceptance of His will, but why a festival – with music and dancing?"

"Jerry, up until now, it was no big deal to be a happy man and a lover of God amidst success and abundance. Ah, but when I encounter misfortune, I have a golden opportunity to show The Almighty that my love for Him is unconditional. I won't pass up such an opportunity! The Talmud says we must thank God for the bad just as we thank Him for the good. I'm happy to be alive! C'mon, let's dance a jig! And dance they did – all night long. Jerry slept the whole next day.

Level tens know how to find the good in everything and everyone. Most people see gray clouds in life, but level tens can see the silver lining.

> A person must seek peace with his fellow human, and seek peace with himself. Inner peace means that one doesn't differentiate between favorable occurrences and unfavorable occurrences, and happily sees the hand of God in whatever happens. – *Rebbe Nachman of Breslev*

Here's another story, about a level ten's relationship with a fellow human, based upon the writings of the renowned 16th Century Kabbalist from Safed, Rabbi Moses Cordovero:

The Thief

It was midnight in the middle of a snowy winter. Old Isaac the Innkeeper heard rustling in the kitchen.

At first, he thought that the noise came from a raccoon or a stray cat. Later, he heard footsteps. Maybe a guest is thirsty, he thought. Then, he heard drawers and closets opening and shutting from the direction of the reception desk.

Isaac dressed quickly and went downstairs. Sure enough, a thief was emptying drawers and closets as fast as he could.

Isaac was twice the thief's size, and could've easily apprehended the midnight intruder. He didn't. Instead, he looked at him in pity.

"You look hungry, my friend. When's the last time you had a decent meal?"

The startled thief was amazed at the innkeeper's reaction. He was caught red-handed, yet his apprehender showed no displeasure, let alone anger. He replied shyly, "Matter of fact, Mister, I don't have a dime. I haven't eaten in two days. Truth is – I'm really hungry!"

In the next few minutes, Isaac prepared a four-course banquet for the intruder. Afterwards, he gave a room and put him to bed for the night. The next day, he fed him breakfast, packed him a two-day's supply of food, gave him five hundred dollars to help him stand on his feet, and sent him with a blessing on his way.

A year later, Isaac received a letter with a five hundred dollar check in it:

Dear Isaac,

Thank you for treating me like a human, and not like a thief. I don't steal, but that night, I really was cold, hungry, and desperate. I had just gone through a painful divorce, and the lawyers stripped me of everything. Now, I'm back on my feet.

Thanks to you, I'm not in jail, nor do I have to live the rest of my life with the stigma of a criminal. Instead, I have a nice apartment and a good job as a mechanic. I want to repay you the $500, but I can never repay you for your kindness. You showed me what a human being can be. You gave me a new life. May the good Lord bless you always.

Yours truly,

Harry Higgins

Level-ten people are so close to God that their behavior seems Divine. Even when people transgress, God patiently continues to sustain them. It's mind-boggling to think how God gives us our pulse and our breathing during the very moments that we go against His will. That's the epitome of patience, compassion, and lovingkindness. It's difficult to imagine a policeman telling an apprehended burglar, "You look tired and hungry; let me get you something to eat and drink." Yet, God acts that way with us every minute of the day. Level tens emulate that very same Divine behavior.

Similarly, as with Isaac and the midnight intruder, even though the thief came to steal, Isaac only saw a human being in distress, and fed him. Not only did he refrain from punishing the poor man, he helped him make a new start. Isaac's compassion literally saved a life.

I once asked a ninety-two year old sage – a level ten – about his amazingly good health and longevity. He answered with a smile, "Simple – I never get angry and never harbor any negative feelings in my heart or brain. Therefore, my heart is sound, my digestive system is normal, and thank God, I don't know what a headache is." This particular individual had lived through poverty and several wars.

I pressed the point a little bit: "How can a person be as happy with the bad experiences in life as he can with the good?" Here's the reply I received:

"Just remember three rules of thumb: First, The Almighty runs the world; Second, The Almighty has infinite love for all of his creations; and third, The Almighty knows what's best for each one of us.

When you combine these three rules, you're left with no reason in the world to worry or to be angry." Worry and the above three rules of thumb simply don't go together. Without worry, you too will be feeling healthy and happy at age ninety-two.

2

The Prancing Buck

*After learning about the levels of anger in the previous chapter,
this chapter will show us the two main causes of anger. Before
we move on, take out that slip of paper that you wrote your
initial anger-tranquility estimation. How accurate were you? No
matter what your present position is, you'll soon feel your initial
progress up the trail to tranquility.*

Welcome to the University of the Trail. In this chapter,
the allegorical wooded foothills of Mount Patience will
serve as our classroom. We'll be searching for natural
phenomena that teach us about the causes of anger. Learning in
the outdoors is an exhilarating experience.

Rebbe Nachman of Breslev teaches that a person should
search for the underlying wisdom behind every creation –
mineral, plant, animal, and human. The Almighty instills infinite
wisdom in the design of every being in the universe. Therefore,
by carefully observing each creation, we absorb God's wisdom.
Divine wisdom heightens our perception and deepens our
insight.

We take so many wonderful gifts in life for granted, because
we fail to observe. Look at a fresh red apple. Exquisite, isn't it?
Do you know the old expression, "an apple a day keeps the
doctor away?" The mallic acid of an apple does wonders for the
human body – it's a natural antibiotic and antioxidant. Eating a
crisp apple is equal to brushing your teeth – not only does it rid
your teeth of trapped food particles, it invigorates your gums and
sweetens your breath. The vitamins, energy, and moisture of the
apple are readily available to the body. The apple tastes good

too. Consequently, each crispy apple is a compact doctor, dentist, dietician, and dining room.

The more you gain spiritual awareness, the more you'll notice the seemingly simple things around you. There's so much to learn. Appreciating the treasures of life is a key to happiness. People who take things for granted never achieve inner peace. They're always angry, because they think that they deserve more than what they have.

This chapter illustrates the two main causes of anger – **arrogance** and **lack of spiritual awareness**. By observing the environment, we'll hopefully gain an interesting insight as to why people suffer from anger and lack inner peace.

> By overcoming arrogance, a person attains wisdom, happiness, longevity, faith, and understanding of Divine secrets. – *Rebbe Nachman of Breslev*

* * *

Let's view an example of nature's classroom, the divine wisdom within each creation. Look at an anthill. Ants teach us three main lessons – honesty, faith, and diligence. Observe closely, and you'll see why.

Ants are invertebrates – they don't have a spine. Most invertebrates overheat and dehydrate in full sunlight; therefore, most of their activity above ground level is either in early morning, in late evening, or in full shade. If an ant tells a lie, his peers execute him immediately.

In bright sunlight, we don't see any ants crawling around. If we were to cast a shadow over the mound, a leader ant would peek his head out of the main entrance and walk around freely in the shade. Then, he'd return to the edge of the hole to call his buddies to come outside and join him. Meanwhile, if we were to remove the object that cast the shadow, and the emerging ants would not find shade, they'd kill the leader ant for lying to them. Ants don't tolerate the slightest form of dishonesty.

An ant lives for approximately six months, yet a grain and a half of wheat is sufficient food for its entire lifetime. If we were to dig down to the central warehouses of the anthill, we'd find about three hundred grains per ant. Each ant gathers enough food for two hundred years!

An ant never stops working, because he has faith that The Almighty will grant him a lengthy life. An ant never steals. The moment he takes a bite from a grain, the grain acquires the unique odor of its owner's saliva. No other ant will dare touch the grain of a comrade. So, by observing ants, we learn about honesty, diligence, and faith. That's what the University of the Trail is all about.

Let's now look at deer. You're correct in thinking that the slightest rustle frightens deer away – that's in a place where people hunt deer. In a place where the county doesn't allow deer hunting, our fawn friends are fearless. They'll walk right up to your back porch, and eat leftovers from a dinner plate just like a house pet. A deer has a keen sense of smell, and if the wind is right, he can smell a grizzly bear or a mountain lion from almost a mile away. So, wherever we see deer, we know that there are no predators in the vicinity.

Predators usually roam around at night. Rebbe Nachman of Breslev says that if a person fears God, he doesn't have to fear anything else in the entire universe. The predators themselves are afraid of a God-fearing person. Later, in chapter three, I'll explain why. I've seen righteous people out in the woods at night many times, without even a penknife in their pockets.

The average person doesn't believe that one can communicate with plants and animals. King David could, and so could his descendant Rabbi Israel Baal Shem Tov. Rabbi Yitschak Luria, the father of Kabbala, not only understood the birds and the animals, but could discern which human was reincarnated in a particular bird or animal, and why.

Have you ever wondered why two farmers feed their cows the same diet, yet one farmer receives more and better quality milk than his counterpart? Or, have you ever wondered why your neighbor's African violets look so much healthier than yours?

Plants and animals have spirituality. They can differentiate between love and hate, or between respect and disdain. A sensitive farmer or gardener can *feel* the need of a plant or animal. Sensitivity to another being is a form of communication, almost like talking.

Insensitive people don't know how you feel, usually because they're too preoccupied with themselves.

An avid houseplant enthusiast can look at your African violets, and tell you that they lack iron – not by virtue of any horticultural background, but by understanding and feeling the needs of the plant. I can't understand an African violet, but I do comprehend an apple tree, a peach tree, or a grapefruit tree. Some say that deer are easier to understand than fruit trees.

Not far from our point of embarkation on our allegorical journey up the trail to tranquility, we come to an area with an abundance of deer; we'll soon see the unforgettable lessons of life that we can learn from observing those very special creatures:

The Prancing Buck: A lesson about arrogance

Old Isaac's Inn and farmstead are in the foothills of Mount Patience. The eighteen-mile trail up the mountain begins at the eastern border of Isaac's apple orchards, and works its way through a forest known as Deer Haven, because of the large deer population. After a mile-long walk into the forest, you reach a clearing by a spring. This is the home of Zachary's clan.

The big buck with the stubs of broken antlers on his head is the patriarchal king of the herd. His name is Zachary. Zachary is thirteen years old – ninety-one by human equivalent – well exceeding the average life span of a deer. Zachary couldn't have reached such a ripe old age in the face of constant challenges from all sides – from the clan within and from enemies without – were it not for his wisdom and strength of character.

"Ohuuuuuuuuuuu!" That's the call of a king buck. Whenever Zachary and the herd reach the spring, no one dares take a drink until the venerable patriarch tilts his head back, raises his voice to the heavens, and thanks God for the water. When King David first saw this same moving sight twenty-nine centuries ago, he was inspired to compose Psalm 42: "Like a buck's yearning call by the stream, my soul yearns for the Lord."

Quietly, in perfect order with no pushing or shoving, the deer move forward to drink – first the fawns, then the does, and finally the young bucks.

"Ahh-hoooooooe!" What's that call from the opposite bank of the stream? Zachary raises his head and perks his ears. He nods in understanding, and paws the gravel deliberately with his right front hoof. Sure enough, another challenger; Zachary encircles the herd, delineating an imaginary boundary and warning the challenger that trespassing is a declaration of war.

The challenger is a robust four-year-old buck, twenty-eight by human equivalent, with the largest, most impressive antlers you've ever laid eyes on. The young does in the herd – despite their respect for their patriarchal king – can't restrain their awe at this handsome stag, and gasp in admiration.

The challenger's name is Dandy. Rather than crossing the line and risking a direct confrontation with the time-weathered Zachary, the cocky stag prances in wide circles around the herd. He flaunts his antlers and attempts to humiliate the king in front of his own clan.

Dandy is a marvelous specimen of deer. Not only is he attractive, he's a superb athlete. He takes a running jump, and leaps six feet high in the air while traversing a distance of over fifteen feet, to the delight of the goggle-eyed does. Dandy sprints to and fro, exhibiting speed of over forty-five miles per hour. Zachary doesn't seem to be impressed, and observes the spry young challenger with extraordinary tolerance.

Dandy stops his antics. With a few short leaps, he climbs to a ledge that serves as his stage, so that the entire herd can view him with ease. "Grandpa Zach", he calls out with insolence, "your time is up. Relinquish the herd to me, and retire peacefully to the mountains. You're an old deer, and I don't want to disgrace you in front of the clan."

Zachary smiles. "Where did you learn ethics, young stag? After your ridiculous display of theatrics, you're suddenly concerned with my honor? Spare the needless rhetoric; you've impressed the fawns but you don't impress me. State your challenge – a fight or a race!"

Dandy stammers at the old buck's candor and quiet confidence. "Maybe I had better not fight", he muses. "Who knows what tricks the old warhorse has? A race is the better idea! I'm definitely three times faster than he is. If he doesn't die of embarrassment at defeat, he'll disappear in the hills and the herd will be mine."

"A race it is!" declares Dandy, "from here in the clearing, up the trail, through the forest, to the finish line at Beaver Creek – a total of eight miles. Agreed?"

"So be it," responds Zachary. "Know full well, young stag, that this race bears the legal ramifications of a fight to the death. You have made a public challenge before tens of witnesses. By deer law and tradition, the loser must leave the vicinity of Mount Patience and the surrounding valleys, and remain an exile for the rest of his life. I offer you one more chance to withdraw your challenge, young stag, so that a moment of arrogance won't ruin the rest of your life."

Dandy smirks, protrudes his chest, and raises his head, flaunting his antlers in a supercilious gesture of disdain. "The worn out old buck is looking for a way out," he smirks, blinded by an excess of pride and vanity.

Dandy calculates that at his average cruising speed of forty miles per hour, he can traverse the eight-mile course in a mere twelve minutes. Zachary, he calculates, can't possibly reach Beaver Creek in less than fifteen minutes.

"Forget it, Gramps, the race is on. You can console your ancient bones that your exile won't last long. Your days on this earth are numbered. I'm giving you a final chance to step down respectfully. Can you still hear at your age, or should I yell louder? Ha, ha, ha…"

Dandy ignores the code of venison etiquette, even at the time of challenge, making an obvious attempt to further belittle the aged patriarch in front of the clan – a heinous moral crime.

Zachary weathers the insult and embarrassment with no anger whatsoever, and responds calmly in an authoritative voice that conveys phenomenal inner strength and composure: "Prepare, young stag. The observers shall take their posts along the way, and the race shall begin in exactly one hour."

The birds chirp all through the forest, across the valleys, and up the mountain, spreading the news of the imminent race. The entire forest becomes a beehive of activity, as the clan deer take observer positions along the trail. The squirrels, rabbits, and raccoons dart up the trees, jockeying for the best position to watch the race. Hundreds of deer from neighboring clans rush to Zachary's domain. Within three quarters of an hour, the entire eight-mile course is loaded with spectators.

Let me describe the course that Dandy chose, the eight miles between the Deer Haven clearing and Beaver Creek: The entire trail is a steady uphill grade. The trail itself is rather wide for the first mile, then the forest thickens, and the trail narrows to a mere two or three feet. For a dense three-mile stretch where the white oaks, the firs, and the wild holly grow, two animals or two humans can't walk side by side.

A hush descends on the forest. All the birds and animals are holding their breath. Jonathan Buck, one of the most respected deer-clan patriarchs within miles has just entered the clearing. He is a middle-aged deer, eight years old, with impressive stature. His antlers are short and stubby like Zachary's. Jonathan is one of several visiting dignitaries chosen to officiate the race.

Zachary takes his position to the right of Jonathan. Dandy descends from his stage on the cliff ledge, and positions himself to Jonathan's left. Jonathan reiterates the terms of the challenge, and both the clan king and the challenger nod in agreement. The officiating buck paws the gravel in front of him three times, and then emits a baritone deer call that reverberates for miles – "Ohuuuuuuuuuu!" The race is on!

Dandy leaves the starting line like a ballistic missile, covering the first mile in a record time of one minute and fifteen seconds, the equivalent to forty-eight miles per hour. The onlookers are delighted. Zachary covers the same stretch of ground in two minutes; forty-five seconds slower than the challenger.

Two gray-black crows, the forest bookies, are now cawing out eight-to-one odds in favor of the challenger, while the squirrels run to get their acorns to place their bets. The forest hasn't seen this much excitement in a long time.

The meadow ends, and the trail enters the forest at the beginning of mile two. By mile three, the woods become especially dense, and the trail narrows to a width of a mere two feet. Dandy darts through the first hundred yards of wooded trail, then all of a sudden...

Crack! Dat-dat-dat! Snap, pop, crack! The clatter of Dandy's antlers clashing with the tree branches resounds through the forest like the staccato of machine-gun fire. The challenger's ostentatious antlers are nearly four feet wide, yet the trail is barely two feet wide. Simple arithmetic reveals that each massive oak and hickory tree – not to mention the surrounding vines, bushes, and undergrowth – is a potential obstacle to a vain stag whose inflated ego is even bigger than his antlers.

Dandy gets knocked around from tree to tree like an erratic billiard ball. A low hickory branch snaps, and whiplashes the fuming young stag across the face. Dandy cringes at the pain, and ducks his head. Suddenly, a second branch snaps, and recoils like a bullwhip across his tail and thighs. The young deer jumps in alarm, and his blood pressure skyrockets.

Like all other arrogant creatures, Dandy can't see the truth. He forgets about the real challenge at hand, and follows the futile dictates of his uncontrollable temper. He declares war on all the trees in the forest, especially on the oak tree directly in front of him.

"OK oak, you're finished!" he threatens. "In two minutes, you're going to be firewood!" Dandy takes a running start, and butts the thirty-inch-thick hardwood with his antlers. The oak doesn't budge.

"Get out of my way, you deciduous dimwit!" Dandy forgets that the oak has been standing in its own rightful spot for the last eighty-five years, minding its own business. He himself is the intruder. Dandy takes another running start, and butts the tree a second time. Not even an acorn falls from the tree. The fuming red-faced stag makes a third attempt to fell the massive oak, without even scratching the tree's bark. Dandy's head begins to throb.

An owl calls down from the top of the tree: "Who, who, who's going to lose? The king just passed you by!"

A startled Dandy watches Zachary disappear in the thicket up ahead. Desperately, the challenger returns to the trail and begins a new sprint, but entangles himself in a labyrinth of vines. The more he tugs, the more his predicament worsens. He hasn't even completed half the course. He hates the sour taste of the leathery vines, but he has no choice: His only chance is to eat his way to freedom. "Wait 'til I cut loose", he continues to threaten, "I'm going to burn this whole forest!"

In the eight minutes that Dandy wrestles with the vines, eating and biting his way to freedom, Zachary covers another four miles at his modest but steady pace of thirty miles per hour. The tables are turning, and the crows are now cawing ten-to-one in favor of Zachary.

The birds, chipmunks, squirrels, and raccoons find Dandy's war with the forest most amusing. Even the bats awaken from their daytime slumber for a first-hand look at the action. The beloved trees are their home; hearing Dandy hurl all sorts of unrepeatable epithets at the trees sorely insulted them at first. But now, watching the haughty stag get knocked from tree to tree emits cries of glee from the treetop spectators.

Have you ever heard a chipmunk giggle or a raccoon laugh? Hundreds of them chiding the frustrated stag from above add considerable insult to the young stag's sorely injured ego.

It never occurs to Dandy, blind in arrogance and burning with anger at every tree in the forest, that the source of his pride – his antlers – is his biggest enemy.

"Hey, silly stag," yells an owl, "if you cut off your antlers, you'll be able to traverse the forest in peace, too."

Such an idea never occurred to the conceited young buck; were he modest, he'd have trimmed his antlers long ago. If his antlers were trimmed, he could have traversed the forest in peace. Yet, if he had sense enough to trim his antlers, he'd have never challenged Zachary in the first place. Now, he'll have to suffer the full consequence of his arrogance and resulting anger.

Dandy reaches the finish line at Beaver Creek dizzy, disoriented, with cracked and broken antlers, a sore neck, and a migraine headache. His time is a full ten minutes slower than Zachary's.

Jonathan and the other officiating deer send Dandy into forced exile. His face is never again seen within a thirty-mile radius of Zachary's kingdom. Venerable King Zachary, the dignified yet unassuming veteran of countless challenges by senseless vain stags, returns home to his clearing amid the applause of thousands of ecstatic furred and feathered admirers.

Zachary doesn't focus on the throngs of well-wishers. He knows that his own limited abilities weren't sufficient to defeat Dandy.

Zachary takes these precious moments of glory, and presents them like a sacred gift to God: "You deserve the praise and glory, my Father in heaven, not me," attributing his victory to Divine intervention.

The venerable venison monarch closes his eyes, while his heart sends a silent prayer of thanksgiving to his Creator: "Though I walk through the valley of death, I shall not fear, for You are with me; Your rod and Your staff – they comfort me. You have set my table before my enemies; you have anointed my head with oil – thank you, God. Who would have believed that a decrepit old buck like me could withstand a challenge from a swift young stag in his prime?

Blessed are you, my Lord, who uplifts the meek and topples the arrogant."

The moral of Dandy's antlers

Let's take a second look at our deer story. Zachary – despite the limitations of age – continues to rule over the clan. He's a more than benevolent monarch, who controls his herd by virtue of his wisdom, experience, and superb character. Even in the most trying situation of public degradation, Zachary remains dignified, composed, and in complete control of his emotions, the sign of a true leader. His brain dictates his decisions, not whim or mood. He prefers an unassuming modesty to a regal crown, and therefore keeps his antlers closely trimmed.

Zachary lives peacefully with the whole world, but nonetheless stands steadfast in the face of tyranny. Like the finest of deer, he is very spiritual and a strong believer in God.

Dandy sorely lacks character development. He is vain and arrogant, concerned only about himself and his physical development. Dandy wastes time and effort on image building, having groomed his fancy antlers to impress others. He lacks the character and leadership qualities to lead a herd, yet his arrogance doesn't allow him to accept the reign of another, more qualified buck.

Dandy's antlers are the symbol and epitome of egotism and arrogance. He is blind to truth; he believes that one hundred year old trees should grant the right of way to his antlers. He's angry at the entire forest.

The forest symbolizes the world, the trees represent other people, and the trail is an allegory of one's personal journey through life. Were Dandy to trim his antlers, he could have traversed the forest speedily, harmlessly, and peacefully. By the same token, when a person deflates his own inflated ego, he has fewer conflicts with others, and goes through life with minimum conflict and no cause for anger.

That's what I meant about the University of the Trail. Back in college, we'd study all night long to pass an exam in Psychology

303 or Sociology 402. A few days later, we'd forgotten nearly everything. On the other hand, we never forget the memorable lessons of observation. By looking at the sharp contrast between Zachary and Dandy, we readily internalize a vital message about ethics, character development, and overcoming anger. All we have to do is keep our eyes open and look for the divine wisdom in every creation. Such lessons in life become engraved in our hearts forever.

Let's further examine how arrogance brings on anger.

The anger equation

Here's how we can describe the cause and intensity of anger mathematically:

$$\text{Expectations} - \text{Realizations} = \text{Anger}$$

The more arrogant a person is, the higher his or her expectations. When in reality, the arrogant people don't receive the homage they think they deserve, or in other words, life's realizations fall short of their expectations, the resulting gap manifests itself in anger.

The expectation scale

No expectations **0** ⟵——————————⟶ **100** *Full expectations*

Here's an example: Imagine a scale of expectations from 0 to 100, whereas "0" signifies no expectations from others, and "100" means maximum expectations from the whole world. A tyrant, for example, is an ego-driven person of extreme arrogance who expects absolute deference from every individual.

Let's assume that the tyrant's expectations from others rate 100 on the scale, since he demands absolute deference. Now, assume that a person receives an audience with the tyrant. That person greets the tyrant politely, but fails to bow down to him and kiss his hand. If such a greeting earns a score of 70, then a gap of 30 points remains between the tyrant's expectations and the person's greeting, in other words, the situation realization. These 30 points of anger are usually sufficient for a tyrant to execute a person. Here's how our tyrant's anger looks as an equation:

The tyrant's expectations	100
Realization	- 70
Anger	= 30

Arrogant people waste considerable time and energy on anger, since their expectations are rarely met. Living with such a person is a difficult tribulation in itself, comparable to walking on eggs without breaking them. Family members of arrogant and angry people frequently suffer from a number of nervous disorders of various degrees, unless they've made a concerted effort on attaining spiritual awareness (see chapter four).

The anger equation also explains why modest people are always happy. A modest person has few expectations, if any, from his fellow human being. Let's assume that a modest person has low-level expectations that score "30" – he's happy as long as people aren't throwing tomatoes at him. A person greets him politely on the street, with a cordial hello that would earn a score of "70", resulting in a negative anger gap of 40 points. Negative anger is happiness, or tranquility. As such, the modest person, with minimal expectations, is constantly happy and tranquil, and a pleasure to live with. Now, let's view this example as an equation:

The modest person's expectations	30
Realization	- 70
Anger	= - 40

Negative anger is, of course, happiness.

The anger equation is a useful tool for self-evaluation. Try your best to be honest and objective about yourself, and score your expectations against the actual situation realizations that you encounter in daily life. You'll gain an amazing insight about yourself.

> All of one's troubles, tribulations, and shortcomings stem from a lack of spiritual awareness. The more one gains spiritual awareness, the more one neutralizes shortcomings.
> – *Rebbe Nachman of Breslev*

Arrogance, as Dandy's antlers and the anger equation demonstrate, is the prime cause of anger. The second major cause of anger is lack of spiritual awareness.

The Furious Worm – a lesson about lack of spiritual awareness

Would you believe that we can learn about faith and spiritual awareness from a worm? We're about to see another very special example of the wisdom in the environment along our allegorical journey:

If you see an apple with a little brown circle and black spot in the middle, don't eat it. There's a worm inside that apple.

Imagine that we're holding such an apple to our ear, and hearing a squeaking noise. There are probably two worms in that apple – the squeaking indicates that they're having a discussion. If we could understand worms, we'd be privy to an eye-opening discussion.

A mother worm lays her two eggs in the core of the apple, and disappears. Wilma, the older sister, hatches a few hours before Wendy. We catch the two sisters in the midst of a heated discussion.

Wendy: The end of the world is near! Do something, Wilma!

Wilma: What are you talking about, silly?

Wendy: I've had it! I can't stand another of those murderous tremors. The darkness and the cold are driving me crazy. This is the end! We're going to die! I can't stand it!

Wilma: Will you calm down, please? You can lower your voice, too. There's a legitimate explanation for the tremors, the cold, and the darkness. If you'll stop creating such havoc and give me your undivided attention, I'll explain everything.

Wendy: *(impatiently)* Go ahead, know-it-all.

Wilma: Must you be so abrasive? Right before I was hatched, Mother explained everything…

Wendy: *(interrupts her sister in a most indignant fashion)* Who and what is "Mother"? What kind of fairy tale are you trying to sell me? Don't you understand, Wilma? The world is ending!

Wilma: Will you please control yourself? Thank you. Now listen: We are worms. We were born inside this apple two weeks ago. Our mother was a mature worm, who laid her two eggs – you and me – and continued her own life elsewhere. Soon, we'll mature, and we'll leave this apple for the outside world as well.

Wendy: You're daft, sister! The world is on the verge of oblivion – the quakes, freeze, and darkness are proof – and all you do is fabricate ridiculous myths about a mother and an outside world…what garbage! You're insane, and you're driving me to insanity as well!

Wilma: I'm sorry about your harsh manner of expression and your fiery temper. If you'd only listen, I can easily explain the tremors, the cold, and the darkness.

Wendy: Theories or more fairy tales?

Wilma: Neither; until this morning, our apple was still attached to the tree. We were born in the summer, on a southern exposure of the orchard with plenty of heat and sunlight, and the only movement we felt was the slight swaying of our apple on its branch in the breeze. The first big jolt we felt this morning was when our apple was picked. The other tremors came from being knocked around all day long by two hikers and their backpacks. The cold and the darkness are from the lack of sunlight.

Wendy: Enough, Wilma. What an imagination! You've lost contact with reality. More stories - apple, sunlight, hikers, outside world - you're seriously grating my already shredded nervous system. You see these moist, sweet walls *(Wendy licks the apple)* – this is the entire universe, our home, and our sustenance. I maintain that the end is near – there's no other logical explanation for the tremors, the cold, and the darkness.

Wilma *(sighs in obvious frustration)*: If so, little sister worm, will you please enlighten me and inform me who created us, and how we got here?

Wendy: Your question is irrelevant. That's not the issue. We are here and nothing else matters except that the destruction of the world is near!

The hikers decide to aid Wilma's almost hopeless cause, lay the apple on the ground, and carefully make an incision with a penknife. Soon, both worms poke their heads out.

Wilma: I told you, Wendy! Look at this tremendous world outside our apple. Notice how miniscule our apple is compared to the world at large. Mmmm, smell those exotic aromas – we can choose from a myriad of delightful delicacies such as fennel, clover, or wild mint. You see, no more tremors; the warmth of the sun has returned. Mother was right...

Wendy *(unable to concede the point)*: Wilma, excuse me, but you have less brains than I gave you credit for. Our universe has been destroyed – here it is cut open before your very eyes. We are now dead, in the world to come...

Wilma: Dead? I'll show you, stubborn sister; there's one way to make you understand *(and bites her sister on a very sensitive place)*!

Wendy: Ouch! What did you do that for?

Wilma: Certainly not out of anger, not like other worms, not to mention any names, but to show you that we're still very much alive. You wasted an entire day with temper and impatience, complaining about the cold and the tremors. If you'd have only listened to me, you could have prevented needless aggravation. Look how nasty you've treated me all day long. Did I deserve it? Have I ever given you anything other than compassionate sisterhood and affection?

Wendy (embarrassed): No.

Wilma: I also suffered from the cold, the darkness, and the tremors. Don't forget, we're in the same boat – I mean, the same apple. The difference between the two of us is, that as the senior egg, I received the oral tradition from mother. Mother taught me spiritual awareness.

Wendy: What do you mean?

Wilma: I knew all about mother, the apple, and the tremendous outside world that you are now witnessing with your own two eyes. Even when I didn't see them, I still believed in them. Because of spiritual awareness, my vistas weren't limited to this apple.

Wendy: Are you trying to tell me that I was blind?

Wilma: Look in retrospect – you refused to believe what you couldn't see. Now that you're on a higher cognizance level – the restrictions of our former environment no longer seal us from the outside world – you can see that everything I told you was true. Here are the sun, the trees, and the outside world before your very eyes. Hey, look at those two giants – they must be the hikers!

Wendy: I really must apologize, big sister. I know that I acted unbearably all day long. Do you forgive me?

Wilma: Certainly I do, sweetheart. I want to teach you a few more things, so that you'll overcome your anger and your negative feelings. The fear and the worry that you suffered are examples of the negative emotional byproducts of anger. Birds of a feather flock together.

Wendy: I don't quite understand. Why was I so angry about today's tremors?

Wilma: Good question; you lacked spiritual awareness. Since you thought that your suffering was random, with no rhyme or reason and beyond your control, you developed feelings of fear and futility, further intensified by your growing frustration. That's the formula for an emotional 4-F profile: Fear, futility, frustration, and finally fury.

Wendy: How would spiritual awareness have helped me?

Wilma: With spiritual awareness, you'd have known that today's events were perfectly planned and completely under the control of a great master Creator for our own benefit. Therefore, you would have been calm and collected like I was. Oh yes, I have a few bruises from the rough ride we took today, but I knew that this was a necessary step toward a bigger and better life. I believed Mother, and you should have believed me, confident that I would never lie to you. Notice how our situation has improved within a few short hours: Solid ground, our choice of a number of new homes, gourmet food – you name it! Are you beginning to understand?

Wendy: Yes, and I'm learning to pay attention to you, big sister. I'm sorry for being so worm-headed. Tell me, though – who's that master Creator that does things for our own good?

Wilma: Every creature distinctly and intimately knows who he is – God. Before Mother left the apple, she spoke to us – her beloved eggs – and said that she must leave the apple before we are born, but that we should never worry, since God will care for us. I can describe the difference between your anger and my patience with two words – spiritual awareness.

Wendy: Explain to me a little more, Wilma.

Wilma: Certainly, dear. Today, while you thought that our tribulations were happenstance, you had nothing to cling to and therefore succumbed to negative emotions. I had Mother's oral tradition – which has been passed down from worm to worm since the beginning of time – and therefore knew that some strange and exciting events, no matter how trying at the time, would ultimately lead to a wonderful improvement in our lives. Spiritual awareness helped me realize that our world was not limited to the walls of the apple in front of our noses. Wasn't I correct?

Wendy *(licks a fennel leaf)*: You certainly were! But tell me something else, Wilma. Who is God? I don't see him...

Wilma: Until a few moments ago, you didn't see the sun, the trees, and the grass either. You've already learned that your former hypothesis of our apple as the entire universe is mistaken. Just because we don't see something doesn't mean that it doesn't exist. Even in the physical world, all sorts of phenomena exist on various levels that we don't see.

Wendy: Can you cite an example?

Wilma: Of course – the air is full of sound waves on different frequencies. We neither hear them nor see them. Humans have these plastic boxes with all types of wires and transistors inside, called radios. By turning on a radio, you can capture the sound waves that are floating around in the air. You can hear people talking, without seeing them. If you have a different type of box, called a television, you can see them too. Let's go one step further: You can never see God, because He's spiritual and not physical, but the more you develop your spiritual antennas, the more you feel and hear Him, rather like a radio broadcast on a spiritual level.

Wendy: I believe you, big sister. I'm hungry – can we have dinner?

Wilma: Certainly, sweetheart. After dinner, we're both going to bed under a nice warm quilt of maple leaves on a soft mattress of pine needles, in the shelter of a fresh mushroom. You'll love our new home in the wide wonderful world of worry-free worms.

> The main consolation of all life's troubles, our greatest hope, and our expectation of pleasure in the World to Come are none other than spiritual awareness. – *Rebbe Nachman of Breslev*

The moral of the furious worm

We oftentimes refer to the environment at the tip of our noses as reality, and deny whatever seems intangible to our sorely limited level of perception. Such lack of spiritual awareness severely restricts both emotional and intellectual growth. A person without spiritual awareness develops feelings of fear, futility, and utter frustration, which lead directly to anger, because he or she fails to see the ultimate benefits of life's difficulties.

Whenever a person regards pain and tribulations as random, inexplicable, and purposeless, life becomes miserable. Spiritual awareness gives us insight and understanding into all our dilemmas, and allows us to channel our emotional powers to a positive, anger-free path.

Jewish spirituality is based on a 34-centuries-old unbroken tradition from teacher to pupil since Moses on Mount Sinai. Many people deny the lessons of spirituality on the grounds of so-called modern enlightenment. Such "enlightenment" is really spiritual darkness, or the lack of spiritual awareness, just like Wendy the Worm.

The higher one ascends the spiritual ladder, the more spiritual cognizance increases. The higher you go, the more you get to know God, and the happier you become. Everyone knows that the best view is at the top of the mountain. That's where you and I are heading.

3

The Grouchy Grizzly

Now that we've learned about the different levels and causes of anger, we'll see how anger damages the quality of our lives.

Angry people wouldn't be such a problem if they only harmed themselves. Bad-tempered people though, like grizzlies, create tension in the environment. Consciously or otherwise, they prevent others from living tranquil lives. Like the old adage says, misery loves company.

Grizzly bears exhibit classic angry behavioral patterns. By observing the habits of a grizzly, one can learn a substantial lesson about anger. See for yourself, as I tell you a story about a bear that lives in a cave near Lupine Valley, not far from Old Isaac's Inn. Everybody in the area calls him "The Grouchy Grizzly of Lupine Valley."

The Grouchy Grizzly of Lupine Valley

Deer Haven, the home of Zachary and his herd, ends a mile from Bear Ridge. Zachary, the cautious venison monarch, maintains a healthy distance from the grizzlies. Bear Ridge overlooks a breathtaking valley carpeted with rare blue and white flowers – Lupines.

The valley is actually a plateau. Its dark gray soil is highly fertile and well aerated, full of pumice – small perforated rocks that resemble sponges. Both the soil and the rocks are of volcanic origin. Local tradition says that the volcano last erupted six hundred years ago, and probably would have erupted again, but it remains dormant in deference to Old Isaac.

Lupines are from the legume family, and first cousins to the pea and the lima bean. They thrive in volcanic soil. At the end of the summer, the fertilized flowers become a pod filled with four or five lima-sized beans. Lupine beans are quite tough and bitter. But, if you boil them seven times, change the water with each boil, and then salt-and-pepper them, you have a nutritious and delicious protein-packed snack.

The Lupine flower carpet is an exquisite creation. All the birds, insects, and animals of the area – except for one infamous, calamity-prone exception – adhere to an honor code that forbids trampling the flowers.

Only the bees are allowed in the flower patch, since they facilitate pollinization and fertilization of the flowers. States that are fortunate enough to host natural fields of Lupine flowers usually grant them official nature preserve status. This magnificent view is certainly worth recording, both on film and in the heart. What serenity…

"**Grrrrrrrowwwl!**" The ground shudders from the thunderous roar. It can only be one of two things – either the volcano is reawakening or Grouchy Grizzly is having his annual war with the bees. The legend about the volcano's deference to Old Isaac is quite reliable, so it's probably the latter.

There he is, trampling the flowers – all seven feet and seven hundred pounds of Grouchy Grizzly – the lone offender of the area honor code.

Grouchy Grizzly is no run-of-the-mill bear. He qualifies as one of the senior professors of the University of the Trail; if we were to have a curriculum catalog, it would list:

> **Faculty of Anger**
> **Anger 202 – The Damages of Anger – Dr. G.**
> **Grizzly   – 3 credits**
> **MWF 9-10, Lupine Valley Hall**

Grouchy Grizzly is a superb lecturer on the damages of anger. He demonstrates everything he teaches.

Most of the birds and animals in the forest are patient and loyal husbands, but Grouchy Grizzly fails to get along with his mate. Don't even dream about him having a peaceful relationship with any of the other inhabitants on Mount Patience.

Once a year, he remembers his she-bear, and makes a conjugal visit. For Mrs. Grizzly, one day a year is enough to contend with a 700-lb. sack of anger and self-indulgence. The following day, she moves back to her own cave by the river to raise her annual cub or two. He lives like a hermit in his own cave on the ridge, not far from here.

Grouchy Grizzly will go out of his way to create conflict. Here's an example:

Old Isaac took Jerry Miller with him on the eighteen-mile hike up from the inn to the top of Mount Patience. Here in Lupine Valley, Isaac taught him about personal prayer (which we'll be discussing later, in chapter nine).

Once Jerry learned the basics, Isaac sent him on his own, and told him to begin talking to God in his own words.

Isaac stood by an old oak tree, and began singing the most beautiful praises to The Almighty that you ever heard, in his own original melodies and in his own words. He has a tenor voice that can make a boulder cry. Jerry once caught him singing in the barn, and all the goats were standing on their hind legs and bleating in enthusiasm.

Back to our story: Jerry walked a few hundred feet away, and began pouring his heart out in personal prayer. Overcome with the beauty of the surroundings, he closed his eyes and let his heart soar. He felt an uplifting of spirits in a way he never before experienced.

Just as Jerry was getting into the spiritual groove – "**Grrrrrrowwwl!**" His heart collided with his large intestine, and his knees began a percussion accompaniment to "When Johnny Comes Marching Home." Approximately two hundred feet in front of him was a snarling, growling grizzly bear of quite intimidating proportions.

Jerry's throat contracted and his mouth was as dry as the Sahara Desert. He thought he was about to be the suggested entrée on a hungry bear's menu.

"**Grrrrrrrowwwl!**" The grizzly began to pace stealthily in Jerry's direction. Jerry's heart pounded like a sledgehammer on a granite quarry.

Jerry glanced up to the heavens with a silent two-word prayer of "Please, God". He glanced over his shoulder – Isaac was as equidistant to his right as the bear was in front of him.

Without saying a word, Isaac waved his hand and summoned Jerry to approach him slowly and calmly. Step by terrifying step, Jerry began inching his way toward Isaac, while the grizzly bear continued to progress menacingly in Jerry's direction.

Jerry's pulse seemed to be as deafening as Niagara Falls. Alternately, he took a step, and the bear took two, gradually coming closer. When the bear was a mere eighty feet away, he roared again, opening his mouth and exposing a full set of pearly white stilettos. Jerry envisioned himself being ripped to pepperoni-sized shreds.

When he finally reached Isaac, Jerry grabbed his hand, squeezing it like a vice. Inexplicably, he felt calm and safe in Isaac's presence.

Isaac looked the bear straight in the eyes, and smiled. The bear was a mere twenty feet away. Slowly, the grizzly circled them seven full times, then walked away to the forest – a most bizarre spectacle. That is, until the next story you're about to hear. *(Why was the bear afraid of Isaac? You'll soon find out.)*

A year later, Isaac and Jerry went hiking again. They spent their first night at the Beaver Creek cabin and continued up the trail the following morning, through the conifer forest to Bear Ridge overlooking Lupine Valley.

At about ten o'clock in the morning, the wind picked up to a near-gale velocity, and foreboding gray clouds darkened the sky. A bolt of lightening struck a massive fir tree not far from them, and split it in half as if it were a Popsicle stick.

Old Isaac knew of a cave close by, near the trail's descent from Bear Ridge to Lupine Valley. Within six minutes, he and Jerry stood at the entrance of the cave. Isaac walked inside and Jerry followed.

The blackness of the cave made a moonless night seem like Times Square on New Years Eve. Jerry pulled a flashlight out of his hiking belt, and switched it on.

Are you ready for this – "**Grrrrrrrowwwl!**" This happened to be Grouchy Grizzly's cave, and he didn't appear to be putting his best hospitable paw forward.

What a predicament – lightning, thunder, a bombardment of hailstones, a killer gale outside the cave, and Grouchy Grizzly inside the cave!

The bear ignored Isaac and growled at Jerry again, but with a little less ferocity than the first time.

Isaac nonchalantly opened his rucksack, and produced a paper bag filled with his famous home-baked oatmeal and honey cookies. He tossed one to the bear, and the bear caught it in mid air. He threw a second one on the floor of the cave, in front of the bear. Grouchy Grizzly moved forward and ate that one too. By the eighth cookie, Grouchy Grizzly was eating out of Isaac's hand, a spectacle worthy of top booking at any Ringling Brothers' arena.

Outside, the storm was worsening. Bolts of lightning literally crackled at the entrance of the cave. Calmly, Isaac sat down on the floor of the cave, resting his back on a boulder. The bear sat down beside him, purring like a pussycat while Isaac stroked the fur of his neck.

Isaac was as relaxed with the bear as a person is with a pet poodle, but Jerry preferred to remain standing. An hour later, the storm subsided.

Isaac suggested that before they leave the cave, Jerry should become friendly with Grouchy Grizzly too.

Usually, a host serves the guests, but if you're a guest in the cave of a grizzly, you serve the host. Jerry pulled a can of smoked sardines out of his backpack, which fortunately had an easy-open top. With trembling hands, he ripped the top off, and set the can in front of the grizzly's nose.

Have you ever seen an ecstatic bear? He devoured the contents of the can with one swift lick, rolled his eyes, and continued purring like a kitten. For dessert, the bear ate another cookie out of Isaac's hand.

Jerry had heard about difficult guests at the inn, who couldn't get along with anyone in the world except for Isaac. His amazement trebled at the sight of an anger-prone, vicious grizzly bear – that can't even exist on nonbelligerent terms with his own mate – eating out of Isaac's hands.

At this point, I'd like to keep the promise that I made earlier, and explain why animals – even predators – are afraid of a God-fearing person.

The scene of Isaac and the grizzly bear makes a similar point as the biblical account of Daniel in the lions' den. People on a high level of spirituality, who are careful about fulfilling The Almighty's commandments, are loved, respected, and feared by all of creation.

> "A person with a heart is respected by all of creation." – *Rebbe Nachman of Breslev*

The more you make spiritual growth, the less you have to fear from anything on earth. When God created Adam, the first human, he blessed him (see Genesis 1:28), saying, "You shall rule over the fish in the sea, the birds in the sky, and the animals on earth."

The above blessing works, to this very day. Humans, God's prize creation, are instilled with a tiny portion of Godliness, their divine soul. Humans have higher spiritual capability than the basic life spirit of a fish, bird, or animal.

The Zohar teaches that as long as the divine soul remains unblemished, it shines, and a divine aura reflects from that person's eyes and forehead. The birds, fish, and animals – insofar as they rarely violate Divine Will but do exactly as they were created to do – are capable of recognizing the aura of divine light reflected from a human's eyes and forehead. They think they're seeing a divine being – like an angel – and therefore pay instant homage.

The contrary holds true as well. Take for example a liar, a thief, a gossip, an adulterer, or an evil-tempered person. Such people lose their divine auras, because their negative deeds tarnish their souls, thereby suppressing the reflection of divine light. The human soul is comparable to a candle; bad deeds extinguish the candle, while good deeds enhance its light. When an animal looks at a human devoid of the divine aura, the animal sees a low-level creature worthy of disdain.

When Cain, the world's first murderer, killed his brother Abel, God punished Cain with exile. Cain was deathly afraid, and said (Genesis 4:14), "Anyone who finds me will kill me." Cain wasn't referring to other humans, for the only other humans alive at the time were Adam and Eve – Cain's parents – from whom he had nothing to fear. Cain was referring to the animals. As a murderer, he had lost his divine aura, and he was afraid that the animals would kill him. Therefore, God printed a letter of His ineffable holy name on Cain's forehead, which would serve as protection from the wild animals (ibid. 4:15).

Isaac patted the bear on the head and climbed to his feet. The sun pierced a hole in the storm clouds, and within a few short minutes, the entire sky was a stunning royal blue. The bear closed his eyes and fell asleep. Isaac and Jerry tiptoed out of the cave into the fresh mountain air and into the sunshine.

Jerry gave a sigh of relief that made his whole body shudder.

Isaac smiled his warm, understanding smile. He appeared as nonchalant as someone who just finished drinking coffee with the next-door neighbor.

Don't think the story of Isaac and the grizzly is so far-fetched. I'll give you another very practical example. The Zohar teaches that when one slanders a fellow human, one not only forfeits one's divine aura, but acquires a spiritual stench of impurity as well. That particular stench arouses the wrath of dogs, with their keen sense of smell. I once saw a dog in a crowded train station that attacked a certain person. Why was that particular person, out of a crowd of hundreds, the object of the dog's fury? Most certainly, that person slandered his fellow man earlier the same day.

Like all angry critters, Grouchy Grizzly is a hypocrite with a double standard. An intruder to his cave, unless accompanied by an Old Isaac, is in grave danger.

If you happen to be picking wild berries, and at that particular moment, Grouchy Grizzly decides that berries are chef's suggestion of the day, he'll attack.

Grizzlies, like angry humans, are so self-centered that they think the entire world belongs to them.

A fisherman once pulled a beautiful four-pound trout out of a mountain lake, within smelling range of a grizzly. The bear thundered down the mountain like a steaming locomotive. The startled fisherman abandoned both the fish and his gear, and raced up the nearest tree faster than the most agile of squirrels. The grizzly ate a lunch of "poached" trout, at the expense of the fisherman who returned from his outing looking ten years older.

Don't think that grizzlies are limited to the Rocky Mountains or to the city zoo. Unfortunately, you've probably encountered plenty of grizzly-like humans on the roads. Today, road rage is a dangerous national problem. Almost half of the fatal accidents that kill 41,000 Americans[17] annually in road accidents can be traced to road rage[18].

A closer look at the abovementioned statistics reveals a startling fact: Anger on the road kills more Americans than combat duty in Baghdad or Kabul! During the 13-month period of November, 2003 – November 2004, 789 Americans lost their lives in Iraq. Yet, an estimated 20,000 Americans lost their lives as a result of road rage.

Who would believe that a U.S. Marine in Iraq might actually be more secure than a metropolitan rush-hour motorist on the

---

[17] NHTSA statistics, 1996-2000

[18] Washington Beltway Study, "Analysis of the Capital Beltway Crash Problem", March 1996

way home from work? True, a lot more people can be found on the turnpikes than on combat duty in the Middle East, yet society has seemingly become desensitized by anger on the roads. Did you ever hear of a White-House demonstration protesting road rage? How many people realize that anger on the roads kills twenty times more Americans than the war in Iraq?!

Many of us have had unpleasant experiences with bullish, irate drivers who try to muscle on the parking place that we've just found, after arduous searching. Such people remind me of grizzly bears stealing a fisherman's trout. My advice is to avoid conflict and let the tyrant have the space. Proving that you're right isn't worth losing your peace of mind over an argument.

4 Important Tips for Avoiding Road Rage

1. Keep right except to pass. Don't speed up or slow down when other drivers want to pass. Let them by.

2. Be courteous. Let other drivers merge and exit. Use your turn signal BEFORE initiating turns or lane changes.

3. Don't take other drivers' mistakes personally.

4. If you make a mistake, say you are sorry. Use a conciliatory gesture such as a wave or peace sign to acknowledge your error.

If the lion is the king of animals, honeybees are the kings of insects. Honeybees are industrious, cooperative, highly respectful of each other, and contrary to popular misinformation, very peace loving. A honeybee won't sting unless its life seems threatened. The hive and combs are the home of nearly fifty thousand bees.

At this point, let's return to Lupine Valley.

All of the birds and the animals, as we mentioned previously, uphold the honor code of the Mount Patience vicinity, which includes preserving Lupine Valley and respecting the honeybees. Grouchy Grizzly blatantly ignores both clauses.

As you can see, there's no lack of food in the area. Grouchy Grizzly is certainly not underweight. Like other angry creatures, he is a slave to his urges, without considering the consequences. Around this time of the year, the aroma of fresh honey drives him crazy. He'll climb up a tree, topple a honeybee hive, and dive into the honey. That's the first shot of the annual bee-bear war.

The bees are furious – they've just now witnessed the destruction of their home. They attack Grouchy Grizzly from all sides. Most of the stings do nothing against the bear's thick hair and skin, but the stings on the tip of his round black nose incite his uncontrollable fury. The bees chase him and he chases the bees – from the forest, down the ridge, and all across Lupine Valley.

Down in the valley, the bees that have been busy collecting pollen from the flowers come to the aid of their cousins from the hive. Such a fiasco usually continues until the entire ten acres of lupines are trampled. Look at the toll of one selfish, angry bear that cares about nothing except for his own base appetites. The area of Grouchy Grizzly's anger looks identical to the path of an Oklahoma twister.

Do you think angry grizzly bears are dangerous? How many people do grizzlies kill every year? One? Maybe two? Certainly no more. Angry humans are much more harmful – to themselves as well as to others, as we are about to see.

The Toll of Human Anger

Grouchy Grizzly does damage to the valley, to the bees, to whoever gets on his nerves, and to himself. Let's examine the damages of human anger, which are far more serious. Here's why:

An animal has a basic vital life spirit, which is comparable to a conventional weapon. A human has a holy, divine soul, from a much higher spiritual level than the animal's basic life spirit, and comparable to a nuclear weapon. Just as a nuclear weapon is far more powerful than a conventional weapon, human anger is much more destructive than animal anger.

Grouchy Grizzly's bad temper causes anguish to everyone he encounters – flora, fauna, or humans. Angry people are the same – they bring pain and suffering to others, especially to those who come in close contact with them, such as family members and colleagues.

As we learned in the previous chapter, the main cause of anger is arrogance. Since arrogant people are self-centered, you won't be able to convince them to change their ways by showing them that they're damaging others – hurting people's feelings, causing them nervous and emotional disorders, and robbing them of their happiness. Angry people are blind to their fellow human.

The angry person, especially on the lower rungs of the spiritual ladder, usually justifies his or her own fiery behavior. Therefore, one of the only methods to encourage anger-prone individuals to mend their ways is to show them the damage they do to *themselves*. That's the focus of the next portion of this chapter.

The Twelve Self-destructive Damages of Anger

One: Damage to the soul

The Zohar teaches that anger is worse than almost all other transgressions. Why? When a person performs an evil deed, he tarnishes his divine soul – the worse the deed, the worse the blemish. Anger, on the other hand, causes the divine soul to leave the domains of the angry person altogether.

In metaphysics as in physics, there is no vacuum in the world. Therefore, when a person's divine soul picks up and leaves, an impure soul from the nether spiritual world – what Kabbalists call "the dark side" – enters the person. As such, the angry person severs himself from God and from holiness, and places himself under the regime of evil forces.

A person's good deeds, such as giving charity, assisting other people, and dealing honestly enhance and strengthen the divine soul. Yet, a moment of unleashed anger can destroy the spiritual gains of months and even years.

Imagine a glass blower that has patiently worked on an exquisite crystal chandelier for three years. If in one quick second, the chandelier is knocked off the worktable, it shatters on the floor in a million pieces. The divine soul resembles that fine crystal chandelier; a moment of anger is liable to destroy it, too.

A dead body is ritually impure. An angry person is spiritually similar to a dead body, since both are devoid of their divine souls. Therefore, atoning for anger is more difficult than atoning for other serious misdeeds.

The blemish of an average misdeed is similar to a dent in a new car – a trip to the body shop and a few hundred dollars can have the car looking like new. Prayer, self-evaluation, and a resolution to try harder are usually enough to recompense for an average blemish to the soul. Anger, on the other hand, resembles a car with a blown engine, that either needs a complete overhaul or a new engine altogether.

Correcting the damages of anger is tantamount to revitalizing a dead person. In order to regain the divine soul, a person must make a major spiritual overhaul.

If you are prone to anger, don't lose heart: Hand in hand, we'll be making that spiritual overhaul in the coming chapters, during the continuation of our journey.

Two: Damage to one's physical appearance

A person's mood directly affects his or her appearance. A face shines with happiness, or becomes dull and lifeless with sadness. The eyes are the windows of the soul; no mascara or eye shadow can replace the beauty reflected by tranquil eyes and a pure, serene soul. Conversely, no eye makeup in the world can compensate for the repulsive look of angry eyes and an impure soul. Simply speaking, tranquility makes you beautiful and anger does the opposite. Nothing in the world is so magically magnetic like a tranquil smile.

People spend phenomenal sums on new clothes, coiffure, and cosmetics. Yet, with one small tantrum, their efforts are wasted.

Imagine a bridegroom spending a hundred dollars for an exclusive haircut, a thousand dollars on a hand-tailored three-piece suit, three hundred dollars on a chic pair of Italian shoes, eighty dollars for a massage and spa, and four hundred dollars for a rented limousine and uniformed driver. He arrives at the grand ballroom of the local Hilton – the site of his wedding – and loses his temper at one of the waiters. Such a groom looks exactly like Grouchy Grizzly! He could have saved the extravagant expense of grooming himself, for a face contorted with anger is just as repugnant as a bear's countenance.

Even so, any normal bride would gladly prefer a groom in a bear costume to a groom with anger in his eyes.

I once had the unfortunate opportunity of seeing a bride lose her temper moments before the wedding ceremony. For some inexplicable reason, she became furious at her sister. Hot tears of wrath began slithering down her cheeks, leaving black, telltale rivulets of mascara smears all over her face. The groom almost had heart seizure – he thought that Dracula's daughter was coming down the aisle in his direction.

Nothing improves a person's appearance like a tranquil soul, and nothing destroys a person's appearance like anger and inner turbulence. People spend fortunes on plastic surgery in order to improve their appearance; a bit of genuine tranquility can make a person more attractive than any plastic surgery can. Think of the pain and money saved in the process!

Three: Angry people invoke severe judgment against themselves

The Talmud teaches that God operates the world according to the "ATFAT" Principle (abbreviation for "a turn for a turn", see chapter six). The Almighty judges a person exactly the way that person judges others. To elaborate, when a person is lenient and patient with his fellow man, God is lenient and patient with that person. Conversely, when a person is strict and exacting with others, God is strict and exacting with that person.

Very often, God shows us a particular situation and asks for our opinion. For example, suppose that we see a flaw or unfavorable behavior in our fellow man, and we comment, such as, "Look at that person's gross ingratitude; he deserves to be punished." Rebbe Nachman of Breslev teaches that such situations are very risky, since The Almighty usually shows us misdeeds that we ourselves are guilty of. The Heavenly Court sentences us identically like we sentence others.

Since angry people call for severe retribution against those who anger them, they invoke the same severe judgments on themselves; that's the ATFAT Principle in a nutshell.

Four: Anger shortens a person's health and life span.

Your personal physician will be happy to enumerate the long list of anger-associated diseases and ailments. The following are a partial list: Heart disease, hypertension, high blood pressure, ulcers, indigestion, and strokes. Anger easily triggers asthma, and severely damages the body's immune defenses.

If your current physical condition will help you reach the age of seventy, get rid of your anger and you'll live 'til ninety. Unfortunately, the converse is also true – anger shortens a person's life span.

Five: Anger damages a person's income.

Two Russian soldiers were once on a training maneuver in the Siberian forest, in the middle of the winter at midnight. The light of the full moon reflected on the snow, so the woods were well illuminated.

All of a sudden, they heard a thud. A distressed wild turkey with a broken wing had fallen from the treetops. Within seconds, two hungry wolves arrived on the scene. One grabbed the turkey by the wing, and the other sunk its teeth in the turkey's thigh. The two wolves began a tug of war. When neither wolf succeeded to free the turkey from the other's grasp, they attacked each other. Viciously and mercilessly, they literally tore each other apart, until one wolf dropped dead on the snow. The victor limped away, dragging the turkey between his teeth and leaving a trail of blood on the snow. A few minutes later, he keeled over and died too.

The gruesome but profound incident conveys a powerful message: The turkey weighed more than twelve pounds; it would have been a more-than-adequate dinner for both wolves. Their greed led them to anger, and their anger led them to violence. As a result, three corpses were left in the snow – the turkey and the two wolves.

The Talmud teaches a consequent rule of thumb from situations like the wolf fight: Wherever you have peace, you have abundance; with no peace, starvation is prevalent.

Often, husbands and wives fume at each other about financial difficulties just like the two wolves over the dead turkey. Such anger is detrimental to their cause, both from a rational and a spiritual standpoint, as follows:

Rational standpoint: When a wife is continuously angry, she seriously weakens her husband, and vice versa. A wife's wrath gnaws at a husband's confidence and self-image, two of his major emotional tools for coping with the commercial and professional world. The more an angry wife bombards her husband, the worse his vocational performance. Consequently, the negative effects of anger manifest themselves in the family paycheck.

When a wife doesn't have enough money to make ends meet, the worst thing she can do is to yell at her husband, especially if he's industrious and holding a steady job. An intelligent wife should encourage her husband and help him believe in himself. A husband with a supportive wife will normally make every effort possible to fulfill all of her needs.

Rebbe Nachman of Breslev teaches another rule of thumb – an anger-free home is a debt-free home.

On the other hand, when a husband is stingy with a wife, he shows her that she's not highest-level priority in his life. When he denies her a new dress for a holiday occasion, on the claim that he can't afford it, yet turns around and buys himself a box seat to the World Series or to the NBA playoffs, he's inciting a major domestic riot. Such actions are an overt declaration that the wife takes back seat to the Yankees or the Knicks; no wife can tolerate the insult of being a second-class citizen in her own home.

A double-standard husband should take my advice and rent a flak jacket and a multi-layered combat helmet from the local Civil Defense headquarters, because shrapnel's going to fly in his house. Stingy husbands soon discover that they don't have enough money for themselves, either. The anger they cause wreaks financial havoc in the home.

Spiritual Standpoint: The Kabbalists teach that the blessings of abundance – income and financial wealth – flow from the upper spiritual worlds to our tangible material world by way of a series of spiritual pipes. One of the predominant "pipes" is the pipe of peace in the home. When anger prevails in a home, the peace pipe becomes clogged or bent, and thereby impairs the flow of abundance. Anger is therefore closely associated with financial loss.

Six: Anger causes sadness.

True happiness goes together with holiness. Anger comes from the dark side, the opposite of holiness. Just as the dark side is the opposite of holiness, sadness is the opposite of happiness. Therefore, whenever anger sways a person to the dark side, sadness sets in as well. Anger and sadness go hand in hand. You can't be simultaneously happy and angry.

Happiness is the best spiritual gauge in the world. The happier a person is, the closer he is to God. Don't confuse the happiness of inner peace and a tranquil soul with short-term thrills from outside stimuli.

People who look for outside happiness by way of various modes of entertainment always discover that when the vacation, the meal at the restaurant, the dance, the film, or the ballgame is over, they return to the humdrum of a gray existence. True happiness comes only from within, in an anger-free environment.

Seven: Anger causes fear.

As we learned in chapter two, lack of spiritual awareness is one of the two main causes of anger. Spiritual awareness and faith go hand-in-hand. A person with strong faith in God fears nothing, since he believes firmly that nothing can happen to him without God's will and consent. My esteemed and beloved teacher Rabbi Shalom Arush often says that fear of God is like one-stop shopping – you don't have to fear anything else: "He who fears One fears no one!"

The contrary is also true. A person with no faith fears everything. Anger and lack of faith go hand in hand. Since angry people lack faith, they usually suffer from a long list of phobias.

Eight: Anger induces stupidity and bad judgment.

Wisdom and good judgment are from the holy side of spirituality. Anger stems from the impure, evil side of the spiritual coin. As in flipping a coin, either "heads" are up, or "tails" are up; both sides of a coin can't be face-up at the same time. Therefore, an angry person waves goodbye to wisdom and to good judgment, and loses much – if not all – powers of reasoning. (See also damage no. 11, below).

When anger overrides reason and ends up dictating national policies, governments waste thousands of lives and billions of dollars on senseless and needless wars.

Nine: Society dislikes angry people.

Do you enjoy the company of angry people? Of course, you don't; no one else does, either. If a person isn't winning popularity contests, he should check one of two things: His temper control or his deodorant, because one of them isn't functioning properly.

Ten: Anger clouds truth.

We've already learned that nothing chases the divine soul away like anger does.

The more a person succumbs to anger, the more his brain loses control over the body. Anger vanquishes the brain like a marauding aggressor. The brain, with the help and guidance of the divine soul, has the ability to discern truth. If the divine soul leaves a person, that person is rendered incapable of discerning truth. In the absence of the divine soul, a person's evil inclination – the coalition of bodily appetites and base urges – reigns exclusively. Such a person makes decisions according to his or her own base desires, and not according to truth.

Simply speaking, a person whose divine soul reigns over the body first seeks truth, and then forms opinions accordingly. On the other hand, when the evil inclination prevails, the bodily appetites motivate a person. Such motivation leads to a fabricated truth, which in turn dictates that person's decision-making process.

Let's illustrate the above principle: Suppose that an anger-prone person has lost his divine soul, and is therefore motivated exclusively by his bodily appetites and his base inclinations. He sees a beautiful married woman. In the absence of truth, he rationalizes numerous reasons why he is entitled to that woman. His thought process is the opposite of truth – first he decides what his appetites are, and then he fabricates a "truth" that allows him to pursue the satiation of his appetites.

A person with "soul control" is the exact opposite: He also sees a beautiful married woman, but immediately tells himself that coveting another man's wife and adultery are two serious breaches of the Ten Commandments, the universal truth accepted by the entire monotheistic world. If that person's brain were a keyboard, his soul would press the "delete" button on any thought of another man's wife. Such an individual first asks what The Ten Commandments say, and then forms an opinion or a mode of action, thereby living his life according to the parameters of truth, and not according to the dictates of his appetites and base urges

Angry people are especially not interested in hearing anything that fails to justify their anger. Anger goes together with spiritual impurity, the opposite of holiness. Truth and holiness are closely connected. Consequently, angry people are far from the truth.

Eleven: Anger causes amnesia.

The physiological and neurological influences of anger are far-reaching. Have you ever noticed how angry people clench their fists and grit their teeth? Such phenomena are the result of nervous reactions, which lead to muscle contractions.

Anger not only causes contraction of muscles, it also causes contraction of blood vessels, which directly bring about a sharp rise in blood pressure and a reduction of oxygen to the brain. Lack of oxygen severely diminishes the brain's ability to function properly.

An angry person's heart has to work twice as a hard as a tranquil person's heart in order to pump the same amount of blood to the body. Anger causes excessive wear and tear on the entire cardiovascular system. That's another reason why angry people are candidates for an early death.

Angry people suffer from a decreased flow of blood to the brain. In extreme cases, anger is liable to trigger a stroke. In mild cases, a person temporarily loses a substantial portion of his thought capacity, and becomes forgetful. As such, anger is a direct cause of amnesia.

Twelve: Anger locks the door to spiritual gain.

The divine human soul is our spiritual engine. Anger, as we learned previously, chases away the divine soul. Expecting to make spiritual gain without a divine soul is like trying to drive a car with no engine – you go nowhere.

You might ask, "What's the big deal if I forfeit spiritual gain? So what if I'm not the generation's symbol of righteousness or a spiritual guru?" The problem is twofold: First, in spirituality, there's no such thing as standing in one place. Either a person makes spiritual gain, or else falls deeper into the pit of slavery to base and bodily appetites. Second, is it prudent to spend an entire life chasing after the body's material desires, especially when the body is so short-lived, while ignoring the needs of the divine soul, especially when the divine soul is eternal? The answer is obvious to any objective thinker.

Life's biggest tragedy is the waste of valuable days chasing insignificant follies, while ignoring the eternal benefits of cultivating the divine soul.

Now that we've diagnosed our temper tendencies, and have heightened our awareness of anger's pitfalls, we're now prepared to grab our anger by the horns and to deal with it. The coming chapters will give us the spiritual tools to eliminate anger from our lives.

4

Spiritual Map Reading

We now begin the second segment of our trail to tranquility. This chapter introduces us to spiritual awareness (SA). The more we achieve SA, the happier we are.

Spiritual awareness is the key to tranquility. Once we become spiritually aware, we easily overcome anger, stress, anxiety, and depression. That may sound like a bombastic claim, but it's really very simple: Emotional disorders stem from misuse of the soul. Spiritual awareness (SA) is the mechanism that properly activates the divine soul. As soon as we begin to use our soul properly, emotional difficulties become a thing of the past.

Our divine soul, centered in the brain and with a relay station in the right side of the heart, gives us a fortified mental ability that far surpasses our basic biological brains. Without SA, we don't scratch the surface of our personal potential.

> There is no such entity as wisdom devoid of spiritual awareness. People think that they can be nuclear physicists or computer engineers without spiritual awareness. They're correct. A person in high tech is no more than a technician, several rungs more sophisticated than a plumber or shoemaker. You don't need wisdom to unclog a drain *or* to send a satellite into outer space. You *do* need wisdom to differentiate between good and evil.
> – *Rabbi Naftali Moskowitz, the Melitzer Rebbe*

Life without SA is like trying to fly a jet airplane with diesel fuel. Maybe the sputtering jet will be able to taxi down the runway for a few hundred yards, but it will never get off the ground. Even worse, unrefined fuel wrecks the jet's engine. By the same token, without SA, a human is emotionally and spiritually grounded. The lack of SA does a lot more damage to a person's life than diesel fuel does to a jet engine.

If your brain is analogous to a jet engine, then SA is similar to highest-octane refined jet fuel. With SA, you'll climb to heights you never before imagined.

Rebbe Nathan of Breslev says that the worst form of punishment after death is people's shame in discovering that they had the potential for fulfilling their wildest dreams, but wasted their time and energy on basic bodily urges. This chapter will help you prevent such a nightmare.

If you're an unpolished gem, SA will make you glitter. Even if you think you're a flawless one-carat diamond, SA will show you that you're actually a rare three-carat diamond, suitable for a king's crown. The more you acquire spiritual awareness, the more you'll expand your spiritual and intellectual horizons. Since spirituality is limitless, spiritual awareness offers you limitless personal potential and happiness.

This chapter answers four basic questions about spiritual awareness:

1. What is spiritual awareness?

2. Why does a person need spiritual awareness?

3. How do I attain spiritual awareness?

4. How do I know if I have spiritual awareness?

Question one: What is spiritual awareness?

Kabbalists cite two types of human intellectual power – **sensual awareness** and **spiritual awareness**.

Sensual awareness is the knowledge and intellectual power derived from activating the five senses – smell, sight, hearing, speech, and touch. Sensual awareness governs thought processes by virtue of experience, extrapolation, and appetite. Here's how:

- Experience – we refrain from touching fire because we know from experience (either our own or other people's) that it burns. Our vocabulary, as well as most of our basic functional knowledge, stems from the experience category of sensual awareness.

- Extrapolation – we believe that the nation of China exists even though we never visited there. Why? We know that the map is honest and accurate about the USA and Canada. We therefore have no reason to believe that the map would lie about China. Also, we've seen people with Oriental appearance who claim that they come from an Asian country named China. Maybe we've also seen magazine articles, photos, or films of China. Our senses gather all their stored information and our sensual brain extrapolates that there is a country in Asia by the name of China.

- Appetite – this is the strongest area of sensual awareness, and often governs decision-making and thought processes against all logic. For example, a bank robber knows that he stands a 90% chance of going to jail, but his lust for money overrides all other sensual intelligence. The same goes for a diabetic who eats sugar, an alcoholic, or a person who covets someone else's spouse.

A person whose brain functions exclusively on the level of sensual awareness can become an engineer, a doctor, or a nuclear physicist, but is still unable to feel the presence of a higher supernatural power. Such a person can also become a philosopher or a theologist, but will remain far from the truth since his or her sensual appetites continue to dictate thought processes.

Since a baby's conditioning results exclusively from sensual awareness, sensual awareness *(actually the regime of the body)* dominates a person's brain, consequently suppressing spiritual awareness *(the reign of the soul)*. As such, many people remain spiritually undeveloped their entire lives.

Since sensual awareness and body are both finite, the body's rule over the soul is tantamount to confinement in a prison. Your soul – which is both eternal and limitless – can't stand confinement. Therefore, spiritual neglect is *the* root of untapped

> Girls receive their first taste of spiritual awareness at age 12, and boys at age 13, since girls mature emotionally faster than boys do. Puberty gives a massive reinforcement to sensual awareness, vanquishing the first sparks of spiritual awareness. Unless a person makes a concerted effort, or comes from a home with high spiritual motivation (such as the Chassidic lifestyle), genuine spiritual awareness during the teen years is rare. Therefore, sensual awareness dominates most people's lives exclusively until they're well in their twenties. As such, the decades-old exclusive regime of the senses is most difficult to overcome.

and misused potential, unhappiness, and emotional disorders.

Spiritual awareness is the knowledge and intellectual power derived from activating the divine soul. Since the divine soul within each human is both eternal and totally spiritual, SA gives us the power to transcend all physical limitations, including time and space. SA widens our intellectual horizons, grants us extrasensory perception, and enables the mind to rule over the body.

The spiritually aware recognize that a supernatural power – God, The Creator, The Almighty, The Holy One, or however you prefer to call Him – is the ongoing creator and sustainer of the entire universe. Moreover, the spiritually aware are capable of distinguishing God's presence within themselves and within every other creation – mineral, plant, animal, and man. Spiritual awareness enhances one's comprehension of oneself and of the environment, and thereby broadens intellectual horizons and expands personal potential.

The dynamics of SA: The more a person activates the soul, the more he or she develops spiritual awareness. The more one attains spiritual awareness, the more one's divine soul develops and thrives. The more a soul thrives, the more intimate a person's relationship with God. The closer one gets to God, the more one achieves inner peace and overcomes emotional ailments.

Since your potential for spiritual self-development is limitless, your potential for inner peace also knows no bounds.

Let's elaborate on the above definition, and examine six important points that a person needs to understand in order to acquire SA:

1. Understanding that the creation of the universe and all of its inhabitants, from the great galaxies to the one-celled ameba, wasn't a random, inexplicable event. The Almighty created the world for a purpose, and continues to sustain all that He created.

2. Understanding that each individual creation has a unique purpose.

3. Understanding that you have a soul within you, a divine spark of The Almighty, which elevates you above all the other creations.

4. Understanding that God controls the universe and all its inhabitants, but grants you the freedom to do good or evil.

5. Understanding that God talks to you personally by way of the stimuli in your environment and the events of your life.

6. Understanding that you have a very special mission in this world.

Ponder each of the above six points for a few moments. If you look close enough, you'll understand a lot more about your own particular task on this earth. Let's now examine the above points in detail:

Point one: Understanding that the creation of the universe and all of its inhabitants, from the great galaxies to the one-celled ameba, was not a random, inexplicable event. The Almighty created the world for a purpose, and continues to sustain all that he created.

The Almighty transcends time and space. He is both infinite and eternal. He has no physical attributes, nor can a human mind grasp His magnitude in the slightest. The Almighty's presence is everywhere, and his love and personal attention for each of His creations are unfathomable.

Over 3,750 years ago, lived a man by the name of Abraham, the first Hebrew and the father of monotheism. As a young child blessed with cogent powers of observation, he scoffed at the folly of idol worship, and began to seek the real master of the universe. At first, Abraham thought that the sun ruled the world. Then, darkness defeated the sun. Maybe the moon rules the world, he thought, and then the sun returned to the eastern horizon and chased away the moon. Later, clouds appeared in the sky and defeated the sun. Then came the wind and blew away the clouds. Abraham looked up to the heavens in confusion, and asked, "Who is the great power that created everything, and nothing rules over Him?" The Almighty answered, by instilling the capability in Abraham's heart and mind to know that God is The Creator of the world.

One may ask, why was the account of young Abraham recognizing the supremacy of The One God recorded only in the Midrash – the compilation of Jewish oral tradition – and not in the Bible? The answer is simple: The Bible doesn't consider such a phenomenon remarkable, because *every* human being has the innate capability of recognizing God. If a person genuinely seeks spiritual awareness, God will be more than happy to assist.

Spiritual awareness directly contributes to happiness. Let's use the human heart to illustrate this point. A person devoid of SA thinks that the heart functions automatically, according to the course of nature. Most people don't appreciate their own hearts. If they realized the intricacy of the heart, they'd jump for joy every time the heart beats, they'd feel happy, and certainly not angry or depressed. Therefore, by taking their hearts for granted, they miss an opportunity to appreciate their good fortune. Lack of appreciation is rooted in spiritual ignorance.

On the other hand, those with SA make the following calculation: The average heart beats 70 times per minute, or 4200 beats per hour. Multiplied by 24 hours, the heart beats approximately 100,000 times a day. Multiplied by 365, the heart beats over 36 million times a year. By the time you reach the age of thirty, your heart has expanded, contracted, and pumped blood through your body over a billion times!

People with fine-tuned SA know that The Almighty is personally responsible for each and every heartbeat. They have 100,000 reasons per day – by pondering the healthy functioning of their hearts alone – to be happy and to express their gratitude. Such people don't know the meaning of anger and depression, and are usually level sevens and higher on the tranquility continuum *(see chapter one).*

Kabbalists refer to two ways that The Creator runs the earth – general supervision and personal supervision. General supervision is the overall global plan, whereas personal supervision controls the tiniest detail of each creation's sustenance on a mind-boggling moment-to-moment level. The more one develops SA, the more one senses divine intervention. The more one senses divine intervention, the more one feels the proximity of God. Nothing in the world grants a person such a wonderful sense of happiness, inner peace, and security as the feeling that God is close by.

Point two: Understanding that each individual creation has a unique purpose.

Rabbi Israel Baal Shem Tov – the early 18th Century Ukrainian Jewish sage, miracle worker, and founder of the Chassidic movement – once explained the above point to a group of disciples who seemed skeptic about it. He took them to the forest, and asked them to observe a simple creation, which they consider useless. They chose to observe a falling oak leaf. It was an unusually warm Ukrainian October morning, and a gentle breeze ushered the leaf out of the forest to a sunny, green meadow. The leaf came to rest on top of a distressed worm that was caught in the hot sun.

The shade from the leaf saved the worm's life. The Baal Shem Tov's disciples were amazed by The Almighty's personal care of a worm, and by the importance of a seemingly insignificant dry leaf.

Over 2300 years ago, the Baal Shem Tov's ancestor King David asked The Almighty why the world needs spiders. The Almighty answered, "One day, you'll find out", and closed the subject.

Alone in the desert, exhausted, his throat parched and limbs in agony, King David fled from his enemies[19]. The enemies pursued him mercilessly, and were about to seize him.

King David had no choice – his last place of refuge was a cave. He crawled inside, and cried out to God from the depths of his soul. He could hear his enemies approaching on horseback.

A large spider began to weave its web on the opening of the cave. After a few short minutes, the entrance to the cave was completely covered by the spider web. The pursuers reached the cave. "He can't be inside there", they said, "Look at that spider web!" The spider saved King David's life, and King David no longer questioned the necessity of each and every creation.

* * *

A mosquito once saved the life of an Israeli infantry platoon during the 1982 confrontation between Israel and the PLO, Lebanon, and Syria[20]. During the first five days of the war, the Israeli spearhead troops fought day and night and barely slept. A

---

[19] See Samuel I, chapters 20 - 26.

[20] The author witnessed this incident first-hand.

ceasefire was declared on the morning of the sixth day of the war. The platoon camped in the shade of an olive orchard, and after the sergeant major in command assigned sentries to four different watch posts, the rest of the soldiers collapsed in utter fatigue. The exhausted sentries struggled to keep their eyes open, but to no avail; they too fell into a deep sleep.

A relentless mosquito buzzed in the ear of one of the sentries, and then bit him on the neck. Reinforcement mosquitoes joined the campaign, with further buzzing and biting. The sentry awoke from his irritated slumber, and saw a rustle in the distance, about 300 yards away. Instantaneously, he opened full fire with his Browning .03 machine gun, exhausting close to 300 shells within twenty seconds. The entire platoon jumped to its feet, and repelled an ambush of Syrian El-Saika terrorists equipped with Russian RPG shoulder missiles that planned to exploit the ceasefire. A mosquito foiled their scheme.

If every mineral, vegetable, and animal is vital to the world, how vital is each human being![21] That brings us to point number three.

Point three: Understanding that you have a soul within you, a divine spark of The Almighty, which elevates you above all the other creations.

Man is above the animal. The soul within him is like its Father in Heaven[22] - **spiritual**, with no physical attributes, and **eternal**.

Here's a simple test to prove what we're talking about: Close your eyes, and think about your childhood in your parents' house. Now travel to a far away site. Think of summer. Now, think of a

---

[21] See point five for more about the purpose of humans in this world.

[22] The Kabbala teaches that the soul is a tiny spark of The Almighty, so holy and sublime that humans are incapable of understanding its essence. Since our souls are part of The Holy One, we often refer to him as "Father in Heaven".

cold and snowy winter. Come back to the present, and open your eyes. Within a few seconds, you've traveled several thousand miles and transcended several decades. That's the power of the divine soul within you.

Rebbe Nachman of Breslev says, "A person is where his thoughts are." As such, it's no problem for a human to jump from one end of the world to another. The great scholars of Torah purified their minds and elevated themselves to an extent that their souls had complete control over their bodies. Since their divine souls overruled their bodies, their minds could function beyond the limits of time and space.

During the mid 1700's, Rabbi Israel Baal Shem Tov lived in the Ukraine, and his contemporary, Rabbi Chaim Ben-Attar lived in Morocco and moved to Israel before his death. As the respective giants of their generation, they had tremendous spiritual contact with one another even though they never met one another in person.

The Baal Shem Tov once sat at his Sabbath afternoon meal with his disciples, when he suddenly remarked, "The light of the west has been extinguished", cryptically referring to Rabbi Ben-Attar. Shortly thereafter, news of Rabbi Ben-Attar's death reached the Ukraine. He passed away on a Saturday afternoon, exactly at the time of the Baal Shem Tov's meal. The Baal Shem Tov's ultra-refined soul could actually feel Rabbi Chaim Ben-Attar's soul leaving this world, despite the tremendous physical distance that separates the Ukraine from the Land of Israel.

Our bodies are composed of matter, like the animals. Our souls are completely spiritual, like the angels. The more our bodies control our souls, the more we resemble an animal. The more our souls control our bodies, the more we resemble an angel.

Man is the only creation in the universe that is both spiritual and material. Man has the potential of reaching great spiritual heights, but if he fails to activate his soul, his body seizes control with its animal appetites. Under the body's regime, man becomes worse than an animal. On the other hand, if one's divine soul prevails over his flesh-and-blood body, one can rise above the level of an angel. When our souls reign over our bodies, we climb to a spiritual altitude where the turbulence of anger ceases to affect us in a negative fashion, like the example of the airplane ascending from the storm clouds to the clear blue sky.

Point four: Understanding that God controls the universe and all its inhabitants, but grants you the freedom to do good or evil.

The Almighty runs the universe on a precision-perfect balance of power between good and evil. Therefore, a person can't use the excuse that he or she is forced to do good or evil. Without the balance of power, there can be no reward or punishment in the world to come, and a person could plead "not guilty" to the worst of criminal acts.

The Bible (Exodus 9:12) says, "And God hardened Pharaoh's heart". Apparently, this is a direct contradiction to the notion of man's free will to do good or evil. Not so. Several times before The Almighty hardened Pharaoh's heart, the Bible states that Pharaoh hardened his own heart, and refused to release the children of Israel who were slaves in Egypt for a bitter two-hundred-ten years. Once Pharaoh refused to heed Moses' plea in the name of God, God decided to utilize Pharaoh's free choice of evil. Pharaoh's punishment included ten miraculous plagues and a host of miracles at the splitting of the Red Sea, which led to worldwide sanctification of God's name.

Each one of us has the liberty to be a Moses or a Pharaoh. Our souls have greater power than a nuclear reactor, and a nuclear reactor can either blow up the world or light up the world. A cancer-research physician takes a scalpel in hand to cure mankind, but a terrorist hijacker uses the same sized knife to hijack a plane and to kill people.

Once we understand the power of free choice that God vests in us, we are prepared to harness our emotions, our talents, our energies, and our desires in order to perfect and refine ourselves to the point where anger and negative emotions become a distant memory. We don't need to change others so that we'll attain inner peace; we only need to exercise our own free will to change ourselves.

Point five: Understanding that God talks to you personally by way of the stimuli in your environment and the events of your life.

The above point, once internalized, is the epitome of spiritual awareness. Once you become aware that God is constantly speaking to you, your entire outlook on life changes for the better. Here's an example:

Case study: "Richard Green" (*imaginary name*) came to me with a marital difficulty. After an initial three years of peaceful married life, his wife Janet – normally kind, considerate, and sweet-natured - began to be quite belligerent. For the last several months, their marriage was on a downhill slide.

I asked Richard a lengthy series of questions, trying to establish the change in his life that triggered negative reactions from his wife. Within an hour, we struck pay dirt.

Four months prior, Richard left his job as the head mechanic of an automobile dealership to open up a garage in partnership with a friend. Richard handled the auto mechanics side of the business, while his partner handled the administrative end. From the start, Richard's partner was padding customers' bills, charging them for parts and services that their cars never received.

Richard was a full accomplice to his partner's misdealing. He knew what his partner was doing; yet, he made no effort to protest. As such, he was bringing home dishonest dollars. The dishonest dollars were an obvious blemish to Richard's soul.

Richard recalled that Janet began being argumentative about the same time that he opened the new business, despite the fact that he was making more money without working longer hours.

God was obviously talking to Richard by way of Janet; her displeasure with her husband was none other than God's displeasure with him. I suggested that he sell his share of the business, or find a decent person to buy out his partner.

Within five weeks, Richard sold his half of the garage and returned to his old job. Janet was still irritable. Richard returned to me complaining bitterly, "Hey, Rabbi – you didn't deliver the goods!"

Richard had sold his half of the business for an $8,000 profit after expenses. I told him that part of the profit was dishonest cash. After he had admitted that his partner usually padded bills by 25%, I suggested that he give $2000, or 25% of his profit, to a crippled children's fund. He agreed. Smiles returned to Janet's face and peace returned to the Green household almost immediately.

Moral of the Green case study: If Richard would have realized from the outset that his wife's belligerence was none other than a repeated message from God, he'd have taken a spiritual inventory of himself. SA counseling showed him that God was communicating with him via Janet, to prevent the terrible spiritual damage that he was doing to his soul. Once Richard corrected his actions, his marital problems disappeared.

SA helps one realize that life's problems and difficulties are actually divine messages. Equipped with such cognizance, a person traverses life with reduced anger and frustration, and enhanced inner peace.

> If a man so deserves, his wife is his ally; if he does not deserve, she is his enemy. – *The Babylonian Talmud*

Point six: Understanding your own special mission in this world.

Imagine a uniformed soldier in the middle of Baghdad. Now, imagine that the soldier doesn't know which side he's fighting for, the USA or Iraq. You ask the soldier what his mission is, and he shrugs his shoulders and says, "I don't know." Sounds ridiculous, doesn't it?

Without SA, a person has no way of knowing what his or her mission in life is.

Do you understand what your own special mission in life is? If not, don't be ashamed; most people have no idea what they're doing in this world. When a person doesn't know what his mission is, he or she becomes angry, frustrated, and constantly restless.

Ask yourself an important basic question: "If I have a divine soul within me, that's a tiny spark of God and both spiritual and eternal, why does God take me away from the bliss of the spiritual realm to send me here, to this lowly physical world?" The answer to this question is vital to spiritual awareness.

Doing good deeds. First, God created the world in order to bestow His loving kindness on man. God gives man the opportunity to do good deeds. Each of us has our own individual mission of good to accomplish, based on the abilities and aptitudes that The Creator instilled in each of us. Once a person pursues his or her mission of good, he or she is ultimately rewarded with a higher, more sublime spiritual status of eternal bliss in the world to come.

Getting to know God. Second, God put man on this lowly physical earth so that man would have to overcome a series of obstacles to acquire faith and spiritual awareness, or simply speaking, to get to know God. By defeating the material obstacles that separate a person from God, such as bodily urges and evil inclinations, man wins a heroic spiritual victory. Again, God lavishes indescribable bliss and rewards on such a soul in the world to come.

You can't accomplish the above two tasks in the spiritual world. The disadvantage of the spiritual world is that personal advancement is most difficult. Because of the suffering, the trials, and the tribulations of the material world, one earns mind-boggling dividends for overcoming material appetites to achieve even the smallest spiritual gain.

Since doing good deeds and getting to know God within modern society's hostile agnostic atmosphere are two difficult tasks, the rewards are tremendous. Spirituality, like gymnastics, is rated according to level of difficulty.

You can perform your two-fold mission of doing good deeds and getting to know God in any career context. Once you begin to fulfill your spiritual mission, you'll be rewarded with enhanced success in all your endeavors.

Question two: Why does a person need spiritual awareness?

Rebbe Nachman of Breslev teaches that anger stems from the lack of spiritual awareness. The more we attain spiritual awareness, the more we neutralize anger. As such, spiritual awareness is the map that directs us up the trail to tranquility.

Life is like climbing a mountain; we begin at the bottom, and gradually work our way up in the direction of the "peak", our goals and aspirations. Negative emotions are the pitfalls along the way, which hinder our progress. The various trails up different parts of the mountain resemble life's options – the daily choices a person must make that influence his or her entire future.

A hiker without a map, or with a map written in a foreign language that he or she doesn't understand, can't possibly reach a destination. By the same token, a person devoid of spiritual awareness lacks direction, suffers needlessly, and never knows which path to take in life. When you're lost, you can't possibly accomplish your goals.

Living in this world without spiritual awareness is like riding a trail bike down a narrow wooded trail on a pitch-black night without knowing that the bike has a headlight. Imagine crashing into a tree, wrecking the bike, incurring a serious injury, and then discovering the headlight switch. What a waste! If the biker would have known that the bike had a headlight – and how to turn it on – he or she could have safely navigated their way through the woods.

The material world is analogous to a dark forest. The course of our lives is a like narrow trail. The bike is symbolic of our body, and the headlight is our soul. The headlight switch is spiritual awareness, which activates the soul. As in the example of the trail bike on a dark night in the forest, if we attempt to get through life without the benefit of spiritual awareness and the divine power of our souls, we are bound to do severe damage to ourselves. Therefore, the key to living a physically and mentally healthful life, and to achieving inner peace, is spiritual awareness.

The more a person lacks spiritual awareness, the more he or she suffers in this world. Again, life devoid of spiritual awareness is like a tourist who can't read a map – a lost soul in every sense of the word. It's truly frightening to think about the number of people who lack direction in life, traveling down random roads and making major decisions in life by chance or instinct, because they've never acquired the skill of spiritual map reading.

When an airplane flies through thick storm clouds, it feels constant turbulence. Flying is both difficult and dangerous, and the passengers – belted in their seats, jolted to and fro, and nauseated from the falling sensation in their stomach – have difficulty performing the simplest of tasks. Suddenly, the plane rises above the clouds to the clear blue sky and the shining sun. The passengers gaze out of the window, and the gray mattress of cloudy turbulence is beneath them. The plane levels off at cruising speed and altitude, and the passengers feel calm and steady like they're sitting in their living room. They now reassume their normal mode of functioning.

Spiritual awareness takes a person above the cloudy turbulence of basic survival in a non-congenial world. Without spiritual awareness, hardship is unbearable. Negative emotions, such as anger, hate, and depression, stem from a lack of spiritual awareness. Let's see why:

Imagine that an Olympic boxing coach grabs a strong young man off the street and throws him in a boxing ring. The coach starts sparring with him, jabs him in the ribs, then in the face. The young man doesn't know what he's doing in the ring or why he's getting punched, and his anger intensifies with every blow.

If the young man were a member of the Olympic boxing team, and knew that the coach was giving him personal attention in preparation for the upcoming Olympics, he would appreciate every minute in the practice ring. He'd also accept each of the coach's jabs with love and understanding.

The identical punch in the face causes anger and hatred to a young man off the street who lacks understanding, but is received with appreciation and understanding by a team member. Why? The team member understands that getting punched is part of the path to becoming an Olympic champion. The goal is well worth the price.

Like the example of the boxer in training, once we attain spiritual awareness, we'll begin to regard our difficulties in life as valuable opportunities for personal growth. Our pain becomes gain, and our anger evaporates like dewdrops in the sunlight.

Question three: How do I attain spiritual awareness?

Entire volumes address this question, but we'll limit ourselves to seven main points, **The Beginners "one-week plan"** for opening the gates of spiritual awareness. Practice one point per day, and soon you'll be able to implement all seven together. By that time, you'll notice a substantial change in your life for the better.

The overall objective of the One-Week Plan is to open our clogged, materially oriented hearts and brains to spirituality. The plan encourages modes of behavior that are conducive to spirituality, while avoiding certain things that are detrimental to the soul.

Let's review our working definition of SA: *Spiritual awareness is the cognitive power one gains by activating one's divine soul.*

The One-Week Plan has two specific functions: First, the plan activates your soul; second, it reduces the influence of bodily appetites on your decision-making process. As such, the plan puts you on the road to spiritual awareness. Let's get started on this important segment of our trail to tranquility:

The Beginners "One-week Plan"

Point one, Sunday: Don't act according to instinct! Stop, compose yourself, and think before you act or speak.

The two equal superpowers within us are the divine soul, which strives to do good, and the evil inclination, which sways us in the opposite direction. The evil inclination's main ploy is to drive us crazy and to keep us on the run, so we'll never have a chance to stop, collect our thoughts, and use our minds.

A person who lacks composure has difficulty in getting close to God. – *Rebbe Nachman of Breslev*

The human mind is the palace of the divine soul. According to Kabbalistic teachings, the evil inclination controls the left side of the heart, the liver, the gall bladder, and the spleen – the centers of animal urge. If we use our minds properly, we activate our divine souls, and the mind reigns over the body. Without using our minds, the body with its animal urges seizes control of our lives.

People are far from spiritual awareness, because they lack composure. In order to gain composure, one must stop for a moment, think, clarify thoughts, and then make an intelligent decision. A champion archer or marksman knows that shooting after taking careful aim, relaxing, and then breathing deeply will be far more accurate than an impulse shot from the hip.

Sunday is a good day to practice point one. Most people are at leisure, and it's easier to slow down and think. Imagine how the quality of our lives would improve if we thought before we spoke. If people would think before they press harder on the accelerator pedal, they'd save a lot of money on speeding tickets and make the roads considerably safer.

You'll quickly discover that the implementation of point one pays immediate dividends, both material and spiritual. To paraphrase an old song from our college days in the seventies, "Don't let the sound of your own wheels drive you crazy". Calm down, compose yourself, think matters over, and then act. You'll be amazed at your enhanced effectiveness and improved awareness. You can't fathom how composure will change your interpersonal relationships for the better.

Point two, Monday: Use your mind in an active mode, not a passive mode.

If he's not driving you crazy, the evil inclination will use an opposite tactic: Have all the leisure time you want, just don't activate your mind. That way, your divine soul never has a say in your life, and you lose all hope of attaining spiritual awareness.

Monday is the beginning of a fresh and challenging week. Decide that you're going to use your mind to full potential. Stay away from external stimulants, such as television and video, which put your mind to sleep and make you lazy. The mind, like the body, needs a good daily workout to stay in top shape.

Rebbe Nachman of Breslev teaches that a baby's mind capacity develops exclusively from stimulation of the divine soul.

If a person never uses his divine soul – if his entire life is devoted to TV shows, spectator sports, and movies – his mind capacity never develops. Rebbe Nachman of Breslev teaches that negative character traits attach themselves easily to an undeveloped mind. As such, a person can reach the age of eighty and remain a spiritual baby, self-indulgent, egocentric, and perpetually angry. Such a person has no control over his or her own life. He or she is an unfortunate slave to the television program guide.

Today, try to put your mind in an active mode. Think of passive entertainment as spiritual cholesterol, which clogs the thought paths of the mind and endangers spiritual health. Read as much as you can. Try to learn new skills. Observe your environment and pay attention to details you normally take for granted. Creative writing and correspondence with a friend are both healthy activities for the mind and soul. Write a poem for your spouse, and put it in a place that he or she will find it. It's good exercise for the mind and does wonders for the atmosphere at home.

Most marital difficulties stem from petty anger and faulty communication. Passive entertainment is public enemy number one to communication in marriage. Many couples are so glued to the television that they never sit down to an intimate meal and a meaningful discussion. I've counseled couples that have been married for years, yet they don't know each other! Misunderstandings are commonplace between two strangers.

Many parents will refuse to answer their child's important question, if it interrupts the ball game or the seven o'clock news. One who prefers a soap opera or tag-team wrestling to the emotional welfare of a spouse or a child is light years away from spiritual awareness.

Rebbe Nachman of Breslev teaches that there cannot be peace in a place devoid of spiritual awareness. Therefore, in a home where the television takes priority to parental attention, dissension, anger, and tension pervade the atmosphere.

Point three, Tuesday: Decide that you'll be happy today, no matter what.

Happiness is the key to mental composure. By being happy, our thinking improves. Sadness puts the mind in exile. Sadness and anger are twin sisters.

You might ask, who doesn't want to be happy? Or, how can I be happy with all my problems?

> If you spend an hour a day crying your heart out to God, you can be happy for the other twenty-three hours. – *Rebbe Nachman of Breslev*

Force yourself to smile. The first three smiles will be artificial, but the fourth will be real, for our sages teach that a person's actions influence his thoughts: If we try our best to be happy, eventually we *will* be happy.

A simple spiritual rule of thumb teaches that happiness comes from holiness, while sadness comes from the evil inclination and the dark side of the spiritual world. A happy person virtually neutralizes his evil inclination, because he has composure and a clear mind. The evil inclination has a hard time defeating a clear mind.

Personal prayer, or talking to God in your own language, is a foolproof method of achieving happiness. We'll discuss that in "point seven" of the one-week plan.

After work or school, today's a good day to do something special that will make you happy, like driving to the mountains or to the beach to watch the sunset. If that's not possible, take a walk in your favorite park or meadow and breathe some fresh air. Focus on the positive aspects of your life. Take inventory of your good points. Think of the myriad of blessings in your life, such as your health, your livelihood, and your home.

An instant happiness ploy. Back in my army days, the intelligence corps received information of a planned terrorist infiltration into Israel by way of the Lebanese border. My platoon was picked to ambush the terrorists, and to prevent the infiltration.

We had to lie in mud from ten p.m. to four a.m. without moving a muscle. At midnight, it began to rain. It was February – Israel's coldest month – and 36F outside. I was soaked and chilled to the bone. I put a piece of flannel in my mouth to keep my teeth from clattering. My feet were freezing and my toes were numb. At that point, I would have given anything for a hot, sweet cup of coffee or a pair of clean, dry socks.

Whenever I feel something trying to pull me in the direction of unhappiness, I use my instant happiness ploy: I make myself a hot, sweet cup of coffee, and think back to that freezing ambush mission in the winter mud of the Lebanese border. I sip my coffee, feeling like the most fortunate human on earth, and wiggle my toes to remind myself of the clean, dry socks I'm now wearing. Instantly, I regain my composure and my happiness.

Design an instant happiness ploy for yourself, too. Think of an extreme hardship you once suffered, and now think how fortunate you are today, without that particular hardship in your life. See how you are instantaneously happier.

Tomorrow, we'll continue our positive mental momentum.

Point four, Wednesday: Observe the world around you, for each stimulus in our lives is a message from Heaven. Contemplate God to the best of your ability.

During work or school today, pay special attention. Don't take anything for granted. Maybe you've been working on a particular project or transaction for weeks, or you've been struggling to understand some difficult material in your studies. Before you begin your day's agenda, say a little silent prayer asking The Almighty to help you succeed. Now, keep your eyes open – you're about to see some amazing phenomena.

The minute you decide to open your spiritual eyes, The Almighty will help you see; to make life pleasant, He'll help you succeed. This is God's way of positive reinforcement for those who seek Him. Be careful to avoid attributing your successes to your own talents or to natural causes, because that's tantamount to closing the door to The Almighty.

Once observation becomes second nature, you'll begin to see how the difficulties in your life are also cherished gifts from

God. Here are a few true examples from a long and exhaustive list (see Chapter five also):

❑ David, a submarine crewman in the Navy, applied for acceptance to the elite crew of a new submarine. He was accepted. The day before the submarine's maiden voyage, David came down with a severe case of the flu. The sub sailed without him. David was heartbroken. Three days later, the submarine sank, leaving no survivors.

❑ Lisa, an exchange student at the Hebrew University in Jerusalem, had an important final exam at nine in the morning. She missed her 8:30 bus by a few seconds, and was so frustrated that she broke out in tears. The bus continued on its route, and two stops later, exploded into a ball of fire. A terrorist bomb killed half the passengers, and crippled the other half.

❑ Arnold, a recent Harvard MBA graduate in finance, was confidant that he'd be employed by a prestigious Manhattan brokerage firm. The company rejected his application. Arnold was devastated. Two weeks later, the company's offices went up in smoke with the rest of Twin Towers.

❑ Janet was certain that Edward would soon marry her. Mysteriously, Edward dropped her and shortly thereafter married a different woman. Three years later, Edward died of cancer, leaving a widow with twin toddlers.

The Almighty granted the above four people a wonderful opportunity for spiritual awareness. Imagine the tragic loss of ignoring the Divine intervention in our lives, and attributing the events around us to a random stroke of fortune!

Rebbe Nachman of Breslev says that a person should seek the innate wisdom implanted in every creation or event. Proper observation means asking the question, "What can I learn from this?" Since all wisdom stems from The Creator, when one connects himself to the wisdom of a creation, he becomes attached to The Creator. When we connect ourselves to God, we receive spiritual awareness.

Point five, Thursday: Try to perform good deeds.

Anger stems from a lack of spiritual awareness. Anger is also the opposite of compassion. The Talmud teaches that God has minimal compassion for angry people. Why? God instills in each person a precious gift of divine holiness – the human soul, created in His own image. Since an angry person – devoid of spiritual awareness – both ignores and starves his own soul, he abuses the divine gift.

Imagine that you purchased a rare crystal chandelier for someone you loved; rather than hanging the chandelier proudly in the middle of his or her living room, the recipient of your priceless gift hangs it in the cowshed, or even worse, throws it on the floor and it shatters in a million tiny pieces. Wouldn't you be upset too?

Conversely, God has unlimited compassion for a person who treats others with compassion.

A ploy for gaining spiritual awareness: Try this ploy. Help a needy person, especially a widow or an orphan. Since you show compassion for the needy, The Almighty will show compassion for you. In order for God to treat you with more than minimal compassion, you must have spiritual awareness. Therefore, if you've performed a worthy deed, and you don't yet have spiritual awareness, God will open your eyes and grant you spiritual awareness in order to qualify you for the gift of increased divine compassion.

The above ploy won't be effective if your motivation is self-serving, such as giving charity for the sake of publicity or prestige. Therefore, try to perform as many good deeds in an altruistic fashion, solely in concern for your fellow human. Shortly thereafter, the waters of spiritual awareness will begin to flow from your soul; all you have to do is to open the dikes.

Giving is holiness. Therefore, when a person gives charity or does a favor for his or her fellow man, he or she connects immediately to God. A good connection with God always facilitates spiritual awareness.

Point six, Friday: Abstain from mind-influencing substances.

Back in my university days of the late 60's and early 70's, folks on campus used to have TGIF (Thank Goodness It's Friday) parties. People were in great spirits, and were looking forward to the upcoming weekend after a week of intensive studies.

Take advantage of your high spirits. Look forward to the joy of a Sabbath and weekend of relaxation. Take a day free of alcohol and of any other mind-influencing substances you may consume. This is important: Alcohol and drugs are two of the evil inclination's favorite traps. Once a person develops the slightest dependence on a mind-affecting substance, he becomes a slave to the evil inclination. A slave can't have two masters; therefore, if a person is a slave to the evil inclination, he can't be connected to God.

Why are alcohol and drugs called "mind-benders"? Try this simple experiment: Take a plastic pipe or rubber hose, and bend it. Notice that light can not pass through such a pipe. That's exactly what substances do to the mind – they bend it, so that divine light can no longer pass through it.

Substances and spiritual awareness never go together. Happiness and spiritual awareness never depart. Therefore, if a person consumes alcohol or uses drugs, he or she will never be happy. Why? Happiness comes from within, and is independent of outside substances and stimuli. Take away an alcoholic's bottle; he won't be happy for long. On the contrary, he'll probably erupt like a medium-size volcano.

Declare that today is a substance-free day. Our sages teach that if a person opens his heart to God in the slightest, even a pinhole, God will reciprocate and open for that person a gate to spiritual awareness as wide as the Los Angeles freeway. [23]

Point seven, Saturday (Sabbath): Talk to God.

If you're Jewish, the Sabbath is the most special day of the week, perfect for attaining spirituality. If you're not Jewish, Saturday is a wonderful day to refresh your emotional and spiritual batteries.

Designate an hour for yourself and try to find a place where no one will disturb you. Talk to God like you'd talk to your best friend, your most intimate confidant. Spill your heart out, laugh, cry, dance, and ask for whatever you want. Release your anxiety. Tell God about your aspirations, your fears, your loves, and your deepest secrets.

Maybe at this point, you're saying, "Hold your horses, I don't yet believe in God. I was never educated in religion". Don't worry, cherished friend; many people with conventional religious training also lack *genuine* belief in The Almighty. Try this test: Find a pleasant place of solitude, and begin talking. Here's the way to start: "Dear God, I've never been aware of You. I desire to know the absolute truth. Could you please send me some answers, and take time to personally reveal Yourself to me?"

The above test works for sincere truth-seekers. God acts quickly on such a request, as tens of thousands of new believers can testify.

---

[23] Drinking wine in the performance of a mitzvah (a religious commandment), such as Kiddush on Sabbath, is of course permissible. Despite the fact, many people prefer to maintain absolute mental clarity at all times, and refrain from wine as well. Grape juice is an acceptable substitute for wine on all religious occasions. Also, the Halachic (religious law) ordinance for getting drunk on the festival of Purim may be substituted by taking a nap.

Maybe you'd like to ask a different question: "I feel ridiculous all alone, talking to the wind. What am I supposed to say?"

Try this: "God, thanks for the one-hundred-thousand beats of my heart in the last twenty-four hours. Thank you also for the twenty thousand breaths I took in the last twenty-four hours. Thank you for my eyes and for my eyesight. Thank you for my ears and for my hearing. Thank you for my job and for my livelihood. Thank you for my home and for my clothes..." The list is endless. Think of all the blessings in life that people take for granted.

Other people's ingratitude appalls us. Yet, we totally ignore millions of favors (remember that the average heart beats more than three million times per month) that God does for each and every one of us.

When people give thanks to God, God opens their heart. Usually, after going down your checklist of thanks, God helps you speak from the bottom of your heart. The satisfaction of a good talk with God is indescribable. People accustomed to speaking with the Almighty save both emotional and physical wear and tear – less anxiety, less worry, less ulcers, and less anger, as we'll see in the coming chapters.

Once you've successfully implemented the one-week plan, you're ready for ESA, the enhanced spiritual awareness workshop. During the workshop, you'll choose a subject that you'd like to strengthen, and work on a particular aspect of SA.

The Enhanced Spiritual Awareness (ESA) Workshop

Our character traits are integral parts of a whole – our personality. Therefore, when we succeed in improving even a lone character trait, we immediately exert a positive effect on our personality as a whole.

Many people ask, "I'm so stressed and nervous all the time; how can I ever be cool and collected? Is it really possible for me to improve my personality?"

We certainly can't wave a magic wand to perfect our personalities. But, by working on the individual traits one by one, we are able to "divide and conquer" bad habits and unfavorable behavioral reactions, including anger, stress, and anxiety. I've had the privilege of seeing many people work patiently and consistently on each of the twenty factors that comprise the ESA, who over the course of one calendar year made dramatic improvements in their lives. You can too.

In the same manner that you devoted a day of the "One-Week Plan" to a particular attribute, go down the following list of twenty factors that affect SA, and devote a day's workshop to each factor. I've seen tenacious spiritual trainees devote a week or a month to a single factor, until it becomes second nature.

The following is a handy tabular summary of the basic factors that are conducive or destructive to SA:

Twenty Factors that affect Spiritual Awareness

Conducive Factors	Destructive factors
1. Faith	Lack of faith
2. Marital fidelity	Adultery
3. Modesty	Lewd behavior
4. Healthy, natural foods	Alcohol, drugs, tobacco
5. Bodily cleanliness	Lack of bodily hygiene
6. Compassion and kind deeds	Cruelty
7. Love and respect of fellow man	Hatred, prejudice, disdain
8. Charity	Stinginess
9. Honesty	Dishonesty, theft
10. Mental composure	Impulsive behavior and reactions
11. Happiness	Sadness

12. Clean speech	Slander, cursing
13. Patience	Anger
14. Overcoming bodily urges	Succumbing to bodily urges
15. Listening to good speech	Listening to gossip or curses
16. Looking at wholesome images	Looking at lewd images
17. Contemplation and soul-searching	Instinctive behavior
18. Personal prayer, thanksgiving	Denial of the soul; ingratitude
19. Reading and learning about spirituality	Passive entertainment, such as TV and movies
20. Judging others fairly, granting the benefit of the doubt	Constant criticizing and condemning of other people

Remember that this book and the exercises within are not "instant coffee" – you can't put a sticky character trait in a microwave oven for 180 seconds and remove it completely corrected. Modern society has conditioned us to look for instant gratification, but character improvement doesn't work like that. The good news is that anyone can follow the ESA and see major changes for the better; the more the perseverance, the more dramatic the changes. At any rate, if this book becomes a workbook for you that you reread and work on all the time, you'll be a big winner.

Now, let's take a brief look at each factor, and see how to utilize an ESA Workshop day for best results:

1. Faith – think about the many times in your life that you were in dangerous situations. Do you really believe that you were randomly saved each time? Think about the world and all of creation. If you believe in a big-bang theory, then who or what caused the big bang? Ask yourself difficult spiritual questions, and try to focus beyond the limits of your body, time, and space. You'll be amazed at the results.

2. Marital fidelity – Maybe you think this is an extraneous category. Remember though, that your thoughts and speech affect your spirituality as well as your deeds. You may be physically loyal to your spouse, but if you even *contemplate* an extramarital relationship, you impair the power of your soul. Today, think about your partner, say nice things, and perform acts of love, consideration, and kindness.

3. Modesty – when you flaunt your body, you blemish your soul. Don't treat yourself like a cheap piece of meat for sale in an outdoor market. Imagine that you are the son or daughter of a great king *(you are!)* and dress, speak, and act accordingly.

4. Healthy, natural diet – today, try to eat with the sole intent of maintaining your bodily health. Prefer grains, fruits, and vegetables to processed foods. Avoid junk foods and fast foods that are high in calories and low in nutrition. Deny your body detrimental substances such as alcohol, tobacco, and drugs. If you can eat naturally and refrain from substances for three days consecutively, you'll experience immediate spiritual gain and a much clearer mind.

5. Body cleanliness – spiritual impurity and lack of physical hygiene are closely related. Wash your hands as soon as you wake up in the morning, every time you visit the toilet, and before eating. Bathe or shower daily, if possible, and wear clean clothes.

6. Compassion and kind deeds – look for the many little opportunities to do favors for people, especially for your loved ones whom you often take for granted. By giving, you imitate Divine behavior and climb quickly up the spiritual ladder.

7. Love and respect of fellow man – look past the other person's appearance. Think how he or she also has a divine

soul, a tiny spark of godliness within them, just like you have. Practice respecting family members, friends, and strangers.

8. Charity – this is one of the fastest ploys in gaining SA. When you show compassion for others, God shows compassion for you and rewards you with SA.

9. Honesty – maybe you never lie; be careful, though, to refrain from saying things that you don't intend, like, "Why don't we get together sometime," when you have no intention of implementing what you say. Careful about all the little white lies you might say during the course of a day. Maintain good relationships with others by way of polite candor instead of diplomatic niceties that aren't true. Be careful to deal honestly with others. Even an unauthorized telephone call at work is enough to blemish the soul. Outright swindling completely destroys SA.

10. Mental composure – review point one (Sunday) of the One-Week Plan, and devote more time to working on carefully weighed decisions instead of impulsive behavior and instinctive reactions.

11. Happiness – this was point three (Tuesday) on the One-Week Plan, but it's so important that it deserves additional practice during the ESA Workshop. Review point three of the One-Week Plan, and keep on plugging. Happiness and SA go hand in hand. You can't be happy and angry at the same time.

12. Clean speech – the use of off-color speech blemishes the soul. Try to express yourself in the same manner that you'd speak to a king or dignitary.

13. Patience – try to understand others instead of losing your temper with them. Remember that your children are neither slaves nor dimwits; treat them like miniature adults. Listen to what others have to say.

14. Overcome bodily urges – don't let your bodily appetites boss you around. Whenever you overcome a harmful bodily urge *(such as eating that second piece of Boston cream pie)*, you strengthen your soul.

15. Listen to good speech – hearing gossip, slander, and lies blemishes your soul. Avoid those who bad-mouth others.

16. Look at wholesome images – just as a beautiful sunset strengthens your soul and brings you closer to God; looking at pornography does the exact opposite.

17. Soul searching and contemplation – take time in the evening to evaluate yourself and to think about the direction of your life. Don't let others drag you into impulsive behavior, or into acting against your better judgment.

18. Personal prayer – review point seven of the One-Week Plan. Personal prayer goes way beyond meditation, and is the fastest, most efficient mode of spiritual gain. Prayer allows us to give thanks for past blessings and to request our needs for the future *(See also Chapter nine)*.

19. Reading and learning – review point two of the One-Week Plan, and use your mind in an active mode. Avoid passive activities such as watching television.

20. Judge others fairly, and grant them the benefit of the doubt – practice avoiding criticism and hasty judgments of others. Imagine that you'll be judged by the same criteria you judge others. *(See also Chapter seven)*.

Prepare an ESA workshop log or diary to monitor your efforts. Attach a copy of the "Table of Twenty Factors" to a monthly calendar, and write down the number of the individual ESA factor you are working on in the space that designates a particular day.

The ESA Workshop is hard work, but immensely satisfying. The more you enhance the conducive SA factors, while simultaneously overcoming the destructive factors, the more you strengthen your soul and improve your character. If you persevere, you'll be making tremendous spiritual gain within a relatively short time.

Because of the spiritual profile of your own individual soul, some factors will be easy for you while others may prove to be a rigorous challenge. Don't lose heart. The reward for correcting a spiritually detrimental attribute is greater than anything you can imagine.

Question four: How do I know if I have spiritual awareness?

This is a question that every truth-seeker asks, both at the outset of his spiritual journey and for the rest of his days. Spiritual hunger is literally insatiable, for King Solomon once said (Ecclesiastes 6:7), "The soul is never satiated". The more a person gains spiritual awareness, the more spirituality he or she desires. Since spirituality knows no confines, there are infinite levels of spiritual awareness. The following eight parameters are a good diagnostic test of a person's spiritual gain, both for beginners and for advanced truth seekers.

Parameter one: Courage, calm, and inner security.

The more a person worries, the more he or she drifts away from God, since a worrier lacks trust in God. Conversely, the more a person trusts in God, the more he or she acquires true courage, calm, and inner security. Since courage indicates proximity to The Almighty, it's a good indicator of spiritual awareness.

Courage doesn't mean confronting an enemy tank battalion single-handed; it means steadfastly doing what's right with no trepidation, even at the expense of constant ridicule from others. Courage also means going with the truth wherever it takes you.

A courageous person's eyes focus on his or her spiritual goals, and not on peer pressure or social pressure. For example, if a 250-pound linebacker from the first-string football team sits down to a meal with his teammates, and is ashamed to say a blessing in front of them when he knows he should, he's a coward despite his twenty-four-inch biceps. Yet, when a fifteen-year-old young lady decides to dress modestly, even at the expense of ridicule or a loss of popularity among her classmates, she exhibits spiritual awareness – the type of courage that signifies closeness with God.

The more a person gains spiritual awareness, the more he or she realizes their dependence on God. Since The Almighty's strength and abilities are unlimited, one who depends on Him doesn't ever have to worry. For example, a person with a high level of spiritual awareness knows that his or her livelihood comes from God; no tyrannical employer can ever intimidate such a person.

People with SA have a good feeling of inner security. They know that if they lose their job, The Almighty has plenty of additional messengers who'll give them a new job. Someone who lacks such understanding worries every time the boss frowns at him, or every time the economic news reports of a recession.

Increased inner strength to do what we believe is right is a sign of spiritual gain. The more we cultivate the spiritual side of our lives, the more we gain courage, calm, and inner security.

Parameter two: Happiness.

Happiness goes together with courage. Just as the divine soul is within a person, true happiness is also within a person, and is independent of outside factors. The more a person nurtures his relationship with The Almighty, the closer he comes to true happiness.

We often fool ourselves with illusions of happiness, such as:

❑ "I would really be happy if my husband made more money".

- "I'd be the happiest guy in the world if I could only get accepted to law school".

- "Boy, would a new Harley make me happy!"

- "If Johnny proposes to me, I'll be the happiest girl on campus!"

All four of the above characters are seriously misleading themselves. The first lady, whose "happiness" depends on a raise of her husband's salary, will never be happy, no matter how much her husband earns. Who's to say that the second, the student, wouldn't be a miserable failure as a lawyer? As for the third, maybe The Almighty refuses to give him a new Harley, in order to save him from a 100 mile-per-hour motorcycle spill. With today's divorce statistics, chances are 50:50 that the young lady in the fourth example and her Johnny will end up in divorce proceedings within the next five years. That's happiness?

Genuine happiness comes from within. A truly happy individual is one who is contented with his lot in life. Positive thinkers focus on the blessings in life, and regard life's difficulties as opportunities for personal growth.

Rabbi Joseph Chaim Zonnenfeld of blessed memory was the head Rabbi of Jerusalem in the early twentieth century, a pious scholar of impeccable character. One morning, he walked through the Arab market on the way to the holy Western Wall. A young prankster, an Arab vegetable vender's helper, threw a tomato at him, which splattered all over his face. The rabbi turned to him, and said politely in Arabic, "*Shukran, hawadja*", thank you, sir.

The lanky young Arab was amazed at the elderly Jew's reaction. "Why are you thanking me?"

Rabbi Zonnenfeld answered, "You could have thrown a rock at me; it was only a tomato – thank you very much."

The Rabbi Zonnenfeld anecdote teaches that outside influences don't affect genuine inner happiness. Since happiness depends on true proximity to God, if you're not happy, you need to make some spiritual improvements to your life. If you've already started, and you're happier than you were last week, then you're making progress on the road to spiritual awareness.

Parameter three: Peace, both internal and external, the opposite of anger.

Peace is directly related to spiritual awareness, since arguments, anger, and cruelty stem from a lack of spiritual awareness. The more we gain spiritual awareness, the more sympathy, compassion, and peace prevail in our lives.

The above anecdote about Rabbi Zonnenfeld applies here as well. A person with spiritual awareness realizes that nothing can occur in the world without God's agreement. Rabbi Zonnenfeld felt no anger toward the vegetable vender's helper; he knew that a heavenly decree dictated that today, a tomato must splatter on his face. Therefore, he made no effort to retaliate, nor did he utilize his spiritual power for a bad cause, such as cursing the prankster. Rabbi Zonnenfeld did better than turning a cheek – he preserved the peace. After the vegetable vender's helper realized that he had degraded a righteous man, he became the rabbi's close friend, and would personally escort the rabbi whenever the latter traversed the Arab market.

An increase in spiritual awareness leads to a decrease in dissension-causing emotions such as anger, jealousy, and revenge. When we defuse the anger, jealousy, and revenge within us, we preserve the peace all around us. As such, spiritual awareness is the number one genuine peacemaker in the world.

When negative emotions weaken, positive emotions strengthen. The tremendous mental benefit of spiritual awareness leads to a higher level of patience and tolerance and a consequently much lower level of anger and impatience.

One of the best litmus tests of spiritual awareness is the peace of your immediate environment. If your home, your marriage, and your place of employment are more peaceful than they used to be, then you can take pride in your achievements, because you're fast gaining spiritual awareness. If the outside world hasn't changed, but you feel less negative emotions, you're still doing an outstanding job. Keep up the good work.

Parameter four: Improved physical and mental health.

Negative emotions take a serious toll on our mental and physical health. Feelings of worry, anger, jagged nerves, hate, and revenge lead directly to cardiovascular problems, digestive problems, lack of sleep, reduced concentration, and severe headaches, just to name a few. Negative emotions cause a long list of indirect problems, such as the physical and mental damages incurred by the consumption of alcohol, tobacco, and drugs, the substances that people use for a temporary, artificial sensation of feeling good.

Thousands of years ago, our sages taught that spiritual awareness heals. Today, any heart specialist will tell you that emotional stress, worry, and especially anger take their toll on the heart. Via spiritual awareness, we alleviate these negative emotions, and consequently strengthen the heart.

Spiritual awareness reduces negative emotions, and therefore lessens the chances of emotionally related diseases such as ulcers, asthma, blood disorders, and miscarriages. Once you feel a general improvement in your overall vitality – the old twitch in your left eye disappears, you know longer feel the knot in your diaphragm, or you suffer a lot less from headaches – you're making great headway toward spiritual awareness.

> True spirituality isn't a mere collection of rosy platitudes that "in-people" like to roll off their tongues at a tea party. True spirituality – particularly *emuna*, the pure and complete faith in The Creator – stands by you during life's most difficult tribulations. If it doesn't hold up under fire – when the bombs are falling all around you – it's not the real deal. True spirituality is practical, like money in the bank. – *Rabbi Lazer Brody, from a broadcast on Israel National Radio*

Parameter five: Body – soul priorities.

Another rule of thumb states that the more a person has spiritual awareness, the more his soul takes priority over his body.

People who favor their bodily appetites over their spiritual needs are totally tied to the material world and devoid of spiritual awareness.

A person with a refined and developed mind loses animal appetites in favor of an insatiable appetite for spiritual awareness and the knowledge of God. For such a person, there's no difference between this world and the next. Why? The privileged souls who earn a portion in the world to come spend their time basking in the Divine light of the Heavenly Presence, which is none other than a sublime spiritual experience of boundless wisdom and understanding which surpasses all worldly pleasures. When you think about God in this world, you approach the spiritual bliss of the world to come.

Self-purification of bodily urges and of base inclinations is conducive to attaining spiritual wisdom and understanding. Therefore, if a person gives highest priority in this world to spiritual growth, then the material world becomes for him or her almost as tranquil as the spiritual world of afterlife. Such a person never dies – his soul simply deposits its physical shell in the grave and then ascends to its rightful position in the spiritual world. On the other hand, those whose entire lives are devoted to the body, lose everything at death. With an undeveloped soul, nothing remains after the body decays in the grave but sorrow and eternal regret.

When you find yourself thinking more about your soul and less about your next meal, you're gaining spiritual awareness.

Parameter six: Giving – receiving priorities.

Charity leads to improved spiritual awareness, as follows: Giving comes from the side of holiness, for God only gives, He never receives. Therefore, when you give, you act in a Godly fashion, and thereby attach yourself to holiness. The more one is attached to holiness, the more one gains spiritual awareness, and vice versa. Parasites, on the other hand, and those who take from others, come from the evil side, the opposite of holiness.

The above explanation is the key to any successful interpersonal relationship, especially marriage. When both sides ask, "What can I contribute to the relationship", they both become givers. Holiness prevails in such a relationship, assuring lasting success. When both sides have expectations of receiving from the other side, the relationship is a disaster, devoid of holiness, doomed to chaos and strife. True peace goes together with holiness. Evil and strife are husband and wife.

The more you gain spiritual awareness, the more you desire to do for others. Concern for others is the opposite of egotism. An egotist is a taker, interested in his or her own benefit, and therefore linked strongly to his evil inclination. Egotism is an iron curtain that separates a person from God. By giving to others, a person neutralizes those innate egotistic tendencies. People who give charity, who perform voluntary services for the community and for those less fortunate than themselves, and who are alert to the needs of others, achieve high levels of spiritual awareness.

Rebbe Moshe Leib of Sassov, Ukraine (1745-1807), one of the great Chassidic masters of his time, devoted his life to increasing his capacity of spiritual awareness. Once, he overheard the following dialogue between two Ukrainian peasants, who met each other in the marketplace:

"Ah Sergey, I'm so happy to see you!"

"Do you really mean that, Alexis?"

"Of course I do, Sergey. You are my dearest friend. I love you more than a brother."

"If you love me so much, Alexis, then tell me what my needs are!"

Rebbe Moshe Leib testified that the above dialogue taught him an amazing lesson in life: Real charity means giving according to the needs of the receiver, and not according to the desires of the giver. Also, true love means sensitivity to another person's needs. Such sensitivity comes from enhanced spiritual awareness.

An old Hebrew expression says, "The tongue has no bone"; the connotation is that words easily roll off the tongue. People often tell each other, "I love you". Do they really mean it? Why doesn't the expression succeed in appeasing an irate spouse? The answer is simple: True love comes from spiritual awareness. A giver is tuned in to the needs of a fellow human, and especially to the needs of someone close, such as a husband or a wife. If both husband and wife can pass the "Ukrainian peasant" test, then their home is surely a Garden of Eden, a haven of spiritual awareness.

Parameter seven: Efficiency

A person with spiritual awareness can accomplish in fifteen minutes what another person cannot accomplish in seventy years.

The following example helps us understand the above principle:

Mrs. Gold gave separate errands to each of her two twin daughters, Sheila and Shirley. She sent Sheila to the bakery, to buy fresh bread and rolls for a festive meal. She sent Shirley to the butcher, to purchase meat. Each of the two stores is an eight-minute walk from the Gold residence.

Sheila walked directly to the baker, selected exactly what her mother requested, paid for the goods, and returned home within half an hour.

Shirley met a girlfriend and chatted for ten minutes. Then, the display in a shoe store window caught her eye. After browsing and window-shopping for an additional hour, she passed by the ice-cream salon. Her mouth watered at the sight of blueberry delight, her favorite flavor. Six other people waited ahead of her, and fifteen more minutes transpired by the time she received her blueberry delight ice-cream cone. When she finished licking her cone, she proceeded to the butcher. By this time, she forgot what her mother ordered. Shirley was forced to look for a public phone, call home, and verify the meat order. She accomplished her task in two and a half hours.

Sheila was five times more efficient than Shirley. Why? Sheila wasted neither time nor energy on her own appetites; she concentrated her efforts on performing her mother's wishes. Shirley, on the other hand, was primarily concerned with her own appetites, which consumed both her time and her energy. Her prime task, buying the meat, assumed secondary priority.

People like Sheila attain spiritual awareness easily. Since they are goal oriented and not appetite oriented, they are much more efficient. Their souls aren't coated with a thick layer of "appetite fat" which blocks out divine light and spiritual awareness. Physical appetites always stand in the way of the truth, because an appetite-oriented person will deny truth if truth requires discarding a certain appetite. Just as appetites and efficiency conflict with each other, truth and efficiency therefore go hand in hand; both signify spiritual awareness.

Parameter eight: When I begin to realize that I know nothing.

A tenet of Kabbalistic and Chassidic thought states that the epitome of knowledge is the knowledge that we know nothing. This concept is worthy of a separate volume in itself. For our present purposes, here's a brief explanation:

The less a person actually knows, the more he thinks he knows. The worst back-seat drivers are usually those who never held a steering wheel in their lives. Every man on the street thinks he can run the country better than the President, and every buck private thinks he can command the battalion better than the battalion commander can. Why? Those who lack knowledge think they know everything. They resemble stubborn little children who think they're smarter than their parents.

The Bible testifies that Moses was more modest that any human who ever walked the face of the earth. Yet, Moses attained a higher spiritual level than any mortal ever. Moses received both the oral and the written law directly from God, and was the only prophet ever who could speak directly with The Almighty, as opposed to the other prophets who received prophecy in a dream or in an allegorical form. Moses nullified all his physical appetites, and his soul completely dominated his body, to the point where he no longer had an evil inclination. Moses was capable of learning with God for weeks on end, without sleeping, drinking, or eating. Although he had a better grasp than any other mortal as to what divine wisdom and power really is, his knowledge didn't scratch the Divine surface. Moses knew the limit of his own capabilities, and therefore was truly modest.

Genuine modesty resembles a clean, empty crystal glass. Arrogance is like a full glass, because an arrogant person thinks he knows everything. If you try and pour a fine wine into a full glass, it will be wasted. The clean, empty crystal glass is the proper vessel to hold a fine wine. Spiritual awareness resembles a fine wine. A modest person, who realizes that much remains to be learned about his or her own divine soul, let alone about God, is a worthy vessel for spiritual awareness.

Summary

Keep up the one-week plan until it becomes second nature. Then, work on the ESA factors one at a time. Once you've improved a factor, move on to the next. The eight parameters of spiritual awareness are a superb self-check of your progress. Review them from time to time, and you'll pleasantly surprise yourself with your headway.

Now that we know how to do a bit of spiritual map reading, we're much more sensitive to the stimuli of our environment, and better prepared to continue on our journey up the trail to tranquility.

The end of this chapter marks the successful completion of the second segment of our trail. We're now ready to begin segment three of our trail to tranquility. In the coming chapters, we'll learn how to be at peace with God, with our fellow man, and with ourselves. By attaining peace on all three fronts, we break the back of anger and other negative emotions. Let's continue on our way.

5

Wild Raspberries

We now begin the third stage of our journey. This chapter is the first of two chapters that will help us make peace with God. Later, we'll learn how to make peace with our fellow man, and most important of all, with ourselves.

Angry people often have a lengthy list of grievances with God. They feel that The Almighty treats them unfairly, or causes them to suffer unnecessarily. As such, they carry a burden of bitterness in their hearts. Bitterness is a serious obstacle on anyone's trail to tranquility.

The objective of the next two chapters is to uproot that bitterness. We'll examine why people experience painful situations in life. Once you understand how *everything* that happens in your life is for your ultimate benefit, you'll be ready to make complete peace with God. Although a mortal can't possibly understand Divine reason, the more you make an effort to observe The Almighty's way of running the world, the more you'll sense His limitless compassion, concern, and love for you. Such sensing is none other than spiritual awareness.

This chapter observes the difficulties in life that are gifts from heaven, designed for personal growth.

Every mineral, plant, animal, and human has a certain special quality that teaches us something about The Creator. Just as an artist signs his painting with his own unique signature, we can find God's signature on every creation in the universe.

Rebbe Nachman of Breslev teaches that the uniqueness of a given being is the sign of the divine wisdom instilled in that being.

Take the beaver, for example. Notice its tail; no other creature on earth has such an appendage. No other animal can build a dam like a beaver can. The beaver in general, and his tail in particular, are the result of an enormous amount of divine engineering. When we observe a beaver, we learn quite a bit about The Creator. The beaver has nothing but positive qualities – he's constructive, diligent, and fiercely loyal to his family.

Practice thinking about the divine wisdom in other creations; it's a wonderful mental exercise that enhances spiritual awareness.

Did you know that the eye of a bee consists of hundreds of miniscule lenses, more sophisticated than any of the cameras in the space and satellite program? All the design engineers of all the major camera and lenses manufacturers can't reproduce the eye of a bee or a housefly. Divine engineering is a tough act to follow.

The Almighty communicates with us by way of the creations in our environment. The more we gain spiritual awareness, the more we understand God's messages. A person who looks at a flower or a tree without understanding its divine message is like a tourist in China who can't understand the road signs.

Wild Raspberries and Mountain Roses

Today, Old Isaac is taking you on an allegorical hike up Mount Patience. You'll be hiking along a breathtaking stretch of mountain forest. This particular leg on your journey is about to teach a very special lesson.

After you traverse Lupine Valley to the east, you cross over a creek. Up ahead is a noble forest of Loblolly pine, poplar, and wild oak. To the right is a thicket of thorny vines. Isaac removes his backpack, pulls out a paper plate, and then high-steps his way into the thicket. You're in for a pleasant surprise.

You have a puzzled look on your face; what's the old man find so special about a clump of stickers?

After a few minutes of clomping amongst the thorns, Isaac returns to the trail. You look at his hands and gasp; they're scratched and bleeding as if he hand-fed a clan of irate cats. You can't understand why he has such a big grin on his face, like a little tike that's just robbed the cookie jar.

When was the last time you ate fresh mountain wild raspberries? Isaac withdraws his canteen from its pouch on his hiking belt, washes off the berries, and checks them for worms. He passes you the plate of the shiny bluish-black berries, which look like miniature grape clusters. "This is a present for you, cherished friend," he says. "Enjoy the sweetness of our beautiful world."

Your eyes roll in delight; you can't remember when you tasted such a delicacy.

I learned in survival school that the nutritionally rich wild raspberries can sustain a stranded hiker for several days if need be.

Isaac takes you up the trail for another half mile, and stops again. He makes another quick excursion into the woods, and returns with two of the most beautiful roses you've ever seen. This time, he has a six-inch scratch that broke the skin on his forearm. "A little souvenir from Mount Patience," he smiles, and presents the roses to you.

You're thrilled with the flowers. Their fragrance surpasses the best of French perfumes. You've seen roses before, but these multicolored gold and crimson beauties surpass anything you've ever seen in a florist shop. Old Isaac knows how to make a person feel special.

You continue up the trail. Every few paces, you take a deep, pleasurable sniff of your mountain souvenir. You ponder the mountain roses, their sunset-colored petals, the five elegant dark green leaves that surround each flower like a goblet, and the threatening razor-sharp thorns on their stems.

I'll bet that you're beginning to understand the connection between wild raspberries, mountain roses, and the scratches on Isaac's hands and arms.

Isaac explains: "The sweet berries and the lovely flowers are gifts from God. An expensive gift usually has a high price tag. In the outback, we don't pay with traveler's checks or credit cards; in the case of the berries and the roses, we have to suffer a little pain in order to attain the prize."

Isaac doesn't complain about the thorns scratching his hands. On the contrary, he wears a big smile.

"Picking the berries and the roses was well worth a few scratches," Isaac says. "Knowing the reward of the pain – in this case, granting a pleasurable experience to a close friend – is the spiritual awareness that prevented me from being angry at the thorns. You can't pick wild raspberries or mountain roses without getting scratched."

Let's take Old Isaac's idea one step further: Suppose you got scratched or bruised on your way up the trail, without finding wild raspberries or mountain roses. Would you be angry at the thorns, or at the rock that you tripped over? Once you've succeeded in developing spiritual awareness, the answer is no. Sometimes, the buried treasure within a painful experience is not as obvious as a wild raspberry or a mountain rose, but that doesn't mean that it's not there. If we look hard enough, we're bound to find the reward.

> "Within every sorrow hides a salvation." – *Rebbe Nachman of Breslev*

The hidden blessings within *every* tribulation resemble wild raspberries and mountain roses: They're usually not apparent at first glance, even though the thorns – our troubles – are always obvious.

Don't let a thorn or two in life discourage you. Your reward is on the way. There are seasons in the year when you don't see fruit on the prickly vines – that doesn't mean they're not wild raspberries. Be patient, and when the time is right, you'll find an abundance of sweet fruit. The same holds true of the thorny times in life; at the time of a painful experience, we don't always know what God is doing to us, but rest assured, the ultimate outcome is always for the best.

Since the dawn of humanity, people have been asking the same question: "If God loves me so much, than why does He make me suffer?" Let's examine the difference between a person who understands why he suffers and a person who doesn't understand, in the following example:

Peter and Paul share the same room in a hospital. They're surprising similar – same age, same physical characteristics, and they both have nine stitches in the exact same place below the abdomen. Yet, Peter is bright and cheerful and Paul is depressed and bitterly angry with The Almighty. Why the difference between the two?

Peter had an emergency appendectomy. After the operation, the surgeon told him how fortunate he was; his swollen and infected appendix was a minute away from bursting, and if that were the case, a massive flow of toxins would have contaminated Peter's bloodstream and threatened his life. Peter is tickled by his good fortune – a new lease on life and a few days of forced vacation to relax and catch up on his reading – all for the bargain-basement price of nine stitches and a bearable measure of abdominal pain.

On a pain scanner, Paul's pain level would score identically to Peter's. Paul though, is trapped in a thick cloud of gloom. While walking through the park, three thugs pounced on him, stole his wallet, and stabbed him in the abdomen.

Peter knows why he's suffering, while Paul doesn't. Peter's knowledge is none other spiritual awareness, which makes the difference between happiness and sadness, between inner peace and inner turbulence.

Imagine that an angel from heaven visits Paul in the hospital, and explains all the reasons behind the mugging. Were Paul to realize that his traumatic experience was no less a gift from God than Peter's appendicitis, he would be smiling too.

The seemingly bad times in our lives are very special gifts from God, usually intended for very special people.

Life's difficulties are *not* the result of negative conduct or actions. The overall purpose of the seemingly bad is to spiritually strengthen a person and to bring him closer to God. Our loving Father in Heaven doesn't want His children to stray away, nor does He want them to succumb to spiritual hibernation. The thorns and briars in our lives wake us up and keep us spiritually on our toes. God utilizes various types of tribulations and trying times to conceal a number of very special gifts, as we will see throughout this chapter.

The more we understand that the thorny times of our lives are divine gifts, the more we love the Divine Giver, and the more thoroughly we uproot the spiritually-destructive latent anger that sometimes penetrates our hearts. With that in mind, let's examine nine commonly concealed gifts amongst life's thorns.

Nine commonly concealed gifts amongst life's thorns

Gift number one: Rescue from death.

Sergeant Sammy Adler, USMC, crouched shin-deep in the mud of the Vietnamese jungle less than a mile from the Laotian border. The Vietcong had been smuggling massive amounts of armaments into South Vietnam by way of Laos. His company's mission was to ambush the smugglers, confiscate the arms shipment, and capture whomever they could for interrogation.

An annoying mosquito buzzed in Sammy's ear, and a leech bit his wrist. He didn't dare slap himself, for the slightest noise could reveal his position to an enemy ambush. The mission therefore called for radio silence, which necessitated the three platoons of Company C to maintain eye contact with each other.

A heavy dawn mist descended on the jungle. The fog was so thick that Sammy barely saw Captain John Willis, his company commander, from a distance of three feet. Willis scribbled a note and passed it to Sammy: "Platoon B, 0800, green east".

Sammy looked at his watch and nodded in understanding. His orders were to crawl over to Platoon B, one hundred yards to the right, and to inform the platoon leader that at exactly eight a.m., all three platoons would leave their present position and approach the Laotian border due east of them.

Sammy slithered inch by inch in the mud. His life depended on his absolute silence. He looked at his watch again – five minutes after seven. He took a deep breath and continued, first an elbow, then a knee, another elbow, then another knee. He stopped dead in his tracks: A roundish brown object, the exact size and shape of antipersonnel mine, was right before his nose.

The "mine", none other than a turtle, stuck its head out and laughed in Sammy's face, and then crawled away nonchalantly. He exhaled deeply in relief, and continued in the direction of Platoon B.

Forty-five minutes expired; Sammy wiped the mud off the face of his watch, and read the time – ten minutes to eight. The fog lifted, but a heavy rain drenched the already saturated jungle.

All along the seemingly endless one hundred yards to Platoon B's position, Sammy kept track of his crawling pace. He counted four hundred movements of nine inches each, the equivalent of one hundred yards. He should have reached Platoon B by now, but saw nothing other than mud and jungle.

A minute before eight: What a mess, Sammy thought. In sixty seconds, Platoons A and C will be moving east, and Platoon B hasn't been informed yet. Where in daylights is Platoon B? Where the heck am I?

"Chikachikachik! Chikachikachik!" The cobra's forked tongue almost touched Sammy's nose. The snake snarled, exposing his two deadly fangs, and braced to an attack position.

Sammy froze – he thought that the pounding of his pulse could surely be heard for miles away. In a few split seconds, he envisioned his entire life flashing before his eyes. What a pathetic way to go, he lamented, killed by a cobra in the muck and mire of a Vietnamese jungle, ten thousand miles from home. He couldn't ask the cobra for a stay of execution until he had a chance to send a postcard to Mom and Dad.

Sammy's M-16 rifle lay in a futile silence beside him. His commando knife remained idle in its scabbard, as did the three assault grenades in his ammo belt. He didn't dare move a muscle. Beads of salty sweat from his forehead traversed his right eyebrow and then dripped down and stung his right eye. Wiping his forehead was out of the question.

Jungle survival school taught him that only a bronze statue lives through an encounter with an irate cobra. I'm a bronze statue, Sammy thought to himself; I'm a bronze statue.

"Chikachikachik! Chikachikachik!" The cobra continued with his head cocked in a foreboding assault position. The snake locked itself like a statue – only its tongue darted periodically to and fro.

The cobra was massive – eight, maybe nine feet long and no less than eight inches thick. It maintained direct eye contact with Sammy. An entire hour transpired, then another hour.

Eventually, the rain stopped and the sky cleared. The sun was in the treetops directly overhead, indicating that the time was approximately twelve noon. Sammy heard the staccato of machine-gun fire and the thuds of mortar shells in the distance. The snake wouldn't let Sammy budge; it had been holding the exhausted, nerve-shattered Marine at bay for four hours already.

Every muscle in Sammy's body cried out in pain. His neck was as stiff as granite, his fatigues were soaked, and the unbearable winter dampness seemed to chill the fibers of his soul.

Another two hours passed. Each minute was a trial of a lifetime. Sammy kept thinking to himself, "One more minute, one more minute. I'm still alive. Hold on, Adler, one more minute! You can stick it out for another minute. Thank you, God, for letting me live another minute."

God? When did He come on the scene?

Sammy surprised himself. He never prayed in his life. His parents never practiced any form of religion, even though his grandparents were religious Jews. Sammy Adler was raised American – baseball, apple pie, The Marine Corp, and nothing else.

The snake seemed to alter its facial expression from threat to understanding. The minute Sammy thought about God, he could have sworn that the snake nodded its head, as if to say, "You're correct, soldier!" At that very instant, the snake uncocked its head, performed a perfect West Point "at ease" and "about face", and slithered away to the thick of the jungle.

Sammy's head dropped like a two-ton anchor. He broke out in a cathartic sob, and his entire body shuddered for a good five minutes, releasing the pent-up tension from within. He looked at his watch – seventeen hundred hours, or five in the afternoon.

Who could ever believe it? A U.S. Marine had just been held for nine hours in the custody of a nine-foot cobra. Were it not for his aching muscles and the leech bites all over his body, he wouldn't have believed it himself.

After several minutes of massaging his legs, he was able to stand. He didn't have much time, for nightfall was less than an hour away. The last nine hours felt like nine years.

Sammy, a superb navigator, began walking in the direction of the company bivouac – exhausted mentally and physically, but alive. He arrived at the clearing by the river, less than a half mile from his company's ambush position, and received the shock of his life: Captain John Willis and the Marines of Company C's three platoons were slaughtered to the last man in a counter-ambush.

The realization of the miracle hit Sergeant Sammy Adler like a ton of bricks: The Almighty had sent a gigantic cobra to guard over him. Were it not for the cobra, he would have returned to his company's position and would have been slaughtered too. Nine hours of unimaginable stress and suffering, with a deadly cobra staring him in the face, turned out to be the blessing of his life, a divine revelation in the jungles of South Vietnam, February 1969.

Gift number two: Enhanced spiritual development.

A good athlete knows that suffering strengthens character and pain makes gain. No one can expect to become a champion sprinter or weightlifter without sacrifice, dedication, perseverance, and aching muscles. Becoming a champion is no easy route.

The laws of the physical world apply to the spiritual world as well. One cannot hope to make spiritual gain without effort.

The principle of tribulations designed to enhance one's spiritual development recurs throughout the Bible. Abraham, the first Hebrew, suffered scorn and ridicule his entire life because of his steadfast devotion to God and monotheism. He was forced to withstand endless insults, humiliation, and threats on his life. He alone carried the torch of monotheism amidst a hostile heathen world. Abraham withstood ten severe tribulations, aimed to test his belief and trust in God. His son Isaac suffered likewise, and his grandson Jacob was tested to the limits of human capability. As such, Abraham, Isaac, and Jacob were groomed to become the fathers of monotheism and to serve as role models for their descendents throughout history, who would be faced with trials and tribulations of their own.

Joseph, the son of Jacob, was scorned and humiliated by his brothers and sold as a slave to the Egyptians. From the depths of his turmoil, he arose as one of the holiest righteous men that ever walked the earth.

The annals of King David, from the circumstances of his birth to his last day on earth, are one long, unpaved road of humiliation, degradation, and suffering. He was the object of incessant derision from both sides of the border – from jealous elements within his people, and from his enemies on the frontier. Even his sons plotted to overthrow him. We ask ourselves, why does the Almighty put His most beloved son – David, the anointed king – to such endless suffering?

Had King David never suffered from degradation and humiliation, he could never have attained the spiritual depth that enabled him to write the Book of Psalms, the greatest and most spiritually strengthening collection of prayers ever written in history. King David, like his forefathers Abraham, Isaac, and Jacob, could honestly say (Psalms 23:4), "Though I walk through the valley of death, I shall fear no evil for You [God] are with me, Your rod and your staff – they comfort me".

Scripture cannot be learned at face value. A closer look at the above passage from the Psalms reveals the entire notion of the difficult, seemingly bad times in life.

King David declares to God, "Your rod and your staff – they comfort me". "Staff" is a leaning stick, like the cane that an old man leans on. As such, "staff" symbolizes the comforting presence of God, which King David could lean on during all his troubled times. "Rod" symbolizes the punishment stick. King David in effect says to God, "Whether You console me and resemble a staff, or whether You torment me and resemble a rod, I am comforted by Your presence." Such a righteous man knows the value of the "rod", which is nothing other than the seemingly bad.

King David, as a three-year old shepherd, killed both a lion and a bear that threatened his flocks. As a twelve year old, he killed the giant Philistine warrior Goliath. David remained undaunted. Only one thought scared him: "Don't cast me away from you, God, and don't remove your spirit of holiness from me" (ibid. 51:13). King David's only fear in life was losing the proximity of God.

Just as a gold-medal Olympic sprinter cannot be a world champion without supreme effort, King David could not have become God's anointed, the head of the messianic dynasty, and role model for subsequent generations to this day, without the many arduous experiences in his life.

When you're able to treat the trying situations of your life as precious gifts designed to enhance your spiritual and emotional growth, then you're well on the way to inner peace.

Gift number three: The "distancing principle" – the gift of proximity to God.

Life's difficulties often exemplify the "distancing principle", as follows: When a baby takes his or her first steps, the parent moves a step back. That way, the baby makes an additional effort to take another stride and to reach the parent. The parent doesn't move away from the baby as an act of hate, heaven forbid. The contrary holds true, for when a parent steps back, the baby's longing for the parent is intensified. Therefore, the baby will invest maximal effort to taking an additional step. If the baby stumbles, the parent's open arms are never too far away to prevent a fall. As such, the "distancing principle" is utilized in parenthood as an act of love, to facilitate a baby's first steps.

We are all spiritual babies who – consciously or not, because of the divine souls within us – long for our Father in Heaven. When we try to get close to God, God uses the "distancing principle", and seemingly rejects us by sending us some type of suffering. If we remember to focus our thoughts on God during the emotional challenge of a difficult tribulation, and remind ourselves that He's always near to cushion a fall, we weather the situation with composure. When we don't lose our wits under pressure, we function successfully in highest-stress situations.

Drill sergeants and athletic coaches use the "distancing principle" to train competent combat soldiers and winning athletes. They can't be "nice" to their trainees. The apparent cruelty of a commander is actually compassion for the soldier in training. An old infantry expression says, "Sweat in maneuvers saves blood in battle", or, "the harder the training, the easier the war". The seemingly bad – the rigor and stress of training – is designed for the ultimate good – to save lives.

Any military instructor or athletic coach must make extreme demands on his trainees in order to build champions. The training of an elite soldier is far more difficult than standard training. Much more is demanded from a Marine or a Green Beret than from a cook or a mail clerk. Likewise, those privileged few who withstand severe tests in life are like The

Almighty's Special Forces. The Almighty puts them through special training to enhance their character development.

Character development leads to spiritual growth. Spiritual growth enables a person to get closer to God. Proximity to God means more Divine light. The more Divine light a person absorbs, the holier his or her soul becomes. The holier a person becomes, the more he or she finds eternal happiness and tranquility of the soul. Tranquility of the soul leads to more spiritual growth, and so forth. This wonderful spiritual upward spiral would be impossible without life's thorn bushes, which generate one's best effort at character development.

Gift number four: Absolution of wrongdoing, using a minor form of anguish as a substitute for major suffering.

God, in His infinite love for His children on earth, oftentimes converts a severe punishment incurred by a wrongdoing to some form of minor grief. Consequently, if a person has accrued heavy spiritual debts that have soiled and damaged his or her soul, God often sends that person a cheap substitute for the painful suffering that would otherwise be required to purify a blemished soul. A minor measure of suffering – embarrassment, insult, or the like – is considered adequate penance, and the person's debt is erased for a bargain-basement price.

Despite our best efforts at good behavior, each one of us harbors a burden of major spiritual debts. The average person relates to his or her soul like a spendthrift with a wallet full of credit cards, thinking he can sign for whatever he wants without ever having to pay. Suddenly, our spendthrift wakes up to an overflowing mailbox of overdue bills, and no cash to cover them. That's when the big trouble starts.

Maintaining a spiritual account that's free of debt is literally impossible while living in this world. Who can sign an oath that they did no harm to their fellow man in the last twenty-four hours? Who can testify that they made no unauthorized use of a telephone or a ballpoint pen without the boss's permission? A penny's worth of stealing is enough to severely blemish the soul.

Who can say that their thoughts, speech, and deeds around the clock are completely according to Almighty's will?

The worst thing imaginable is to complete our tour of duty in this world, only to enter the Heavenly court of justice with an accumulation of unpaid debts that have blemished our divine souls. That's like going to a White House reception with muddy shoes and soft-boiled-egg stains on your collar. What an embarrassment!

Nothing in the world cleanses a person so completely and quickly as a bit of minor suffering, such as insult, shame, and embarrassment. The following parable elaborates on the principle of minor anguish as a substitute for major suffering:

Cooper's negotiation with an Angel of mercy[24]

An angel of mercy appeared before Jerry Cooper, the successful owner of a popular gourmet deli in Long Island, respected member of the community and vice president of the local Lions Club, age 47, a superb golfer with a 6-stroke handicap, and at the prime of his life.

Angel: Mr. Cooper, dear friend, I'm sorry to inform you that your account in Heaven is severely overdrawn. Your spiritual checks are bouncing, and your debts are way past due. The Accusing Angel in charge of spiritual banking is demanding that The Almighty call in your markers. You're in very big trouble. Since The Almighty loves you so much, he sent me to arrange a consolidation of debts and a payback schedule for you. Your credit is no longer good upstairs. You either come to a debt arrangement with me or deal with a representative of the credit bureau from the severe judgment side. Those guys are rough.

Mr. Cooper: How acute is the situation?

---

[24] This allegory is a dramatization of a principle taught by the great 16th Century Kabbalist, Rabbi Moses Cordovero, from Safed, Israel.

Angel: Deferring payment is impossible. The Heavenly Bank has already granted you more than sufficient grace time. Instead of working on your praying and your good deeds, you've been working on your putting. The golf may be good for your body, but it's not helping your soul. The Heavenly Bank demands severe repentance and 713 fast days, in order to get your soul cleaned up of the excess spiritual fat. If sin were cholesterol, you'd have been pushing up daisies long ago. Starting immediately, you have five years to pay.

Mr. Cooper (making a quick calculation in his head): Hey wait a minute – that's more than 140 fasts in a year! How can I fast three times a week? Without Sabbath and holidays, that's fasting every other day! I'll look like a piece of spaghetti! Not even an angel is capable of fasting if he were standing behind the counter, serving smoked whitefish, onion bagels, and steamed corned beef all day long. Where'll I have the strength to work, to function on a normal basis? Hey, you're called an angel of mercy? What's going on here?

Angel: No problem. No need to give up the golf or to fast. I can exchange the 713 fast days for 713 days of a severely bleeding ulcer. Either way, you won't have the desire to eat.

Mr. Cooper: Heaven forbid! A bleeding ulcer! Have mercy on me!

Angel: I *am* an angel of mercy, Mr. Cooper. Okay, I can shorten the period of suffering, yet get your debts paid for. How about a massive heart attack? You'll spend 713 hours in an intensive-care unit. That's only a month.

Mr. Cooper: Oh no! Who'll handle my business? I'm smack in the middle of wedding season. Look at this pad full of orders for platters and catering. Who's gonna prepare all that? How can there be a Long Island wedding without Cooper's chopped liver and chicken schnitzel? What about my family?

Angel: You're worried about your family? I see here in your file that you have six kids. You know, I can get your account cleared and establish a new credit rating for you in exchange for one of your children. That way, no suffering for you and the wedding platters get completed on schedule. No need for the bride and groom to go without Cooper's chicken schnitzel. A deal?

Mr. Cooper (speechless, tears of fear choking his throat, finally beginning to realize the seriousness of his predicament): Please, I beg you in the Name of our compassionate Father in Heaven, not my kids...oh please, dear angel, not in my lifetime...

Angel (passes a clean pearly white silk hanky to Cooper): Sure, dear friend, I understand. I'll tell you what – let's examine your financial profile *(the angel opens up another portfolio)*. According to the latest printout, The Almighty has been good to you. Your assets – the business, your investments, the land in south Jersey, the bungalow in the Catskills, your home, the three cars, the savings accounts, together with all the insurance equity – Perfect! Exactly seven million, one-hundred-thirty thousand dollars... Each required day of fast can be redeemed for ten thousand dollars. How tidy! You lose all your assets and you're clean as a whistle – no heart attacks, no ulcers, and good health for the wife and children. Fair enough?

Mr. Cooper: What are you talking about – my home, my business, my savings and investments, all down the drain? Out on the pavement at my age, with no roof over my head? What about the kids? You know how expensive tuition is at Brandeis? How's my big girl going to finish her degree? Who'll pay med-school tuition for my son at Johns Hopkins? Do you expect me to set up a tent on the front lawn of the synagogue? With all the Divine wisdom in Heaven, can't you come up with a better suggestion?

Angel: Excuse me, Mr. Cooper, but your reactions are quite irrational. Haven't you realized how grave your situation is? For 47 years, you've ignored your soul. Do you know what 47 years of spiritual neglect does to a soul? Do you know how difficult it is to cleanse a badly tarnished soul? I have one more proposal for you, but I'm sure you won't want that either...

Mr. Cooper: No, wait! Let me hear it! Anything's better than losing my health, my children, or my livelihood. I don't have the willpower or the strength for fasts and self-torture.

Angel: This is my last offer. This coming Sunday morning, the Deli will be jammed with people. The Governor's wife will be waiting for her weekly order of smoked fish, and half of Giants' starting lineup will be there for their traditional coffee and Danish, getting fired up for the Redskins game. The financial editor of the Times, the anchorman from Fox news, and the chairman of Chase Manhattan will be at an adjacent table with their bagels and lox. People will be out on the pavement waiting to get in.

All of a sudden, an irate lady – whom you've never seen in your life – will charge into the deli like an insane buffalo, with a wormy pint container of potato salad that she claims was purchased in Cooper's deli. She'll be yelling at the top of her lungs, cursing you and your deli, with a barrage of insults in three languages. Your face will turn bright red, then completely pale. Your pulse will rise to 150, and your blood pressure will almost blow a gasket. You will undergo seven minutes and thirteen seconds of the worst humiliation you've ever known. Now, if you so much as emit a peep from your mouth – if you display the slightest sign of anger – you fail the test.

On the other hand, if you're smart enough to accept seven minutes and thirteen seconds of insult and embarrassment with patience and humility, realizing that The Almighty is doing you a major favor by sending this deranged lady with her venomous mouth to the deli, all your sins shall be atoned. Your slate in Heaven shall be wiped free, and your soul will be whiter than a snowflake. You get continued good health, a healthy family, and a more-than-substantial livelihood.

I'll fill you in on a little secret: By accepting the anguish with a smile, at exactly seven minutes and fourteen seconds after the beginning of the test, the guys in the white coats will appear punctually on the premises to remove the mad lady with the wormy potato salad. All the suffering will do an about face in your favor. People will have tremendous respect for your self-control and strength of character. Best of all, the embarrassment will completely cleanse your soul, and your spiritual deficit will disappear. But don't forget – the seven minutes and thirteen seconds will feel like a fiery furnace. Not a peep of protest, complaint, or anger. Agreed?

Mr. Cooper: Yes! Of course! Bring on the insults! Welcome embarrassment! Hurray for humiliation! Let's get the show on the road! I hope she throws the wormy potato salad in my face!

Aftermath of the Cooper story: The deranged lady *did* throw the wormy potato salad in Jerry Cooper's face. Cooper winced, but gave a whispered thanks to The Almighty for His lovingkindness. The test was tough, but he passed.

Cooper's domestic life took a major turn for the better. His wife felt a new flame in her heart for her patient and loving husband. Even the Brandeis daughter and the med-school son, who used to look down on their deli-peddling daddy's short fuse, shared new respect for their father's tranquil deportment. The customers adored him as much as they savored his triple-decker hot pastrami on rye. The deli became the in-place on Long Island.

Once a year, on the anniversary of the wormy potato-salad episode, Cooper would give free coffee and donuts for anyone who agreed to insult him. That's what he called, "soultime – my annual cleanup day".

The moral of the "Cooper and the Angel" story: Whenever you suffer aggravation, insult, embarrassment, or humiliation, **don't lose your temper!** Close your eyes and smile. Imagine that you've just completed plea bargaining with an Angel of Mercy, and that your ever-loving compassionate Father in Heaven has agreed to waive a decree of cancer, a major car accident, or bankruptcy in lieu of a few minutes of aggravation. Now, breathe deeply, exhale, open your eyes and smile. Don't let anyone or anything rob you of your tranquility. Be happy. Realize in your heart that you've just made the deal of your life. All your spiritual debts have been paid for a bargain-basement price. The Almighty is superbly proud of you.

Gift number five: To qualify a person for a special blessing.

Our bodies operate on the principle of contraction and expansion. By contracting and expanding, the heart pumps blood to all parts of the body. By contracting and expanding, the lungs breathe air. The same holds true for the spiritual: Our "ups" and "downs" in life are none other than spiritual expansions and contractions. Just as the lungs or the heart cannot be in a perpetual state of expansion, a person can't expect a trouble-free life of "ups", or continuous success.

> "The world is round, and rotates. So, if you're on top of the world, don't be arrogant, because soon you might be down. If you're on the bottom, don't be sad, because you've got nowhere to go but up." – *The Melitzer Rebbe*

Our "downs" in life correspond to the contraction mode of our heart and lungs. We can always encourage ourselves with the knowledge that contraction leads to expansion, that our beloved Father in Heaven never disappoints us. Every mother knows that the happiest occasion of her life – the birth of her child – follows labor contractions, which are the sharpest pains imaginable. Sometimes, The Almighty sends difficult "contractions", or troubles in life, before a tremendous "expansion", a gift of some sort. The following case is a living example of this principle:

Alan and Sue Sharff: "Al and Sue" (*imaginary names*) are a Sunday magazine's cover-photograph couple: Attractive, successful in their respective careers, popular in the community, good athletes, and compassionate to their fellow man. They love each other like a pair of turtledoves. Yet, seven years after their wedding, they hadn't yet been blessed with children.

The Sharffs spent thousands of dollars on medical treatments, with no success. The doctors called them, "enigma of the year". Apparently, they should have been healthy candidates for parenthood, but month after month continued to suffer bitter disappointment.

The Sharff's eighth wedding anniversary was a few weeks away. Al came across a magazine article about fertility problems, and one particular point of advice caught his eye: A change of environment and a total relaxation situation enhances fertilization.

Al thought for a moment: What's a drastic change from the boring plains of Winnipeg, Manitoba? The Swiss Alps! He dialed Swissair, booked two round trip tickets to Zurich, and started planning the surprise trip of Sue's life. That afternoon, he came home with a dozen white carnations, Sue's favorite carryout Chinese food, and a legal size envelope sealed with a yellow ribbon – airline tickets to Switzerland – date of departure, September 30, 2001.

* * *

Less than three weeks after the tragic "Nine-eleven", the heinous destruction of the Twin Towers in New York and the attack on the Pentagon in Washington, D.C., the entire intelligence community of the free world was preoccupied with hunting the heinous El Qaida terrorists. On the morning of October 1, 2001, the highest security hotlines between Mossad headquarters in Tel Aviv, Scotland Yard, the CIA, Canadian Intelligence, and Swiss Intelligence were humming nonstop. Bin Ladin's right-hand man, the second most dangerous terrorist in the world, had succeeded in slipping out of the United States by foot, over the Canadian border.

According to Mossad intelligence, El Qaida's number-two man reached an Arab embassy in Ottawa, and was outfitted with a fresh identity, a new cover, and a Canadian passport. The elusive terrorist even looked like a Canadian – light complexion, blue eyes, rusty brown hair, and six feet one inch tall. To further baffle his pursuers, the Mossad communiqué wrote, he was purported to be traveling with a female companion with blond hair, Scandinavian features, tall and slim, under the cover of husband and wife. "Their suspected destination is a safe house in London or Zurich. Zero-hour," the communiqué concluded, "act immediately."

The skeptical desk-jockeying bureaucrats of Canadian Intelligence treated the Mossad's communiqué like a shuttlecock, tossing it back and forth from office to office, as if hunting terrorists was a Sunday afternoon game of badminton in the backyard. By the time somebody took the initiative to tighten security at Canada's international airports, the terrorist and his female companion were more than halfway across the Atlantic Ocean.

* * *

Al and Sue Sharff descended the steps of the Swissair 747 that flew them from Toronto to Zurich. They filled their lungs with a deep breath of the invigorating Swiss air. A shuttle bus carried them to passport control. They looked at each other, filled with excitement and anticipation about their upcoming trip. This was their first trip together to Europe. Their thoughts were far away on snow-covered peaks and glacier-fed lakes.

Al and Sue reached the passport control window, and casually handed their two passports to the officer in charge.

The Swiss are surgically efficient. The passport control officer examined the Sharff's passports and then looked at them with a well-trained expressionless poker face. He pressed a red button under his desk. Within seconds, a dozen Swiss plainclothesmen pounced on the Sharffs.

Three Swiss security agents knocked Alan to the floor. A fourth jammed a police-special .45 caliber pistol to Alan's temple, warning him in French and in Arabic, "One move and you're dead".

Alan could barely breathe. His face was smashed to the floor and close to four hundred pounds of Swiss Internal Security agents were sitting on his back, nearly ripping his arms out their sockets with a double hammerlock.

Out of instinct, Sue went berserk. Two agents grabbed her from behind, while a third handcuffed her. She screamed, "Alan, my God, they're killing my Alan!" One of the agents covered her mouth and yanked her head back. She bit his hand with the ferocity of a wounded she-bear. A hand came from nowhere and slapped her so hard that her ears rang. She screamed once more and fainted, falling like a dead weight in the agents' hands.

"Looks like our man", one of the agents said into a mini-transmitter. "He's got the blond with him. We're bringing them in".

Alan and Sue spent their next two hours on the cold metal floor of a windowless high-security van on the way to SIS headquarters, bound by the hands and feet like two slaves. Every bump in the road tormented them. Sue cried in pain with each additional jolt. Hot tears of frustration trickled down Alan's cheeks; he couldn't stand hearing his wife in such pain, yet there was nothing he could do to help her. Who could believe that such torture and degradation was happening in Europe, 2001, and to them! Who could imagine such a nightmare?

The journey seemed like an endless descent to purgatory. When they finally arrived at the Swiss Internal Security compound, they were shoved into separate, dark isolated cells for another hour. Finally, the interrogators arrived. For the next six hours, they were interrogated separately. Sue was so disoriented, that she began to believe the stories of her accusers. "Maybe I really am a terrorist accomplice?"

The Swiss sent in a fresh interrogator every thirty minutes, but the Sharff's were denied food, water, and even a visit to the toilet. They both suffered from excruciating headaches and exploding bladders, victims of Swiss penal efficiency and white-collar torture.

Alan denied repeatedly that he doesn't understand a word of Arabic, only French and English. "My name is Alan Sharff, born and raised in Winnipeg, Manitoba," he insisted.

Swiss Internal Security wasn't convinced; Al's height, weight, blue eyes, and reddish brown hair fit the terrorist's description perfectly. The El Qaida terrorist's name, which appeared near the top of every Interpol wanted list in the Western world, was none other than – Ali Sharif! It seemed obvious to the Swiss that a terrorist mastermind like Ali Sharif would choose an easily-remembered cover name such as Alan Sharff.

Another hour transpired. A black Mercedes with a diplomatic license plate pulled up in front of SIS headquarters. The Security Liaison officer from the Canadian embassy arrived with the dossier of former Flight Lieutenant Alan Sharff, RCAF. As a former navigator in the Canadian Air Force, Alan's identity could be verified quickly, by a mere comparison of fingerprints. The Canadian SLO threatened to make an international issue out of the SIS fiasco, treating two innocent Canadian tourists like convicted terrorists without even making a third grade identity check. "Lucky that you didn't shoot the Sharffs," growled the incensed Canadian security liaison. An embarrassed team of SIS officers released the Sharffs within the next thirty minutes.

The Swiss government tried their best to placate the Sharff family, and reimbursed them for the plane tickets. Neither Alan nor Sue had any desire to remain in Switzerland for one unnecessary minute. They spent the night gratis in the grand suite of the Zurich Airport hotel, and flew home to Canada the next morning.

Alan took Sue on a wonderful consolation vacation to the Canadian Rockies. Nine months later, Sue gave birth to a healthy, eight-pound baby boy.

The Sharffs revisited: If Alan and Sue hadn't suffered the thorny experience of Switzerland, they might have continued for years in parentless frustration. Their own cuts and scratches were a necessary prerequisite before receiving their own rare mountain rose, the birth of their son.

At the time of this writing, little Joey Sharff is a plump, rosy-cheeked toddler of two. Sue is now expecting again. Ask the members of the Sharff family if they're still angry about the Swiss trauma. They just laugh and look at each other lovingly. "Are you kidding," they exclaim, "our little Joey is worth a hundred Swiss traumas!"

Gift number six: To save us from undesirable people.

King Solomon says (Proverbs 18:3), "Scorn is the companion of the evil, and shame accompanies disgrace."

The above proverb teaches how to identify undesirable people: First, they're full of contempt. Second, they have nothing nice to say about other people. Third, they're constantly on the lookout for other people's flaws, as future ammunition to disgrace them in public.

An old Yiddish expression literally translated says, "The hat burns on the thief's head." In other words, a thief thinks that everyone steals. People tend to project their faults on others. Since an undesirable person is loaded with faults – he or she is usually arrogant, dishonest, untrustworthy, extremely insecure, and very angry. Such people project all of their faults on others and then try to elevate themselves by degrading their unfortunate victims.

Many times, a good person becomes involved with some new acquaintance, unaware of the true nature of the latter. God guards the unwitting, and in His infinite knowledge knows that such a relationship will be detrimental to the good person. God therefore sends the good person a double dose of sharp thorns. Here's what happens:

The Almighty exposes the undesirable person, who does something painful or damaging to the unwitting person. In such a case, the thorns are a gift from God, an urgent message to warn the unsuspecting that such a relationship has dangerous prospects, and should be terminated. The well-known folk adage says, "If you play with fire, you get burned." If you associate with undesirable individuals, then you can expect to suffer.

Gift number seven: To prevent spiritual stagnation.

Stagnant water smells bad. It also attracts mosquitoes, snakes, and unfavorable microorganisms. Flowing, or fresh water, always smells good. Such water is drinkable, and it is a suitable environment for fish. Since every entity of the physical world –

mineral, vegetable, animal, and human – receives its vitality from a spiritual life spark, the laws that hold true in the physical world also apply to the metaphysical. A spiritually stagnant person exudes a spiritual stench, which repels good angels and attracts evil forces. On the other hand, a person who makes constant spiritual progress projects a sweet and fresh spiritual aroma which attracts good angels and repels evil forces. A truly righteous person is capable of smelling such a spiritual scent.

A good athlete thrives on daily progress. A long-distance runner wants to knock a few seconds off his previous best time and a weightlifter tries to lift a little more weight than he lifted yesterday. In the same way, a spiritual person tries to get closer to God every single day.

God assists those who have trouble making spiritual progress in the following manner: He sends them a gift that resembles a wild raspberry thicket. The sharp stickers are always obvious, but oftentimes the sweet fruit is concealed.

The Almighty frequently rescues a person from spiritual stagnation by sending him or her some terrible insult or humiliation. If the recipient is cognizant enough to accept the verbal abuse with no anger or negative reaction, then he or she graduates to a higher spiritual level. Insult, embarrassment, and humiliation – as we learned in the Cooper story earlier in this chapter, are always preferable to sickness or financial loss.

Rabbi Yechiel Michel of Zlatchov. Once, the renowned Baal Shem Tov, founder of the Chassidic movement, visited one of his prize pupils, the holy Rebbe "Michel'e" of Zlatchov. As they stood on the steps of the synagogue, a peasant walked past and hurled a string of insults at Rebbe Michel'e. "Who was that?" asked the Baal Shem Tov.

Rebbe Michel'e answered, "He walks past the synagogue every day and 'greets' me in such a manner, then disappears".

The Baal Shem Tov smiled, "How lucky you are, Michel'e, to have a daily spiritual cleansing like that!"

Rebbe Yechiel Michel of Zlatchov, one of the greatest sages of the last three hundred years, never suffered from a day's spiritual stagnation in his life.

Gift number eight: To prevent us from becoming emotionally dependent.

Periodical thorns in our lives – especially tribulations of insult, derision, embarrassment, or degradation – are actually a rare gift from the Almighty. If everyone were to constantly praise and honor us, we'd become addicted to the point that we'd be dependant on others for our daily "fix" of acclaim. Emotional dependence on others is the worst form of poverty. Compliment seekers walk around with an extended palm begging for a bit of praise or honor, just like a poor man begs for a coin or two.

When a "praise-aholic" – a person who is addicted to compliments and praise – suddenly receives the opposite, such as criticism or verbal abuse, his or her life becomes a bitter misery. Such a person is an emotional handicap in every sense of the word, and difficult to get along with. Praise-aholics harbor extreme feelings of hatred toward anyone who dares to criticize or insult them. Their heart burns with anger, and their soul is in constant turmoil. Praise-and-honor addicts can never achieve inner peace, unless they overcome their addiction.

God doesn't want us to become to become emotionally handicapped, nor does He want us to become praise-aholics. Therefore, from time to time, He sends us a dose of verbal thorns – malicious criticism, insult, or humiliation – to keep our ego in line and to perpetuate our emotional health.

Rabbi Zev of Zabriz. Rabbi Zev was one of the five sons of Rabbi Yechiel Michel of Zlatchov *(see Gift number seven, above)*. Rabbi Zev was a holy man, scholar, and miracle worker in his own right, with thousands of followers in the Galician district of Western Ukraine.

Rabbi Zev's clapboard house of prayer was adjacent to his modest apartment. His wife, a razor-tongued shrew to say the least, would often embarrass him in the middle of a sermon or lesson in front of hundreds of listeners. Usually, she'd say something like, "If all those people knew how stupid you really are, they'd go home and do something productive, rather than listening to your foolishness!"

Rabbi Zev would only smile, take a deep breath, and continue with his sermon. But, his followers and pupils were outraged. "Rabbi, we can't stand hearing the *Rebbetzin's* (Yiddish, for "rabbi's wife") blasphemy. Your clerical honor demands that you divorce her. You could have your pick of a hundred better women than her!"

Rabbi Zev shrugged his shoulders, and once again smiled sheepishly: "Thank you for your concern, dear friends, but if I get rid of her, who will give me my daily dose of anti-arrogance medicine? I keep her for the health of my soul!"

Gift number nine: To help us utilize our potential.

When very special people suffer, they mobilize untold inner resources of spiritual strength. Oftentimes, they are unaware of their own capabilities. A Special Forces' expression says, "You can't get juice from an orange until you squeeze it."

Sometimes God sends very special souls to this world, and inserts them in normal bodies. God then applies an enormous amount of pressure on them, for two purposes:

1.   To show the tremendous potential of the human spirit, as a shining example to others;

2.   Under pressure, a person taps his or her deepest reserves of inner strength to make a tremendous contribution to society.

Let's view an example of the above principle:

Rita Richards[25]. Rita graduated at the top of her class at the University of Texas, majoring in radio and television. She started

---

[25] Names, places, and circumstances altered.

her career with a small, local radio station in the Texas panhandle, and within a few short years, became the anchorwoman of Atlanta's most popular television evening news program. Rita's career was blossoming. Her husband Tommy, a frustrated former Longhorn defensive end, spent three seasons warming the benches of a losing AFL team. Before the opening of his fourth season, he was cut from the squad and became a free agent that nobody wanted.

Rita's life soured; she became the brunt of Tommy's frustration. He moped around their apartment drinking beer and becoming nastier by the day. The minute he raised a hand against her, she left their luxury condo and began divorce proceedings. The divorce was a nerve-racking mess that was dragged out for twelve months.

Rita began consoling herself with gin and tonics. Before long, her breakfast, lunch, dinner, and between meal snacks were gin and tonic. Miraculously, she managed to give her nightly, authoritative and convincing delivery of the seven p.m. news, but she was fast becoming a functional alcoholic.

When the divorce proceedings were finally terminated, Rita went home to visit her parents in Dallas. On the flight from Atlanta to Dallas, she sat next to a lovely woman, a dentist, who by a stroke of Divine Providence was a member of Alcoholics Anonymous in Atlanta. Rita couldn't believe that such an intelligent, personable, and pleasant individual was a former alcoholic!

"Believe me, sweetheart," the dentist said, "People think that alcoholics all lay in gutters – not true. You'll find alcoholics among society's most influential and affluent members. Rita, start helping yourself. You are a very special individual; people trust in you. Soon, you'll be able to help a lot of other people!" The dentist was right.

Rita became a regular at the Atlanta branch of AA. Two months after her first meeting, she drank her last gin and tonic. She served as an inspiration to all the other members. Rita used her skills to put the mission and the message of AA in the forefront of Atlanta's consciousness. Here's what happened:

During a commercial break in the middle of the seven p.m. news, the local news editor passed Rita the following bulletin: "Three-car collision claims the lives of seven: Four teenagers, and an out-of-state couple with their eight-month old baby. Three others critically wounded. Police authorities attribute the accident to drunk driving."

Rita narrated the bulletin in her normal delivery tone. A tear welled in her eye. The attentive and experienced director zoomed in on her at full-face close-up, as she began the most dramatic impromptu narrative that Atlanta ever heard:

"Seven human souls, each a special gem, were robbed this evening of their right to live. Dear Atlantans, alcohol is a robber and a murderer. We've got to delete it from our lives. I know – I'm a former alcoholic myself, and were it not for Alcoholics Anonymous, who knows what would have become of me…

"If you've been drinking, put your car keys back in your pocket. Think of your loved ones. Look at the sparkle in your children's eyes; don't they deserve healthy, sober parents? Give AA a toll-free call at 1-800-749-0500. If you don't get an immediate answer, call Channel Four at *(the director flashes channel four's phone number on the bottom of the screen)*…you can talk with me personally. Whatever you do, put that bottle back on the shelf. Better yet, spill its contents down the drain, and use it for a vase. Put a rose in your empty bottle, in loving memory of the seven Atlantans who lost their lives this evening. And now for tomorrow's weather…"

The station was mobbed with congratulatory phone calls: "Right on, Rita!" or "thank goodness, somebody's got a worthwhile message", and "keep up the good work, Channel Four; we love Rita!" Rita personally spoke to fifty-four help seekers within the next three hours. Channel Four news skyrocketed to the top of the local ratings.

Over the years, Rita has personally sponsored hundreds of former alcoholics, helping them rebuild new lives. She's saved tens of couples and dozens of children from the gloomy fate of broken homes. Her force of character, her integrity, and her passion to help others has made this world a better place. More than anything else, she's a role model with a cogent message – with The Almighty's help and your best efforts, you can accomplish whatever your heart desires.

Spiritual analysis of the Rita Richards story. Let's observe the marvels of Divine intervention in Rita's life: Rita was born with a talent for broadcasting, which enabled her to be in the forefront of the public eye and to influence others on a grandiose scale.

Tommy was the first thorny element in Rita's life. Tommy's downhill career and negative traits became a surgical scalpel in The Almighty's hand to expose Rita's own weakness, a tendency toward drinking. Had Rita not been exposed to the extreme stress of Tommy's abuse and the difficult divorce, she may have spent the rest of her life as a casual drinker and a superficial second-rate announcer.

The Almighty forced Rita to take a vacation, and to visit her parents in Dallas. The dentist, a remarkable individual and perfect role model for Rita, was a former alcoholic herself and an active member of AA. Divine Providence had the two ladies sit side-by-side on the flight that proved to be the turning point in Rita's life.

The seemingly bad tribulations of a compulsive drinking habit forced Rita to mobilize her reservoir of untapped inner strength in order to overcome the alcohol. She emerged victorious, and became a shining example for others, fulfilling her true mission in life to the best of her abilities. Without life's thorns, Rita would have never attained such a high spiritual level and such a rewarding life of service to her fellow man.

Rita revisited: A mutual friend introduced Rita to Abbey Gold. They married a few weeks thereafter. Abbey's five-feet seven inches and slight, one-hundred-fifty-pound frame is a striking contrast to Tommy. Abbey, an accountant, is a kind and considerate partner who cherishes his wife. Rita comes home in the evening to home-cooked gourmet dinners and fresh flowers on the table. Were it not for the thorns of her first marriage, she would never have chosen an anti-macho type like Abbey. Rita says that the three best blessings in her life begin with the letter A – The Almighty, Abbey, and Alcoholics Anonymous. Rita gets straight A's in life, having successfully completed the long voyage from total turbulence to inner peace and genuine fulfillment.

Spiritual awareness helps us to arrive at a crystal-clear conclusion: Everything that God does is for our absolute good. Geared with such essential cognizance, we can't possibly be angry about anything.

6

The Panicky Pigeon

This chapter is the second part of our reconciliation plan with God. Chapter Five compared life's difficulties to a thorny wild raspberry thicket or a mountain rose bush – you have to weather the thorns in order to obtain the fruit or the flower. This chapter discusses the type of suffering that a person induces by his or her own actions and teaches how to prevent it. By the end of this chapter, you will hopefully be at complete peace with God – no more grievances and no more anger.

Self-induced Suffering – an unlocked jail

Now, we're resuming our allegorical hike up Mount Patience with Old Isaac. We'll soon learn how self-induced suffering resembles an unlocked jail.

The Panicky Pigeon

Isaac takes you the rest of the way through Raspberry Forest and up the mountain trail to an elevation of about 5500 feet. Shortly before sunset, you reach your prearranged lodging for the night, a quaint hunter's cabin with a redbrick fireplace and a breathtaking view.

Looking down the mountain, you can see the miles of progress you've made up the trail since you left Old Isaac's Inn. What a wonderful feeling of accomplishment – you've climbed, learned new things, and grown. You're not the same as you were at the outset of your journey. Nevertheless, you can't sit on your laurels – there's still ground to cover. Isaac recommends that you rest up here for a day and then continue on your way up the trail to tranquility.

The pine-scented mountain air is indescribable, and since the weather's a bit warm for this time of the year, you and Isaac decide to sleep with the windows open. You both fall into a deep, satisfying sleep to the serenade of crickets, tree frogs, and an old hoot owl, the self-appointed governor of this neck of the woods.

Before daybreak, you awake to a frantic flapping sound. A pigeon has randomly flown in your window, and the poor little bird is panic-stricken. It flies from one wall to another, and thinks that you've trapped him inside the cabin.

You try to calm him down: "Look here, pigeon, we're not even out of our sleeping bags yet! Nobody's set a trap for you. Open your eyes – the two windows are wide open!" The pigeon won't listen. He ricochets from one wall to another like a billiard ball. After a few minutes of frightened flight around the cabin, the pigeon is exhausted. He comes to rest on the fireplace mantel.

Isaac tries a different strategy. In his best cooing accent, he says, "Fulluhoo – hullabaloop – hoodulahoo". The pigeon acknowledges his message, nods, and flies out of the adjacent window.

You pop up out of your sleeping bag in amazement and ask, "What did you tell the pigeon? Isaac, do you really know how to communicate with a pigeon?"

"I simply told the pigeon to calm down and follow the light. The minute he took my advice, he was a free bird again instead of senselessly colliding with the walls of an imaginary prison," Isaac explains.

Let's think about the lesson of the panicky pigeon. The pigeon flew into the cabin on his own free will. Once inside, it felt confined and threatened, like a prisoner in jail. The windows were open the whole time, and it was free to fly away whenever it wanted, but the bird was so stressed that it couldn't see the light.

The pigeon story reminds me of self-induced suffering. Self-induced suffering resembles a prisoner that was thrown in jail on a ten-year sentence:

For weeks, the prisoner wailed, complained, knocked his head against the wall, cursed his misfortune, and was angry at the whole world. One day, in the peak of frustration, he pounded on the door of his cell. Suddenly the door flew open.

The astonished prisoner peeked outside, and saw that the corridor of the jail was empty – not a guard in sight. Still apprehensive, he tiptoed his way to the jailers' office and to the front door. No one stopped him; he simply walked away to freedom.

Confinement in a jail with an unlocked door is senseless. Yet, people confine themselves to a prison of needless inner turbulence every day. A substantial amount of our suffering in life is self-induced. Therefore, once a person realizes that certain actions induce trouble in life, and learns to refrain from those actions, the trouble disappears. No law says that you *have* to suffer so much! You can terminate a good portion of the anguish in your life with the ease of walking away from an unlocked jail.

The concept of self-induced suffering is easy to understand: A heavy smoker that suffers from shortness of breath, a chronic cough, high blood pressure, and frequent headaches, is daft to blame The Almighty for his or her ills. The Almighty didn't design the human lung to be tar and nicotine proof. If your car were malfunctioning because you gave it the wrong type of fuel, or used frying oil instead of motor oil, would it be fair to be angry with your service mechanic or with the auto manufacturer? Obviously not.

The smoker, if he or she really desires, can walk away at any time from the nicotine prison, and regain good health within a few short weeks. Shortly after discarding the cigarettes, ailments begin to disappear. A person doesn't need a high level of spiritual awareness to realize that cigarettes are a health hazard; federal law requires printing a warning on every pack. Yet, many people choose to ignore the surgeon general, the AMA, and their body's own warnings, and continue their life of needless suffering, like a lethargic prisoner in an unlocked jail.

A person with developed spiritual awareness understands that even self-induced suffering, like a cough or shortness of breath resulting from smoking, is also a gift from God. The Almighty sends those ailments as messages to his beloved children, which in effect say, "You shouldn't be smoking! Stop doing damage to yourself!"

In all fairness, giving up cigarettes – or any other habit – is not an easy task. For some, it's a war. Many other types of self-induced suffering are subtler and more difficult to detect and to eradicate from our lives. We can't win a war without effective weapons. In the war against self-induced suffering, we need a cogent plan of action.

The remainder of this chapter is divided into two sections: Section one is the Three-Stage Plan for preventing self-induced suffering; section two discusses twelve common causes of self-induced suffering.

Section one: The Three-Stage Plan for preventing self-induced suffering

The three-stage plan for preventing self-induced suffering is the key to self-improvement. Once you learn to use the three-stage plan, your life will change dramatically for the better. Here's what the plan offers:

1.   Prevention of self-induced suffering.

2.   Immediate relief from existing self-induced suffering.

3.   Better interpersonal relationships, both with family and acquaintances.

4.   Improved productivity and career satisfaction, more success and therefore an improved income.

5.   Improved vitality, better mental and physical health.

6.   Increased happiness and a major improvement in the quality of your life.

7.   Less worry, more self-confidence.

8. A closer relationship between your body and your soul, and therefore a closer relationship between you and The Almighty, Who's waiting for you with the open arms of a beloved father.

9. No more anger and a lot more tranquility.

The more you practice the "One-Week Plan" and the Enhanced Spiritual Awareness (ESA) Workshop that you learned in Chapter Four, the better you'll be able to implement the three-stage plan for preventing self-induced suffering.

Self-improvement is similar to fighting a war

The body and the spirit are constantly at war with each other, until one defeats the other or until a person's last day on this earth. For an alcoholic lying in the gutter, the war is over; his evil inclination and his body have totally vanquished his spirit and his divine soul. For a pious righteous person, the opposite is true; by devoting one's life to spiritual perfection, the soul succeeds in subduing the evil inclination and base urges. Consequently, the righteous person's soul completely controls his or her capitulated body.

Most of us are somewhere in between; our bodies and our souls are engage in pitched battle on a daily basis. Whenever the body gets the upper hand, the soul suffers. When the soul suffers, a person feels inner turmoil, stress, and anger. The three-stage plan is a critical weapon in the war for inner peace, and a giant step up the trail to tranquility.

What are the three stages in eliminating self-induced suffering?

The three stages in eliminating self-induced suffering are:

1. Observation

2. Self-evaluation

3. Implementation.

Here's how they work:

Stage one: Observation

A person should always look for the innate wisdom implanted in every creation or event. Proper observation means asking the question, "What can I learn from this?" Since all wisdom stems from The Creator, when one makes a mental connection to the wisdom of a creation, he becomes attached to The Creator. When we connect ourselves to God, we receive enhanced spiritual awareness.

Let's translate the above concept to practical terms. Pick up an orange. Have you ever examined the Divine wisdom of an orange? Look at the beauty of its skin – an experienced team of packaging engineers, graphics artists, and product development technologists couldn't have invented a more attractive package. What a superb color! The skin of the orange is permeable to oxygen, yet guards the fruit from contamination. The orange provides an abundance of vitamin C. The winter, when a person most needs vitamin C to combat colds and the flu, is the exact time of the citrus harvest.

The Divine wisdom behind the creation of an orange is actually God speaking to us. How? Suppose we're walking down the fruit isle of our local supermarket on a cold February afternoon, and a gorgeous display of tangerines and golden Valencias catches our eye. The impulse from our eye goes to the brain, and a command from the brain stimulates the flow of saliva in our mouth. A little voice in our head says, "Buy some oranges today". That's our beloved Father in Heaven speaking, Who wants his cherished children to have some extra vitamin C. When we observe well enough, we find God in every mineral, plant, animal, and human. Every being has its own unique and timely message.

The world around us is God's way of talking to us. That's the secret of **observation**, our first stage in eliminating self-induced suffering.

Now, let's focus on how observation helps eliminate self-induced suffering. Compare the difference between two neighbors, Herbert and David. Herbert lacks spiritual awareness and never tried to develop his powers of observation. David is the opposite – he observes his environment and tries to understand the wisdom within each creation and event.

Herbert and David drive on the same road to work. Both had two cases of flat tires in one week. David noticed that in both instances, nails had punctured his tires, and that the flat occurred in the proximity of a construction site. David decided to drive to work via an alternate route. As a result, the phenomena of flat tires and the accompanied aggravation ceased.

Herbert continued to drive on the same road, to waste valuable time changing flat tires, and to spend his hard-earned money on tire repairs. The third time he had a flat tire, he pulled his car over to the side of the road, flew into a rage, and started kicking the deflated tire.

David, like other experienced spiritual observers, appreciates the messages that The Almighty sends him. David's spiritual antennas receive God's messages loudly and clearly: "David my son, don't travel this road any more. Litter from the construction site is all over the place. That accounts for the nails that caused you the two flat tires. Take an alternate route to work."

That was only part of the message. Later that week, a fatal, ten-car accident occurred on the same road, at the exact hour when David usually drove past. When David heard the news, he wrote a big check for charity and thanked his beloved God with all his heart. Herbert was one of the drivers involved in the accident.

God doesn't punish – he educates. The flat tires and the nails on the road were God's way of speaking to Herbert and David.

David paid attention. By combining his power of spiritual awareness and cogent observation, he perfectly understood and appreciated the heavenly message.

Herbert missed the boat. He was angry with God, and his anger constricted his thought processes. Instead of putting his powers of reasoning to work, Herbert vented his frustrations by kicking his flat tire. Worse than that, failure to heed important stimuli in his environment led to his involvement in a serious collision.

> The agony of tribulations stems from the lack of spiritual awareness. When a person has spiritual awareness, and looks at the ultimate purpose of tribulations, the sorrow of suffering vanishes. – *Rebbe Nachman of Breslev*

When we experience suffering in life, the first stage of action is observation – slow down, open our eyes, and look for the wisdom behind the suffering. An educational message from God hides within every case of self-induced suffering. Once our mind connects to the wisdom behind our suffering, we connect with God, and enable ourselves to process His message.

Let's add a real-life example: "John and June Rivers" (imaginary names) had extreme marital difficulties, and were on the verge of divorce. At the last minute, they came to me for counseling. I taught them the "Three-Stage" Plan, and explained how to observe. John noticed that whenever he criticized June, a quarrel followed. He promised to make a one-month trial, and no-matter-what, refrain from criticizing his wife. He kept his word.

After a week of apprehension, June began flowering in her new, criticism-free environment. By the end of the month, she was a new woman and a loving wife. John had nothing more to criticize and the marriage was saved!

Had he never learned to observe, John might have held a grudge against God, blaming The Almighty for the misery of his marital lot. In such a case, he would have been like our panicky pigeon or like the prisoner in the unlocked jail. The minute he stopped criticizing his wife, he left his cell and became a free and happy man.

Stage two: Self-evaluation.

After observation comes the stage of **self-evaluation**.

Self-evaluation is the art of judging yourself. It's not easy, but it's certainly rewarding. Self-evaluation is an entire courtroom within your mind – judge, jury, witnesses, defending attorneys, and prosecutors.

Everything you've observed in stage one comes to stage two as evidence. The better the evidence, the better your mental court can reach a just decision. A civil court refuses to accept flimsy evidence and untruthful material. Why should you?

Self-evaluation is a phenomenal tool in life. Experienced self-evaluators excel in their relationships with others, because first and foremost, they're happy with themselves. Since cogent observation is the prerequisite of self-evaluation, self-evaluators are attentive to their environment, aware of others, and good listeners as well. As a result, most people feel strong affinity for self-evaluators.

Rebbe Nachman of Breslev teaches that self-evaluation is the best prevention of future suffering.

Here's how The Talmud describes the spiritual dynamics of self-evaluation:

A heavenly court judges the world in general and each person in particular, every single day. All court decisions must receive the final approval of The Almighty, Who is much more merciful and compassionate than the court is. Frequently, God delays the implementation of an unfavorable decision against a person, to give that person an opportunity for self-evaluation.

When a person mends his or her ways, God cancels the verdict altogether. Double jeopardy is illegal in the heavenly court. Therefore, when a person admits guilt after self-evaluation, he or she has in effect conducted his or her own mental courtroom. The heavenly court is no longer allowed to try the case. If the court has already tried the person, but has not yet activated the sentence, then the sentence is nullified.

If a person makes no change in the behavior that led to a guilty verdict, then the spiritual sentencing manifests itself in some type of affliction in this world. The resulting suffering from a person's own deeds is therefore self-induced.

The prevention mode of self-evaluation – judging yourself before the heavenly court judges you: The minute a person begins to evaluate himself, God sends an urgent message that forbids the Heavenly court from passing judgment on the self-evaluator. Again, The Almighty prohibits double jeopardy. When a person judges himself truthfully, the Heavenly court is not allowed to touch the case.

When a person decides to improve in some way, two things happen: One, The Almighty grants the person's decision the validity of a Heavenly court decision. Two, all punishment is cancelled. As soon as a person *decides* to improve – even if the decision hasn't been fully implemented – God no longer needs to use punitive stimuli to stimulate that person's improvement. Also, God takes keen interest in a person's self-evaluation, and always listens when a person judges himself. Consequently, self-evaluators are close to God.

The elimination mode of self-evaluation – judging yourself after the heavenly court judges you: Truthful self-evaluation can also cancel existing suffering, but with a lot more effort. As in medicine, preventing sickness is easier than curing sickness. Rebbe Nachman of Breslev emphasizes though, never despair! If you believe that it's possible to ruin your life, believe that it's possible to repair your life!

Let's examine two examples of self-evaluation; the first before a heavenly verdict, and the second after a heavenly verdict has already taken effect.

Example one: Self-evaluation before a heavenly verdict. Don Adams, CPA, is trying his best to cope with the tax-season workload. His secretary buzzes his office; a representative of the Crippled Children's Fund is on the line, waiting to speak to him. Don refuses to take the call – taxes come first.

Don returns to the file at hand, tries to work for the next half hour, but can't concentrate. He sits back in his chair, takes a deep breath, and closes his eyes. Mental court is now in session...

Don Adams' Mental Court Hearing

The prosecution begins, reminding Don that he's made more money this year than any previous year in his career. He's enjoyed great health. "Where's your gratitude? Mr. Too-busy doesn't have three minutes to hear the needs of crippled children! Where did you get the time to go bowling last night? For that, you weren't too busy," claims the mental prosecutor.

Mental court now hears the side of the defense: "A person has the right to a few hours of exercise and relaxation after eleven hours of tax returns. As far as good health and good income – true, I concede."

Don was ashamed of himself. What a shabby defense. True, I had time for bowling but I didn't take time for charity. Am I really such an ingrate? How many people in the world have my good fortune? I should be more sensitive to others less fortunate, like the crippled children of our city...

The judge summarizes the case, and tells the jury to come to a quick verdict. The mental jury deliberates for eleven seconds, and the jury spokesman declares: Don should immediately phone the Crippled Children's Fund, and pledge five hundred dollars. The judge raps with his gavel, case is closed. The total time elapsed in self-evaluation – five minutes.

Don returns the call to the Crippled Children's Fund, apologizes for not taking their call, and pledges five hundred dollars.

Meanwhile, he doesn't realize what's transpired in the Heavenly court. His refusal to take the charity call triggered an immediate demand for heavenly justice. The heavenly prosecution claimed that such a person doesn't deserve health and wealth. Just as the court agreed to accept the case, an urgent message arrived from The Almighty – halt the proceedings! The case is out of your jurisdiction! Don Adams is in the middle of judging himself...

Later that evening, Don mails a check to the Crippled Children's Fund. He feels elated. If he knew the extent of suffering that his competent self-evaluation prevented, he'd be dancing all night.

Example two: Self-evaluation after a heavenly verdict: Margie Wilson lost her job as quality-control inspector of a plastic goods manufacturer after sixteen years with the firm. Her boss informed her that the company's streamlining program called for a forty percent layoff of the production crew.

Margie's face turned a bright crimson. She quickly reached her boiling point: "Streamline?!" she shrieked, "If you want to streamline, then why don't you cut back on the fleet of cars that the freeloading office staff drives! What's going on here? You people care more about chunks of metal than you do about your personnel!"

Margie was furious, heartbroken, and confused. Instead of driving home, she drove to the beach. She walked barefoot on the shore, and let the late-afternoon winter sun and the saltwater breeze sooth her. The shore was deserted. The beauty and tranquility of the Pacific coastline made her feel very close to God. Her mind felt crystal clear.

Margie picked up a clamshell, and examined its inner loveliness. "Time to examine myself," she thought. "Help me understand, dear God, why I got fired." She gazed at the waves in the distance, and let her mind wander. At this point, her mental court session began...

Margie Wilson's Mental Court Hearing

The prosecution presented the following evidence: Margie's daughter Pamela, a sophomore at Berkeley, came home a month previously during semester break. She asked to use her mother's new car. Margie reluctantly agreed, but gave her daughter a stiff warning to be careful with the car.

While Pamela and two girlfriends were having lunch at a local restaurant, a careless truck backed into the car, parked outside in the restaurant lot, and dented the back fender. The truck vanished.

Pamela came home in tears. She was deathly afraid of her mother's reaction. Her worries were justified.

When Margie saw the dent, she flew into a rage that would have registered 7.5 on the Richter scale. Pamela tried to explain what happened. Her furious mother cut her short, admonished her, and accused her of fabricating the hit-and-run story.

"Mom," Pamela pleaded between sobs, "Did I ever lie to you? Mom, please, does a fifty-dollar dent in a fender take precedence over your daughter's feelings, your relationship with your own flesh and blood? I-I can't believe that my own mother cares more about a chunk of metal than she does about me!"

A chunk of metal! "That's it!" thought Margie, her hands trembling and a cold sweat breaking out on her forehead. "I deserve what I got. What a thoughtless, heartless mother I am! Pamela's words were almost identical to what I told the personnel manager. I hated what the company did to me, yet I did the same thing to my own daughter. I got a taste of my own bitter medicine. Thank you, God, for helping me understand Your infinite wisdom and justice. Help me to be a better mother. Help me delete the anger from my life!"

The next day, Margie drove three hours down the coast to Berkeley, and surprised Pamela with a care package of her favorite goodies. They spent an unforgettable afternoon together. Margie apologized from the bottom of her heart about the car episode. Pamela lacked words to express her gratitude at her mother's thoughtfulness.

A week later, Margie received a call from the personnel manager: "Margie, the company wants you back. You'll be paid for last week's layoff, and as of tomorrow, your salary increases by ten percent. A deal?"

Margie closed her eyes and thanked God. The Almighty, by virtue of Margie's self-evaluation, repealed the heavenly sentence of two years unemployment.

Stage three: Implementation.

Once you've started to observe your environment and to evaluate yourself, you're ready to add stage three, **implementation**. Implementation means converting the healthy conclusions of your self-evaluation into action. Implementation uproots the causes of self-induced suffering by making the needed changes for a happier life.

Implementers are always close to God. Here's why:

Premeditated implementation is the opposite of impulsive behavior. Impulsive behavior leads to speech and action with no previous forethought. Implementation, on the other hand, is the result of self-evaluation. Self-evaluation is one's personal mental courtroom.

The mind and the divine soul take active participation in self-evaluation. The divine soul is a timeless, infinite part of God within a person. Therefore, when a person acts after thorough self-evaluation, he or she translates a divine thought into an earthly, physical action. Such a person includes God in his or her carefully premeditated action, and therefore succeeds.

Impulsive people neutralize and paralyze their own minds and divine souls. Impulsive speech and behavior are usually the result of base inclinations. For example, when a person "puts his foot in his mouth", in other words, when he or she speaks without thinking, the evil inclination is responsible.

One thing is worse than impulsive speech: impulsive action. As we learned previously in Chapter Four, the evil inclination does everything he can to prevent a person from mental composure. When a person loses composure, he or she makes mistakes. Composure is therefore a critical prerequisite for self-evaluation and premeditation.

Impulsive speech and behavior are frequently responsible for self-induced suffering. Implementation takes the reins of a person's life out of the irresponsible hands of the evil inclination, and raises one's speech and deeds to a higher spiritual level. As such, implementation mends the damage done by one's evil inclination.

Let's take another look at the respective cases of Don Adams and of Margie Wilson, and see how they implemented their mental-court decisions.

The following three-stage process of observation, self-evaluation, and implementation will prevent your life from looking like a slapstick movie of unfortunate mishaps:

Stage	Don Adams	Margie Wilson
Observation	I'm blessed with superb income and health. When I really want to do something, I make the time.	How ugly when people prefer a chunk of metal to a human being.
Self-evaluation	If I were truly grateful for my own blessings, I'd be more sensitive to the needs of others. I have to work on that point.	I'm guilty! I did to my daughter what the company did to me. I'm so ashamed of myself.
Implementation	Immediate return call to the charity fund, a generous pledge, and same-day payment.	Surprise visit to Pamela, apology, care package, propitiation, and reconciliation.

Section two: Common causes of self-induced suffering

An ounce of prevention is preferable to a pound of cure. This section of our chapter illustrates some common causes of self-induced suffering. By familiarizing ourselves with harmful, trouble-inducing behavior and speech, we learn to stay away from trouble. Attaining inner peace begins with preventing the type of troubles that incur anger and suffering.

Let's preface this section with a question that people frequently ask:

When I suffer, is God punishing me?

Many people have the mistaken notion that suffering comes from a vengeful God. Nothing is further from the truth.

When a father reprimands his six-year old son for eating an excess of taffy, is he vengeful? Certainly not. The child at this point of life lacks sense, and has not yet experienced the double trauma – to his mouth and to his bank account – of a root canal and an expensive crown. The father wishes to spare the son of future suffering. The child's short-term sorrow at losing his candy and being scolded by his father are much less painful than a rotten-toothed future.

On the surface, the father appears to be cruel, depriving little freckle-nosed Harvey of his piece of taffy. On the long term, the father is the epitome of compassion. He is saving his son from future painful injections to the gums, uncomfortable drilling in the mouth, repeated visits to the dentist's office, and the exorbitant amount of time and money consumed in the process.

God desires to save us – his beloved children – the horrible fate of spiritual decay that leads to spiritual "cavities", impure blemishes in our divine souls. Aggravation and suffering are designed to awaken us from our spiritual slumber, and to initiate a process of self-evaluation so we can correct what needs to be corrected. Just as a toothache conveys the message that we need to check our teeth immediately, life's difficulties are heavenly memos telling us to evaluate ourselves and to repair the flaws in our behavior.

The minute we react properly to The Almighty's "telegram" – a particular stimulus of anguish – and we make an effort to mend our ways, no further telegram is needed. Consequently, the source of aggravation disappears from our lives, as we learned in section one of this chapter. The nasty foreman or the nagging wife suddenly makes an about face. We no longer have a reason to be angry!

The "ATFAT" Principle – A turn for a turn

"ATFAT" is the abbreviation of "A turn for a turn". In other words, The Almighty treats us in the same fashion that we treat others. The ATFAT principle, like all the other magnificent methods that The Almighty uses to run the world, is evident both in the laws of physics and in the laws of metaphysics, or more simply stated, both in the material world and in the spiritual world.

ATFAT is one of the first laws a beginning physics student learns: For every action, there is an equal and opposite reaction. For example, the greater the rear combustion of a jet engine, the greater the forward thrust of the airplane. Or, the more an archer draws the bowstring, the more distant the flight of the arrow.

The spiritual world functions in the same way. A person reaps what he or she sows. God programs the world in this way for educational purposes. The cause and effect relationship between candy consumption and dental cavities, or between smoking and lung cancer, is identical to the cause and effect relationship between creating anguish for one's fellow man and suffering anguish in return.

By utilizing the three-stage plan of observation, self-evaluation, and implementation, we harness our mental faculties to understand the root of our suffering. Once we uproot the cause, suffering vanishes. Once the suffering vanishes, anger evaporates. Once we become accustomed to anger-free lives, then future stress situations don't cause us to lose our composure. We achieve a positive behavioral pattern that leads to tranquility.

Let's examine a case study that illustrates the power of The Three-Stage Plan:

Case study[26]. Mrs. Brown hosted a weekly study session in spiritual development for the neighbors in her condominium. Eventually, seven ladies became regular participants, and each made significant spiritual gain. Mrs. Black became jealous of Mrs. Brown's status as group leader and spiritual guide, and one-by-one, convinced the other participants that Mrs. Brown lacks competence and expertise.

Mrs. Black initiated a scheme to humiliate Mrs. Brown. After the first few minutes of a subsequent group meeting, Mrs. Black stood up and said, "I'm sorry, but this meeting is terribly boring." The other participants stood up as well, and all seven ladies left the meeting. The humiliation was devastating. Nevertheless, Mrs. Brown forgave the others in her heart. She sincerely bore no malice.

Within ten days, Mrs. Black's two-year-old daughter was hospitalized with a strange infection in her bladder.

Mrs. White, another of the participants who failed to protest against the sinister humiliation of Mrs. Brown, spilled boiling water on her three-year-old son, who was hospitalized with second-degree burns. Mrs. Gray's three-year-old daughter contracted meningitis. Mrs. Green's two-year-old son broke a leg. Instead of devoting their time to spiritual development, the former participants of the class were now devoting their time to hospital visits and sick children.

---

[26] Names are circumstances changed for obvious reasons; the author personally witnessed the chain of events described here, as spiritual guide and counselor for "Mrs. Brown".

Mrs. Gray's child was regressing terribly. She was the only member of the group who utilized the Three-Stage Plan to make a connection between the humiliation of Mrs. Brown and the sick children. Her child's situation was critical. Mrs. Gray left the hospital and her child's bedside, and raced over to Mrs. Brown's house; she threw herself at Mrs. Brown's feet and begged her forgiveness.

"I don't have to be your spiritual instructor," Mrs. Brown said, "I was only trying to do for my neighbors what others did for me. Keep up your spiritual development, Mrs. Gray; if you don't take your soul away from God, then He certainly won't take your children away from you. Of course I forgive you, and you have my blessing for your child's speedy recovery."

To the amazement of the entire medical staff at the local hospital, Mrs. Gray's child made a dramatic comeback, and regained full health within a few weeks.

Mrs. Gray shared her observation, self-evaluation, and implementation with the other ladies. As soon as the others apologized to Mrs. Brown and received her forgiveness, their children also overcame their respective sicknesses. Even Mrs. Black asked Mrs. Brown's forgiveness. But, as the instigator of the whole unfortunate affair, her child continued to suffer from inexplicable periodic infections. Only after Mrs. Brown prayed fervently in behalf of Mrs. Black's daughter, did the child recover completely from the bladder ailment.

Twelve common causes of self-induced suffering

One: Hurting another person's feelings

Case study, "The Broken Engagement[27]": Stanley Freeman was introduced to Marla Potter, a lovely girl, both personable

---

[27] This is an actual case that the author heard from a member of the "Freeman" family; the names and certain details are changed for obvious reasons.

and intelligent, from a very similar religious and social background. After a few short dates, Marla accepted Stanley's proposal of marriage. Joyfully, they informed their parents. The Potters invited the Freemans to a traditional toast, and together with the young couple, the engagement became official.

At the time of their engagement, America was in the midst of a postwar economic recession. Marla Potter's father, a welder, had been laid off his job at the shipyards because of a severe federal cutback in shipbuilding. The Potters couldn't afford a fancy engagement party at a hotel or ballroom, so they opted to have it at home. Marla Potter, her mother, and her aunts worked for a solid week preparing an array of ethnic delicacies for the engagement buffet. The engagement was scheduled for Wednesday night, June 7, at eight p.m.

Richard Freeman, Stanley's older brother, a sailor in the Navy at the time, received a four-day furlough and flew home on Tuesday afternoon, the day before the engagement. That evening, he accompanied Stanley to Marla's house. Mr. Potter, a navy veteran himself, occupied Richard with sailor scuttlebutt. The womenfolk were busy cooking and baking for the morrow, and the entire house smelled like a Lithuanian bakery. Marla Potter served the men beer, kielbasa sausage, and fresh bread hot from the oven, and then returned to the kitchen to help her mother and her aunts.

Stanley and Richard came home after what seemed to be a delightful evening at Marla's house. Their parents were waiting up for them, eager to hear Richard's impression of his future sister-in-law.

Richard asked his parents cynically, "Mom, Pop, when did your eyesight begin failing? Why didn't you write me? I would have mailed you my paycheck so you could get proper eye care."

"What are you talking about, Richard? Our eyesight is fine," they answered.

Richard yelled so loud that he almost shattered the wine glasses in the living room buffet: "THEN WHAT IN THE

HECK ARE YOU LETTING STANLEY BRING SOME FOUR-EYED PIZZA FACE INTO THIS FAMILY! SHE'S THE HOMLIEST THING I'VE EVER SEEN! YOUR GRANDCHILDREN WILL LOOK LIKE CHIMPANZEES WITH HORN-RIMMED SPECS!"

Stanley buried his face in his hands. Richard swayed his mother and his two teenage sisters.

"Richard's got a good point", said the mother.

"Yeh, don't go through with the engagement," chimed the sisters, "Richard's right. She's an ugly duckling. Stanley, don't give us an ape-looking sister-in-law. We're a family, not a city zoo!"

Mr. Freeman protested, "What about family honor? We never go back on our word."

"C'mon, Pop", sneered Richard, "this is Jersey City, not Vilna!"

For the next eighteen hours, doubt gnawed at Stanley's heart. Richard wouldn't let up. "Stanley, are you that hard up that you have to marry a four-eyed hatchet face? Man, her specs are thicker than a beer glass! You won't be able to show your face in public. People will be asking, what's wrong with Stanley Freeman? Why'd he settle for some wilting wallflower? You're gonna have to move to Saudi Arabia, where they make women walk around with covered faces!"

Stanley's defenses crumbled. At seven-thirty p.m. the following evening, he informed his family that he can't bring himself to marry a girl with thick eyeglasses. The family argued for an hour. The father protested vehemently, but Richard, the mother, and the sisters were on Stanley's side. The father was overruled.

Richard declared victoriously, "I'm treating everybody to a consolation celebration of wine and pasta at the Napoli. Let's go!"

The father refused to participate. "Somebody's got to be decent enough to inform the other side. Go dine at the Napoli if you all want. I'm going to meet Mr. Potter. It's a matter of honor."

* * *

By eight thirty, Marla Potter's house was packed. All the relatives and guests had arrived, except for the groom and his family.

Eight forty five – Stanley and the Freeman family were still nowhere in sight.

Nine o'clock – Marla's heart told her that something was drastically amiss. An uncontrollable tear trickled down her cheek. She told her mother and father that she felt weak, and that she was going upstairs to lie down for a while. A heavy sense of humiliation felt like a ton of concrete on her chest, and she could barely breathe.

At nine fifteen, the doorbell rang. Mr. Freeman stood ashen-faced on the front doorstep. Mr. Potter opened the door, took one look at his prospective in-law's fallen countenance, and knew that the engagement was off. Potter stepped outside, beyond earshot of the relatives and guests, and closed the door behind him. "What's going on? My Marla's sick with embarrassment. Where's Stanley?"

Freeman couldn't control the flow of tears. He stuttered, and then poured his heart out: "In the old country, a word was a word. My son has broken his word. He has shamed our family name. I have no control over him. I'm so ashamed. I beg your forgiveness."

Potter answered calmly, "Don't worry, Mr. Freeman; I believe in God, not in violence. I'm not going to shoot you, and I'm not going seek revenge for the disgrace to my daughter. The good Lord obviously doesn't want this match to take place, and I trust His Divine judgment. I suggest you do some hard praying for your family. They need it. Good night."

Potter stepped back inside the house and closed the door. He looked at the guests, and then at the tables piled high with delicacies. He spent his last dime buying new clothes for the family. Days of planning and preparation, not to mention the money, had gone down the drain. All that remained was a sick feeling of humiliation. "The engagement's off," he declared.

* * *

I suggest you do some hard praying for your family. The words echoed again and again in Mr. Freeman's ears as he morosely walked home. The family had not yet returned from the restaurant. He opened the front door, turned on the hall light, and removed his hat and coat. *I suggest you do some hard praying for your family.* Those haunting words wouldn't stop. He plugged in the coffee pot, and the phone rang.

"Hello, I'd like to speak with Mr. Irwin Freeman," the voice requested.

"What can I do for you?"

"This is County General Hospital speaking. Your family's been in a car accident. Please come over right away."

Richard and Stanley Freeman drank too much wine with dinner. On the way home from the restaurant, Richard, driving the family car, swerved instantaneously to the opposite lane, directly in the path of a heavy truck. The truck smashed the driver's side.

Richard was killed on the spot. The two sisters' faces were lacerated to a bloody mess. Despite subsequent years of repeated plastic surgery, their faces remained scarred and frightening. Neither of the two ever married. The mother spent the next four years in a wheelchair, until she died of a bitter, broken heart.

Stanley was catapulted out of the front windshield. Miraculously, his life was spared; his broken shoulder and broken hip healed eventually, but his concussion left him with permanently damaged vision. Stanley, who humiliated Marla because of her glasses, ended up wearing thick glasses and

suffering from terrible headaches and blurry vision until the day
he died thirty years later.

Marla wasn't heartbroken for long. She met a successful
optometrist, and married six months later. Her new husband
fitted her with contact lenses, which were new at the time,
making her a very attractive woman. Thirty-two years later, she's
a mother of five with more than a dozen grandchildren, happily
married, and content. The Almighty gave her a much finer
husband than Stanley Freeman.

Moral of the case: Notice the underlying currents of ATFAT
in the above case. Richard Freeman ruined a young lady's life (at
the time), so he lost his own life. The two sisters called Marla
ugly, and contributed to ruining the engagement, so they became
ugly and never had an engagement. Stanley didn't want a girl
with glasses, so he himself wore thick glasses to the day he died.
All the suffering of the Freemans was self-induced!

Two: Negligence in performing a good deed.

Rabbi Chaim of Chernovitz[28] teaches that good deeds are the
food, clothing, and shelter of the soul. The soul is a spark of
Godliness, to which we allude to as 'the King's daughter'. One
who is negligent in performing good deeds resembles a crass
country bumpkin that marries a King's daughter: He should feed
his dainty bride fine farina muffins, but he serves her stale black
barley bread. Instead of clothing her in silk robes, he dresses her
in a burlap sap. He changes her soft bed of silk sheets for a
mattress of hay and straw. When the princess is incapable of
further suffering, she runs home to the palace. Once the king
sees how miserably mistreated she is, he takes swift retribution
on his country bumpkin son-in-law.

The soul thrives on the spiritual nourishment of good deeds.
When the body neglects the soul, the soul cries out to The

---

[28] Late 18th Century CE Chassidic master, author of "Be'er Mayim
Chaim" and leading disciple of Rabbi Yechiel Michel of Zlatchov

Almighty, who ultimately sends some form of aggravation or suffering as a reminder to the body, the allegorical crass son-in-law, not to neglect the needs of the soul, the allegorical King's daughter.

By trying our best to perform good deeds, we prevent needless suffering. When we prevent needless suffering, we move up the trail to tranquility.

Three: Negligence in developing one's spiritual self

Animals eat, drink, and procreate. They also live positive, productive lives, providing society with meat, milk, wool, leather, and fur. Many types of animals serve as means of labor, transportation, and recreation. Dogs fulfill important functions, such as aiding blind people, serving in police units, and participating in rescue missions.

A human who simply eats, drinks, and procreates, despite the fact that he or she has a productive job and utilizes leisure time for sports or other positive recreational activities, is still no better than a horse. Horses eat, drink, and procreate, do productive tasks on farms and cattle ranches, and serve as a source of recreational enjoyment to their owners. So, is a person superior to a horse?

A person void of spiritual ambition – a thirst for truth and a yearning for self-realization – is no better than a horse. A horse, like a human, has a basic animal soul. The divine spirit and soul, which God instills in a human, is the *sole* point of human superiority over the animal.

When humans utilize their divine spirit and soul to rise above base inclinations, to seek The Almighty, and to behave in a godly fashion, they begin to fulfill their real purpose in life. But, when people misuse or neglect their divine spirit and soul, they are inferior to an animal.

An unblemished soul – one who refrains from transgressing and does God's will on a daily basis – possesses a Divine aura which is reflected by the eyes and the forehead, and casts fear on all of creation, even on man-eating animals.

God blessed Noah after the flood and said (Genesis 9:2), "I have instilled the fear of you in the animals on land, in the birds in the sky, in the creatures on earth, and in the fish in the sea." When people sin, or when they do nothing to develop their spiritual self, their divine soul tarnishes. A tarnished soul lacks the power to generate the holy aura of divine light. Animals and other creatures have no fear of a human devoid of the Divine aura.

The divine soul is a part of God within us, the spiritual platform that elevates a human above the level of an animal. If the soul is misused or uncultivated, then the human loses his spiritual advantage over the animal.

Misused Potential

"Using a neurosurgical scalpel for peeling potatoes doesn't make the potatoes smart; it only dulls the scalpel." *Rabbi Lazer Brody, "Rabbi Rambo Says..." The Jewish Post and News, September 24, 2003*

Imagine that a custodian of a hospital enters the operating room, and takes one of the brain surgeon's fine sterile scalpels for peeling an apple. If caught in the act, such a custodian would surely lose his job. Using an expensive precision instrument for such a mundane task is not only a terrible waste – it's a severe degradation.

By the same token, reducing the soul from its lofty spiritual level to the grade of a mere battery cell that triggers basic emotions and bodily functions is a bitter insult. The degraded soul cries out bitterly before God, "I can't live within a human animal." In turn, the person with the abused soul soon experiences some form of abuse – derision, insult, or embarrassment.

Four: Wrongdoing

God frequently sends a person aggravation or suffering as the result of some transgression or wrongdoing. Again, this is certainly not a form of punishment. On the contrary – the purpose of suffering that follows a transgression or a wrongdoing is to bring a person to the point of self-evaluation, or soul searching.

Soul searching is the first step toward atoning for a wrongdoing. Atonement cleanses the soul. A cleansed soul is a suitable vessel for Divine light. The more Divine light a soul absorbs, the closer it gets to God. As such, the suffering that triggered the initial self-evaluation is a gift from Heaven designed to return a stray soul to the proximity of God.

The Almighty therefore uses suffering as a spiritual vacuum cleaner whose task is to remove the old dust swept under a person's spiritual rug. A house may be satisfactory with no visible dirt, but a soul must be kept spotlessly clean inside and out.

Five: Sadness and ingratitude

Sadness and ingratitude induce suffering.

If people would ponder the myriad of miracles that the Almighty performs for them personally each minute of the day, they would certainly dance for joy.

Sad and depressed people quickly forget, or fail to acknowledge, all the good that The Almighty does for them. The average adult heart pumps 100,000 times a day. The average adult lungs breathe 20,000 times a day. Each heartbeat and each breath are a gift from God. Every command from the brain via an amazing nerve impulse to a part of the body is a Divine miracle, and our brains send out billions of these commands every day. A human with a functioning brain, heart, eyes, limbs, and lungs owes God several billion thanks each day, even before counting the endless number of additional blessings, such as family, food, clothing, and shelter.

No mortal can possibly express sufficient gratitude to God. We humans become gravely insulted when a spouse, friend, or neighbor doesn't properly thank us for one small favor. Many of us live by a double moral standard – we demand a lot more respect and gratitude from others than we're willing to give to God.

The root cause of sadness is ingratitude, and ingratitude is an insult to God. If a person were to insult a mortal king, he or she would face severe retribution. Our loving King in Heaven doesn't punish, He educates. God engineers that people behave toward us in the same manner that we behave toward Him. For example, if our children or our spouses are ungrateful or disrespectful to us, then we have probably exhibited ingratitude or disrespect toward The Almighty. The ATFAT principle – a turn for a turn – is God's way of teaching His children.

Six: Lack of trust in God

A lack of trust in God indicates a lack of spiritual development. A neglected, undeveloped soul remains dormant at best. Normally, those who lack trust in God develop an inclination for wrongdoing, anger, and inner turbulence.

Case study: Robert Bond, a route salesman for one of the beverage companies, fell into financial difficulties. Working honestly, he averaged about sixty thousand dollars annually. He estimated that another fifteen thousand dollars per year would bail him out of his financial straits. Bond rationalized that an honest salesman can't get ahead in the world. The nagging little voice of his greedy evil inclination harped, "God is giving you sixty grand. You need seventy-five, pal. God's laws are too restricting. Take the law into your own hands!"

The storeowners on Bond's route considered him trustworthy. Sometimes, when they were extremely busy, they'd accept their new beverage deliveries without counting the cases too closely. Bond took advantage of the situation and began billing his customers for stock that they never received. The more he stole, the more he developed an appetite for stealing.

Once, Bond delivered an eighty case order to a large supermarket, but billed them for ninety cases. He knew that the department manager was lax in checking him. What he didn't know was that the chain store's detective was on the premises that particular day.

The detective caught Bond red-handed. The supermarket chain threatened to prosecute. The beverage company hushed the matter, appeased the supermarket chain with a considerable sum of money, and fired Bond on the spot. Bond forfeited twenty years of severance pay and benefits to stay out of jail.

For a week, Bond faked the flu. Once he became fed up with sitting at home, he told his wife that he left his job.

Mrs. Bond didn't understand why her husband left such a fine, secure job after twenty years with no severance pay. When she called the sales manger of the beverage company, Bond's direct superintendent, she discovered the real reason. Subsequently, Bond became the object of incessant verbal abuse from his wife. Their marriage is deteriorating.

Epilogue: At the time of this writing, "Bond" *(imaginary name)* is still unemployed, and wastes valuable hours in idleness. He's angry and depressed, yet he refuses to accept spiritual counseling. He is solely responsible for his own suffering.

Seven: Flattery

Flattery does not mean telling your wife that she looks beautiful in her new dress, or complimenting her on the delicious dinner when really, it was no more than mediocre. Flattery means telling an evil person how wonderful he or she is.

The prophet Isaiah says (Isaiah 5:20), "Woe to those who call evil good and good evil, to those who put darkness as light and light as darkness, to those who put sour as sweet and sweet as sour".

Case study: Joan Anderson[29] was the personal secretary of the vice-president of a major British banking firm.

When the president of the bank announced his imminent retirement, a covert power struggle began between the vice president and the chief operating officer (COO). The vice president was an individual of honor, willing to let his professional accomplishments speak for themselves. The chief operating officer was a heartless conniver, thirsty for power at all costs.

Joan listened attentively to the whispering in the corridors. Most of the senior employees believed that the COO would be appointed the new president, because of his forcefulness. She concluded that the COO was the favored candidate, on whom she'd place her bet.

Joan's lust for advancement led her to arrange a clandestine luncheon with the COO. She told him what a wonderful man she thinks he is, and in exchange for the promise that she would be his personal secretary when he became president, she would plant insidious rumors about her current boss's qualifications. The COO agreed to the deal with no hesitation.

During the coming weeks, Joan neglected her own desk in the vice-president's office. She spent extensive time in the COO's office, both during office hours and after hours. She already considered herself the presidential secretary, and thereby succeeded in alienating several of her coworkers.

Joan's plan backfired. News of intrigue and unethical conduct on behalf of the COO reached the ears of the chairman of the board. He and the other members of the board quickly concluded that the vice president was the better candidate.

On the eve of the new fiscal year, the board of directors announced that the vice-president had been appointed president

---

[29] The author heard this story from one of "Joan Anderson's" coworkers at the bank. Names and circumstances changed for obvious reasons.

of the bank. The COO was advised to honorably resign with pay and benefits. The new president promoted a talented secretary from the foreign exchange department as his personal secretary, while Miss Joan Anderson, demoted to licking envelopes in the mailroom, became the joke of the bank.

Eight: Arrogance

King Solomon says (Proverbs 16:18), "Arrogance precedes downfall." This ever-so-brilliant statement serves as mold for all of history.

Pharaoh, ruler of Egypt, the world's superpower of 3400 years ago, considered himself a deity. His arrogance reached a new pinnacle when he declared (Exodus 5:2), "Who is God that I should pay attention to Him?" That hapless expression triggered the subsequent downfall of Egypt.

The list of arrogant tyrants who ruled great powers, yet suffered tragic downfall, is exhaustive. King Solomon's expression, "Arrogance precedes downfall", demonstrates the timelessness and universality of truth. The previous generation witnessed the downfall of the Nazis, who had seized virtual control over all of Europe. This generation has witnessed with its own eyes the downfall of the communists in the USSR, who for seventy years trampled human rights and put millions to their death.

On a personal level, arrogance creates a barrier between a person's soul and God. Such a barrier blocks out divine light. With no divine light, a person can't possibly achieve inner peace.

Arrogance is *the* key symptom of an angry and an unhealthy soul. If the arrogant person mends his haughty ways, his divine soul recuperates and his spiritual life improves. But, if a person continues in the stubborn path of arrogance, his life becomes increasingly miserable. An arrogant person is never happy.

God wants us to be happy. He therefore sends us warning signals whenever we display arrogance. In many cases, some form of suffering is a flashing yellow light from Heaven, warning us to take corrective action against our arrogant tendencies.

Nine: Verbally abusing one's fellow man

One who causes embarrassment, humiliation, shame, insult, or pain to another individual can expect the like in return. Verbal abuse is a boomerang.

By the letter of Talmudic Law, one who makes a habit of degrading, embarrassing, and insulting other people is considered a menace not worthy to dwell on this earth. Therefore, if a verbal abuser becomes the brunt of verbal abuse, he should be happy, because God in His extreme mercy has granted an extremely mild sentence.

At the time of the Holy Temple in Jerusalem, one who shamed his fellow man was subject to excommunication, until he appeased the shamed person. Excommunication itself is a severe humiliation. Today, religious courts don't excommunicate verbal abusers, since so many people are so careless with their tongues. If a religious court had to try every case of verbal abuse, its docket would be bottlenecked for the next twenty years.

Since the earthly courts lack the capability of trying and punishing offenders, the Heavenly Court oversees the enforcement of the prohibition against verbal abuse, and sentences the offender. Often, the decree is implemented immediately, and the verbal abuser becomes the victim of some sort of verbal abuse, a prime example of ATFAT-based justice.

Nearly every case I've ever counseled of insolent and disrespectful children is rooted in parents who are guilty of disdain. A parent's contempt for other people serves as a behavioral role model for a child. In true ATFAT style, parents eat the bitter fruits of their own bad example.

Ten: Setting a trap for others

King David said (see Psalms 7:16) that one who digs a pit to ensnare one's fellow man eventually falls in that very same trap.

In regard to our subject at hand, a person who attempts to upset or anger his fellow man exposes himself to similar damage.

The above principle operates on the lines of an interesting spiritual phenomenon, as illustrated by the following classroom situation:

Victim of the classroom prank

Bill and John, schoolmates, weren't the best of friends. Bill wanted a good classroom laugh at John's expense, so during recess, he planted some well-chewed bubble gum on John's seat, and then left the classroom.

Meanwhile, Ronnie had misplaced his lunchbox, and had returned to the classroom to look for it. While searching the entire classroom, he juggled the chairs, and unwittingly moved John's chair to Bill's desk.

Several minutes later, the bell rang and the pupils returned to class. Bill had a sly grin on his face, eager to see John's reaction of disgust, which would obviously ignite an explosion of laughter in the classroom. Bill sat down behind his desk, and SQUISH! The class breaks out laughing – even the teacher can't contain himself. Bill fell prey to his own trap.

Moral of the classroom story: God arranged that Ronnie misplace his lunchbox in order to foil Bill's plan. Ronnie could have moved the bubble-gummed chair to any one of thirty other desks in the classroom, but God arranged that the chair find its way to Bill's desk. God also diverted Bill's attention when he sat down, so that he wouldn't notice the bubble gum. This is one small example of the Almighty's intervention, even to the smallest detail of our daily lives. Many are the emotional terrorists whose bombs of degradation and ridicule blow up in their own faces.

Eleven: Buffoonery

When a person ridicules or jokes at the expense of others, God will send the jokester ridicule in return.

Jokesters, artists of buffoonery who specialize in hurting others, sever themselves from God. The Almighty is disgusted by buffoonery that is used as a weapon against others.

The abovementioned classroom story is a relevant illustration of the clown suffering from his own clownery.

Twelve: Taking pleasure in another person's sorrow

Those who derive pleasure from another person's sorrow eventually suffer from their own sorrow.

Case study: "Woodland Mall" was a large shopping center comprised of eighty different stores. Three of those stores sold electrical appliances – "Ernie's Electric", "Bargain Bay", and "Reliable Rudy" (imaginary names). One night, an electric fire broke out in the mall, and by the time it was extinguished, Bargain Bay was a charred total loss. Ernie Allen, the owner of Ernie's Electric, rushed over to meet Richard Burns, the owner of Bargain Bay. "Rich, you've always been a gentleman and a fair competitor. That's worth a lot in my book. Anything I can do to help get you back on your feet – just name it". Burns was overwhelmed by Allen's gesture.

Unlike Ernie Allen, Rudy Garfield's reaction to the Bargain Bay misfortune was one of glee. "Reliable Rudy" was counting his additional electric eggs before they hatched. One less competitor meant more sales – or so he thought. He made no effort to hide his satisfaction. He told one customer that Burns was running a losing business anyway, so he probably "Burned" himself out to collect the insurance: "Ha ha, you get it – Burns burns his Bargain Bay basement," laughing at his own sick punny joke.

Reliable Rudy didn't laugh for long. A week later, on a busy Friday morning before the holiday season, the store was packed with customers. Two well-groomed men in dark business suits approached Rudy. They flashed their wallets, each one displaying a federal inspector's badge. "Please show us the invoices of your most recent color-television shipments," in a polite but no-nonsense tone.

Rudy stammered, "Can't this wait until closing time?" The senior of the two officers shook his head in the negative. He produced a legal-size envelope from his breast pocket.

The officer said in a low but very serious voice, "This is a federal court order authorizing the search of Reliable Rudy's. If you are able to produce immediate proof that the color televisions you have in stock were all purchased from a bona fide wholesaler – that means an invoice with each and every serial number – than we'll beg your pardon and wish you a nice day. If not, we have no choice but to close you down. Sales are over for today."

Rudy's face flushed, and then paled an ashen gray. He pulled out a few old invoices from a desk drawer, but none of the serial numbers matched the current stock. The junior officer began clearing the store, while the senior officer remained with Rudy.

The customers were enjoying the action. One lady asked, "Hey officer, what's he suspected of, theft or smuggling?"

A middle-aged man wearing a Yankees cap snarled, "Now we know the secret of Reliable Rudy's prices – he's a crook!"

A freckle-faced fifth grader asked his father, "Daddy, is Mr. Rudy going to jail?"

No less than a dozen comments reached Rudy's ears by the time the last customer left the store. Rudy had never been so embarrassed in his life.

The word spread around town that Rudy was suspect of selling smuggled goods. His wife was embarrassed to go to the grocery store. His two children refused to go to school. His lawyer plea-bargained to keep him out of jail, and Rudy agreed to a fifty thousand dollar fine and a three-year suspended sentence for any similar offense.

The moral of the Rudy story: Only a cruel and angry person enjoys seeing the misfortune of a fellow human. Cruelty and anger result from spiritual impurity. Spiritual impurity attracts verbal abuse. Rudy's joy in seeing his competitor's disaster exposed his own deep-seated spiritual impurity, manifest also by his illegal dealings. The evil forces created by his bad thoughts, speech, and deeds assumed tangibility in the form of court orders, federal inspectors, and chiding customers that come to haunt him.

Summary

The ATFAT principle is significant to every moment of our lives, since it reminds us that each of our actions creates an equivalent spiritual reaction. A good spiritual reaction resulting from a good deed brings joy to our lives. The opposite causes suffering.

Whenever we suffer, we should apply the Three-Stage Plan immediately. The Almighty grants tremendous spiritual assistance to those who observe, self-evaluate, and implement. In most cases, our lives take an immediate turn for the better, anger becomes a thing of the past, and we make major progress up the trail to tranquility. Having come to peace with God, we're now ready to make peace with our fellow man, so let's move on to Chapter Seven.

7

Hardboiled Eggs

The previous two chapters showed us how to make peace with God. This chapter shows how to make peace with our fellow man. By making peace, we uproot anger and neutralize the turbulence in our lives.

Imagine an innocent person unfairly tried in a kangaroo court of some tyrannical regime for a crime that he or she didn't commit. Isn't that upsetting? Often, when we hear news about an evil dictator who executes people without a fair trial, we clench our fists in frustration. We ask ourselves how such heartless individuals are allowed to walk the face of the earth.

We readily see the despotic tendencies of others. Seeing ourselves is a trickier task. During my first year in rabbinical seminary, my faculty counselor pulled a trick on me. He asked, "Lazer, would you like to see what a tyrant looks like?" I answered in the affirmative. He removed a small leather wallet from vest pocket, and said, "Look here."

I thought that my counselor was going to show me a photograph. Instead, he flashed a little passport-photo sized mirror in front of my face. I saw my own astonished image and asked, "Am I really a tyrant?"

"Of course not, Lazer, but your anger comes from tyrannical tendencies." The counselor's point went straight to my heart. From that moment on, I decided to redouble my efforts to eradicate any traces of anger in my life.

The Five Similarities between Angry People and Tyrants

While working on my own soul searching, I found five basic similarities between a tyrannical kangaroo court and a person who harbors anger against his or her fellow human.

This chapter illustrates the five points of similarity, as follows:

1. Angry people and tyrants base their judgments on superficial or circumstantial evidence.

2. Angry people and tyrants violate the principle of innocence until proven guilty. They never grant the benefit of the doubt, and therefore consider the accused party guilty until proven innocent.

3. Angry people and tyrants make judgments on the basis of insignificant or incomplete evidence. Often, they fail to consider a key fact that could completely overturn their verdicts against the accused.

4. Angry people and tyrants base their judgments on stereotypes and preconceptions, and often reach conclusions before examining the evidence.

5. Angry people and tyrants frequently project their own weaknesses, insecurity, and character flaws on others, and then arrive at mistaken conclusions accordingly.

With the help of the above five points, we arrive at a single significant conclusion: **We harbor anger against our neighbors, because we fail to judge them fairly**. If we were to judge our fellow man with the same understanding and lenience that we judge ourselves, all of our anger would dissipate like chaff in an October wind.

By ridding ourselves of tyrannical tendencies, we give others a fair trial in the courtroom of our mind, and thereby avoid the pitfalls of potential anger against them. Nothing improves the quality of life like an anger-free heart.

Let's take a closer look at each of the five points.

Point one: Anger based on superficial or circumstantial evidence.

Hardboiled Eggs

Less than eight miles as the crow flies from Old Isaac's inn, is a little hamlet by the name of Purity Springs. Downtown Purity Springs is a two-hundred-foot-long cobblestone street with clapboard sidewalks on both sides. A small post office, a farmers' supply store, and a camping goods store are on one side of the street, and the Forest Ranger's office, the general store, and a skiing lodge are located on the other side. If you ever ride through Purity Springs on a fast horse or on a trail bike – and you blink – you'll miss seeing the town.

Willy Weatherbee owns and operates the general store. He is an amicable, stout little fellow in his early sixties, with a shiny bald head, wire-framed bifocals, a pencil behind his ear, and a clean white starched grocer's apron around his waist. Folks never saw Mr. Weatherbee with anything other than a pleasant smile; that is, until his fresh eggs started to disappear.

Mr. Weatherbee has a small homestead on the outskirts of the hamlet, and like many others in the area, raises chickens and grows fruit trees. He takes special pride in his laying hens, which lay a conglomerate of one hundred twenty eggs daily. Willy displays his fresh eggs on the sidewalk in front of the store, in open paper-mache cartons of a dozen eggs each.

Willy is a stickler for detail. His store is spotless, and the cans on his shelves stand at attention with the precision of a Marine Corps honor guard. At any given moment, he can quote his exact inventory, from nuts and bolts to ketchup and mayonnaise. A missing fresh egg could therefore cause him an acute case of insomnia.

By tradition, the stores in Purity Springs close down for a lunch break and siesta from one p.m. to three p.m. each afternoon. The owners don't bother to lock up, for there's never been a case of theft in the history of the hamlet. If you ever need something urgently during lunch break, just walk in the store, take what you want, and leave a signed IOU or cash payment by the cash register. Willy doesn't mind at all.

One day, Willy came back to the store after lunch break, at his usual two minutes before three o'clock. Before siesta, he had five crates of eggs left in stock. Now, the upper crate of the egg display was empty. He rushed inside the store to see if anyone left him payment for the twelve eggs, but found nothing by the cash register. His pulse quickened and his face flushed with concern – what happened to the twelve eggs? The mystery of the missing dozen eggs monopolized Willy's thoughts for the remainder of the day.

Later that evening, Mrs. Weatherbee sensed a change in her husband's usually pleasant disposition. Willy's favorite dinner of hot biscuits, chicken and dumplings, and apple delight failed to improve his somber mood. He seemed detached; his thoughts were elsewhere, certainly not at the dinner table. His fork toyed with his dinner, but he had no appetite. "What's the matter, Willy? You haven't touched a morsel!"

Willy stammered, and then looked at his wife with a Presidential state-of-emergency gravity, and declared, "Somebody stole twelve eggs today, during lunch break."

"There must be some mistake. I can't believe a thief would come to Purity Springs," his wife commented.

"I'm certainly not mistaken about a dozen disappearing eggs. Maybe the thief didn't come to Purity Springs; maybe he's here among us!"

Nothing Mrs. Weatherbee said calmed or consoled her distraught husband. Willy spent a sleepless night, tossing and turning from side to side. Not even a hot cup of his wife's lovingly prepared warm milk and honey eased his fraying nerves.

The next morning, a red-eyed Willy Weatherbee defiantly displayed a fresh ten dozen of his farm-famous eggs. As a matter of principle and tradition, he refused to lock up for lunch break, and left the display of eggs on the wooden walkway in front of the store as usual. Sure enough, when he returned at two minutes before three, another twelve eggs were missing, with no sign of either promissory note or payment by the cash register.

Willy was furious. He began a mental survey of his neighbors. It can't be Kirk Mitchell the forest ranger, he thought, because at this time of the day, he patrols the Deer Haven area. Harvey Clarington, the postal clerk, is one of the most respectable folks I ever met, thought Willy, and an honest public servant whom I've known for forty years; it can't be him. Roger Smith, owner of the farmer supply store, has twice the hens that I do; he doesn't need my eggs. Randy Willis, owner of the camping goods store, doesn't eat any animal protein. He also doesn't sell foodstuff, so it can't be him.

One name remained on Willy's list – Dwayne Hodges. Dwayne was a relative newcomer to Purity Springs. Three short years ago, he bought the skiing lodge and the slope franchise from Bernie Beadle. Hodges, a phys-ed graduate from the University of Montana in Missoula, was a former member of the US Olympic skiing team. Willy never seemed to have much in common with the newcomer. Hodges, a good thirty years younger than him, was a longhaired, earring-donning product of a new generation that Willy didn't understand.

"It's definitely Hodges", huffed Weatherbee, pounding his plump pinkish fist on his oak butcher block. "The newcomer probably is serving hot fresh omelets at the lodge, on my expense!"

Later that afternoon, Hodges entered the general store with a long list of needed supplies. Willy's adrenalin level reached dam-breaking proportions. He couldn't even look at Hodges, much less greet him with a minimal "howdy" or "good afternoon".

Hodges spent three hundred dollars on groceries and supplies; at the cash register, Willy debated whether to charge him for the missing eggs or not. He decided not to –

this Hodges fellow looked leathery tough, and Willy was afraid of a violent reaction, thinking that if a person can steal, he can commit assault and battery, too. Hodges paid cash, and returned to the lodge.

For the third day in a row, another dozen eggs disappeared during lunch break. Willy was flabbergasted, and on the verge of an emotional meltdown. As Divine Providence would have it, Jerry Miller went to Purity Springs that same afternoon, to purchase some hardware articles from the general store.

At five after three, Jerry pulled up on one of his quarter horses in front of the general store. Mr. Weatherbee was outside on the store's front veranda, counting the eggs. Jerry dismounted, and smiled warmly, "Howdy Mr. Weatherbee! It's been a while since I've seen you. How are you feeling?"

"Don't ask," he grunted over his shoulder. All of a sudden, he turned around, and his sullen countenance made an about-face. A bright look of hope lit up his eyes. "Hey, Jerry – didn't Old Isaac tell me that you were a Green Beret in Vietnam? Weren't you trained in shooting and in hand-to-hand combat?"

Jerry blushed. He never talked about his military background. Nevertheless, he answered politely, "Guilty on all three counts, Mr. Weatherbee, but a lot of water has flowed down the Mississippi River since then."

"Listen, Jerry: I'm willing to pay any amount you ask…"

Jerry couldn't believe what he was hearing. Kind Mr. Weatherbee from the Purity Springs general store wanted to put out a contract on Dwayne Hodges, the suspected thief! Jerry mumbled, "You're trying to hire me as a hit man? Has the world gone bananas? Is this Mount Patience, 1996, or the south side of Chicago, 1932? Have I been hit on the head? Are you all right, Mr. Weatherbee?"

In a gush of uncontrollable emotion, Willy poured out his troubled heart, and told Jerry all about the missing eggs and his suspicions.

"Listen carefully, Mr. Weatherbee", Jerry said as patiently as he could, "I'm not a soldier any more; I'm a simple horse farmer that loves both animals and humanity. My goal in life is to help others, not to harm them, heaven forbid. I won't step on an ant, much less harm a fellow human. Even as a soldier, I never used force unless I was attacked or unless my life was endangered. Try to calm down. I'll testify for Dwayne Hodges. I give you a million percent guarantee that he's not a thief. Champion amateur athletes live by an honor code. Hodges wouldn't sell his honor for a dozen eggs."

"Then how do you account for my missing eggs?"

"There's got to be some other explanation. I'll tell you what – if you'll let me use your telephone, I'll call Old Isaac and fill him in. Better yet, why don't you call him? I'm sure he'll have some good advice for you," Jerry suggested.

"Why didn't I think of that?" Willy raced to the phone by the cash register.

Willy Weatherbee phoned Isaac and told him the whole story. Isaac replied, "Listen Willy – let's try fooling the thief. When you go home tonight, boil a dozen eggs until they're good and hard, and make sure the shells aren't cracked. Tomorrow, before you go home for lunch, place the carton of the twelve hardboiled eggs on the top of the display. I promise you that we'll catch the thief within twenty four hours."

Willy was thrilled – Isaac never broke a promise to anyone. He did exactly as Isaac told him to do. That evening, he prepared twelve perfectly hardboiled eggs, and packed them in a regular egg carton. The next day, shortly before siesta time, he placed the hardboiled eggs on the top of the egg display, and skipped home for lunch with the glee of a second grader eating crackerjacks. Like everyone else in the valley and around the mountain, Willy had complete trust in Old Isaac.

Isaac's twenty-four hour promise was fulfilled within a mere two hours. When Willy returned to the general store after lunch, at his usual two minutes before three, he found a tremendous five-foot long blacksnake, lying lifeless by the egg display. The snake, a passionate connoisseur of fresh eggs, was responsible for the previous days' theft. Once more, he swallowed the eggs whole, but this time, they were hardboiled. The snake choked to death.

Thrilled, Willy called the inn to inform Old Isaac of the good tidings. "How did you know the thief was a snake, Isaac?"

"Willy, people around here are honest, and they certainly don't need to steal eggs. Furthermore," replied Isaac with his characteristic modesty, "The Almighty solves mysteries, and He enlightens my thinking. A human thief would have taken the eggs with the carton in one fell swoop. An egg-loving animal, like a raccoon or a weasel, would have toppled the entire stack of eggs, and then eat three or four of them. Only a big snake could've swallowed whole eggs without damaging the rest of the stack, while leaving the carton behind."

Isaac was a lot less joyous than Willy was. "I'm sorry the snake had to die. Blacksnakes are beneficial to the environment. They eat rodents, and as long as a blacksnake is in the vicinity, poisonous snakes stay away." Isaac sighed, "Better a dead snake than an angry Willy, especially when the victim of your anger did you no harm."

Willy Weatherbee learned his lesson from Isaac's quiet admonition. He felt sorry for the blacksnake, and even worse about his false accusations against Dwayne Hodges. Willy was thoroughly ashamed. Imagine – he was actually willing to pay money to have Hodges executed!

Moral of the hardboiled eggs story: The world is loaded with anger because of quick and unfounded judgments reached by flimsy or circumstantial evidence. What we see is not always what we get, and often, reality is the opposite of the superficial facts that meet the eye.

If Willy hadn't reached a hasty conclusion, he would have seen how illogical his suspicions against Dwayne were, especially since Dwayne made an expensive cash purchase on the day of the second theft. Once people make snap judgments, they close their minds to truth. The missing eggs could have developed into a feud that would have destroyed the wonderful tranquil atmosphere of Purity Springs. Most of the anger in the world is based on such quick, circumstantial decisions.

Willy should have called Isaac from the beginning of the stolen-egg episode. Likewise, a person who has suspicions against someone else should delay coming to mistaken conclusions, and try his best to uncover the truth. When in doubt, one should seek advice from a wise person with good discretion. A wise person knows how to judge others fairly, and can often shed light on sides of an issue that the angry individual never considers.

Once we discard our superficial and circumstantial judgments against others, we rid ourselves of anger against our fellow man. Anger is the prime barrier to inner peace. So, once we judge others fairly, we take a major stride forward on our personal trail to tranquility.

By judging others fairly, we create an environment of justice and truth, thereby making this world a much better place to live. As such, every individual has a mind-boggling potential to improve the human condition on earth. Think about it.

Point two: Denying a person the benefit of the doubt, and therefore considering him guilty before he has a chance to prove otherwise.

Let's illustrate this point with another story from Old Isaac's inn:

Old Isaac and Sir Edgar Pritchard

Sir Edgar Pritchard is an extremely wealthy, but frugal, investment banker. He divides his time between his main residence in Manchester and his office in London. More than that, I don't know much about him except that he suffers from respiratory ailments, which the damp air of Manchester and the smog of London aggravate even more.

Sir Edgar's personal physician once visited Old Isaac's Inn, and suggested that the crystal clear air of the mountain environment would be beneficial to Sir Edgar's health. Sir Edgar's personal secretary made a long distance phone call to Old Isaac, and inquired about renting a room for his employer.

Sir Edgar was thrilled to discover that a week in Old Isaac's inn would be cheaper than an overnight in a Scottish mountain resort, and booked the reservation. He found Old Isaac, the inn, and the entire surroundings enchanting, and came home feeling like a new man. Since his first stay at the inn ten years ago, Sir Edgar has become one of Isaac's annual guests.

Old Isaac makes everyone feel like nobility. He was always especially careful about honoring Sir Edgar in a manner befitting a gentleman knighted by the Queen of England.

Normally, Sir Edgar arrives at the inn by way of the Limousine shuttle service from the airport, escorted by his valet and his personal secretary. Usually, before the chauffer has a chance to open the door of the limo, Old Isaac rushes down the front porch steps of the inn to greet Sir Edgar and to help him out of the car. Sir Edgar savors the warmth and sincerity of his host's welcome, a heartwarming beginning to a lovely week of relaxation in the exhilarating mountain setting.

In July of 1998, Sir Edgar arrived for his annual week at the inn. Even at ninety years old, Isaac hurried down the front steps of the inn. Without opening the door, he waved a perfunctory hello, rushed over to Jerry Miller's waiting Jeep, and drove away in a cloud of dust.

Sir Edgar fumed. The old innkeeper seriously slighted him. A moment of wrath wiped the ten previous years' cordial greetings from his mind (*remember chapter three, damage number 11, "anger causes amnesia"*).

"How dare the crass old innkeeper ignore me like that," Sir Edgar thought, "how often does nobility frequent these shabby premises?" He considered returning to the airport, but he was exhausted from his journey, and the idea of additional travel seemed appalling. He nodded his head, and the valet took his luggage inside the inn.

Rebecca, Isaac's wife, had a table set with her best white linen tablecloth, porcelain tea service, a carafe of fresh brewed tea, and an assortment of homemade cookies in anticipation of the arriving guest. The mountain hospitality somewhat mollified Sir Edgar. Still, the thought of being slighted by the old innkeeper perturbed him.

The whine of a siren and the screech of skidding tires startled Sir Edgar. He looked out the dining room window, and saw a forest ranger's dark-green patrol vehicle pull up in the front driveway. Kirk Mitchell came bounding through the front door of the inn. "Isaac! Where's Isaac?" he yelled.

Rebecca wiped her wet hands on her apron, and rushed from the kitchen through the dining room, to the entrance foyer of the inn. "Mr. Mitchell, Isaac's already on his way to Peace River with Jerry Miller. He knows about the lost child. Jerry's two sons found the parents, and they called Isaac before they called you." Kirk Mitchell left the inn in a bigger whirlwind than he entered.

Sir Edgar raised a brow at the tumult. "What's going on, here? Who was that man in the brown uniform? What's all the fuss about?"

Rebecca, overwhelmed with concern about the missing child, answered incoherently, "A family from Germany...our guests...they went rafting...in the whitewater...we didn't want to worry you with our troubles, Sir Edgar...*Oy vay*, their raft turned over! Their eight year old son...their only child...he's missing!"

Sir Edgar cleared his throat. The pieces of the puzzle began coming together to form an eye-opening picture. "Let the authorities search for the lad. What's an old chap like Isaac chasing off into the woods for?"

To Rebecca, Isaac was no old chap; he was her knight in shining armor. Her eighty-year old heart still skipped a coquettish beat every time she looked at him. Yet, Rebecca wasn't insulted by Sir Edgar's insensitive comment; she knew that he meant no harm.

Rebecca answered patiently, "No one, not even the forest ranger, knows this mountain and the river as well as Isaac does. He stands a better chance than anyone of finding that child. The Almighty knows how he cherishes life, especially human life... Dear God in Heaven, blessed Creator, please spare that child...oh, excuse me, Sir Edgar. The Peace River Rapids area is dangerous. I'm going back to the kitchen to pray until Isaac returns home safely with the lost child."

Sir Edgar was overwhelmed by the inner strength and quiet conviction of the 102-pound withered sack of skin and bones that was Isaac's better half. He couldn't imagine his own wife steadfastly backing him or praying for *his* well-being.

He remained alone in the dining room. His personal secretary and his valet had taken the luggage upstairs, to his favorite room with the breathtaking view. At first, he scoffed at the idea of the old innkeeper running off to the woods to save a German child. Sir Edgar still had painful memories of the blitz, as a six year-old child in London of 1939. "The war's over," he pondered, "but I wouldn't go out of my way to rescue a German."

People say that the walls and the rafters of the inn are soaked with Isaac's compassion and kindness. The atmosphere of the inn dining room, together with the quiet solitude, put a hairline crack in the wall of Sir Edgar's emotional castle. He gazed in the bottom of his teacup, and felt a warm flush of shame on his cheeks. Sir Edgar hated to admit an error, but remembered a quotation from Shakespeare's Hamlet, when Polonius said to Laertes, "But above all, my son, to thine own self be true." True, he pondered, the biggest liar is one who lies to oneself.

The picture was obvious. Isaac neither slighted him nor insulted him. Isaac had no time to spend on the pomp and procession of the royal red-carpet greeting that Sir Edgar felt entitled to. Isaac was rushing to save a life, and willing to risk his own life in the process.

Sir Edgar was suddenly blessed with a moment of truthful insight – "Yes, German or not, a child's life takes precedence to my momentary self-indulgence. My anger at Isaac is unfair and unfounded; I should have given him the benefit of the doubt. Look at the nobility of his deeds."

Three hours later, shortly before sundown, Isaac and Jerry Miller returned to the inn with a teary but elated Jurgen and Anna Heller, together with freckle-faced eight year-old Johannes wrapped in a blanket at their side. Outside of a chill from his sopping wet clothes and a bellyache from eating too many wild raspberries, the child was fine. When his family's rubber raft turned over, Johannes was immediately thrown ashore; the foaming whitewaters dragged his parents for another half a mile before they succeeded to reach an overhanging log and pull themselves to safety.

As you might have expected, Isaac was the one who found the little boy, napping on a bed of pine needles. Later, Kirk Mitchell commented that if they hadn't found the boy by nightfall, the predators would have; a lone little boy couldn't have survived the night. In short, Isaac saved a life.

Moral of the story: Sir Edgar, like other egocentric people, has difficulty seeing beyond his own inflated image. Oblivious of the world around him, he takes no initiative in trying to find out why Isaac was in such an uncharacteristic hurry; he comes to the premature conclusion that the innkeeper deliberately slighted him. Sir Edgar fails to give Isaac the benefit of the doubt, and forgets about Isaac's ten previous years of flawless service. Only when the situation becomes obvious – that Isaac has embarked on a mission to save a life – does Sir Edgar begin to judge Isaac fairly.

Most life situations resemble icebergs – less than 10% is visible to the casual viewer, and another 90% is below the surface, hidden from the eye. Any ship captain knows that if he doesn't consider the massive, below-surface hidden part of the iceberg, he's liable to wreck his ship. The same holds true in most life situations: Decisions made on the basis of scant superficial facts are usually tragically erroneous. Giving a person the benefit of the doubt is like believing that there's more to an iceberg than what appears on the surface.

Amazingly, people discover more than justified reasons for their fellow man's inexplicable behavior once they grant the benefit of the doubt.

Point three: Failing to consider a fact that could overturn a verdict.

Lisa Kaye and the Cookie Quandary

Lisa Kaye is an effervescent advertising executive from San Francisco and the life of the party wherever she goes. She's also an annual guest at Isaac's inn. One Sunday evening by the fireplace, she riveted the other guests to their seats with the following story of her unforgettable business trip to Chicago:

Lisa's meeting with a client ran overtime. When they finally completed their negotiation, she looked at her watch and double-checked her plane ticket; the departure time of her return flight to San Francisco was in less than two short hours, so she had no time to lose. She flagged a taxi, and promised the driver a ten-dollar tip if he could get her to the airport on time.

The taxi zigzagged its way through traffic jams, ice, and sleet, arriving at the airport twenty-five minutes before takeoff. After a mad rush to the check-in counter, she discovered that the flight was delayed for half an hour. Her sigh of relief was certainly worth the extra ten dollars she paid the driver.

Lisa checked in, and then took the escalator to the departures lounge. Suddenly, she realized she hadn't eaten all day long. Hunger pangs clutched her stomach, but she didn't have time for a meal in the cafeteria. She opted for the vending machines, and purchased a soft drink and a stack of chocolate cookies.

The lounge was packed. Lisa surveyed the entire room, and couldn't find a place to sit. Finally, someone vacated a seat by a two-person table. She sat down, and a well-groomed white-haired gentleman smiled at her from across the table. She popped open her can of soda, and said,

"Cheers!" Her tablemate flashed another warm smile in return. She then opened the stack of chocolate cookies that was on the table, pulled out the tightly packed first cookie, and began munching on it with delight.

To Lisa's amazement, her tablemate – with neither prior notice nor permission – extended his gold cufflink-sleeved arm and withdrew a cookie for himself. What's going on here? She couldn't decide whether the man was trying to make an overture, or whether he was simply too cheap to buy his own cookies.

Lisa took a second cookie. The stately gentleman with the amicable disposition smiled again, and withdrew another cookie for himself. She could feel her blood pressure skyrocketing. This fancy-looking gent in his gray tweed suit with his gold watch is nothing other than a cheeky old man! Where does he get the audacity to invite himself for snack time, and at my expense?

Defiantly, Lisa grabbed a third cookie. For the third time, she received the same warm smile in return. The gentleman then took another cookie for himself. She had never seen such gall in her entire life!

The announcement came over the loudspeaker, calling the San Francisco-bound passengers to board immediately at Gate 23. One cookie was left in the package. The white-haired gentleman took the last cookie, broke it in half, and with another toothpaste-commercial smile, offered one of the halves to Lisa. She nearly screamed, snatched the half cookie out of his hand, and ran to catch her plane.

The whole way to Gate 23, she kept shaking her head from side to side in disbelief, astonished at the nerve of people. "I've seen wise guys in my time," she mumbled, "but that cookie snatcher tops them all!"

She boarded her plane, found her seat in the plush business class section of the aircraft, and stored her overnight case in the compartment above her head. She belted herself in her seat, and then opened her purse to pull out the paperback that she had started to read on the flight to

Chicago. An unopened stack of chocolate cookies stared her in the face. She shrieked in horror.

"Is everything OK?" inquired a nearby stewardess.

"Oh no, I-I mean yes; I accidentally bit my tongue", Lisa answered feebly.

Tears of embarrassment and frustration welled in her eyes. She accused, tried, and convicted an innocent, cordial, and well-mannered gentleman of crimes he never committed. She was incensed with him, as if he were nothing better than a rude and audacious miser of dubious morality! What a turn of events – she herself was guilty of everything she accused him!

"You, Lisa," she scolded herself, "are the piggish intruder! You ate his cookies!" Even more frustrating, she didn't know the man's name or address, so she could at least send him a letter of apology.

The moral of the cookie story: Such an amazing story leads to one cogent conclusion: **A key missing fact can completely overturn our bad judgment of a fellow human**. In the bustle of the crowded lounge after her mad rush to the airport, Lisa didn't notice that she had dropped her own cookies in her handbag. Her anger at her tablemate was based on the mistaken premise that his cookies were hers.

What Lisa considered the epitome of gall, was really a hallmark of virtue, kindness, generosity, and patience.

Don't ever judge another person unless you're sure you have all the facts. Chances are that your anger at your fellow man is based on utter misinformation.

Point four: Judgments based on stereotypes and preconceptions.

The Repaid Loan. Julio Gonzales[30] was the first Mexican American to graduate Summa Cum Laude from the School of Law at Georgetown University. After his admission to the District of Columbia bar, he was also the first Hispanic attorney to be accepted for clerkship at the prestigious Connecticut Avenue firm of Webster, Baxter, and Jones.

Julio's diligence, dedication, and integrity were apparent from his first day on the job. He functioned in his bottom-rung status with dignity, performing the most menial of tasks with seriousness. The senior partners began to pay close attention to Julio, thinking that his clerking days were numbered.

Julio had been with the firm for six months when he received a call from El Paso, Texas, informing him that his father was gravely ill, and urging him to come home immediately. He opened his frayed billfold and found a mere twenty-dollar bill. His checking account was bone dry, for he just paid a three-month advance on his newly rented studio apartment near Georgetown. He needed at least five hundred dollars for the round trip to El Paso, and payday was ten days away.

Julio asked the executive secretary for a five-minute audience with Mr. Paul Baxter. The senior partner received him readily and cordially, and complimented him on his progress. Julio explained his problem, requested permission for a short leave of absence and a five hundred dollar advance on his coming paycheck. Baxter granted the former request, but denied the latter, explaining that wage advances are contrary to the firm's policy. Julio's disappointed expression seemed to ask, "How am I supposed to get home to see my dying father?"

---

[30] "Julio" (names and places changed) and I became good friends through a mutual client, a prison inmate whom I was counseling and he was defending in court.

Mr. Baxter was a father himself, and sympathized with Julio's situation. "I'll tell you what, Gonzales. I'll give you a private, no-interest, five hundred dollar loan for thirty days. You can repay me from your next paycheck." Baxter pulled out a locked metal strongbox from one of his desk drawers, opened the miniature combination lock, and withdrew five one hundred dollar bills. He then drew up an IOU, which Julio signed. Baxter folded the IOU, placed it on top of the cash, and returned the strongbox to its drawer. Julio thanked him profusely.

Julio reached El Paso the day before his father died. He arranged for the funeral, and stayed a few more days to console his mother. A week later, he returned to Washington, D.C.

The young attorney welcomed his heavy workload, which diverted his grief from the loss of his father. The minute he received his next paycheck, he wrote his own personal check for five hundred dollars to the order of Mr. Paul Baxter. Julio looked at his watch; it was six thirty in the evening, and most of the staff had already left the office. "Maybe the boss is working late," he thought. He decided to peek inside Mr. Baxter's office door.

The door was open a few inches, and Julio sheepishly stuck his head inside. Baxter was engaged in a heated phone conversation, but he gestured for Julio to come inside. "Under no circumstances," Baxter said forcefully, "we won't accept a compromise...excuse me, one moment, please." Baxter covered the mouth piece of the telephone with his hand, and raised his head, "What is it, Gonzales?"

"Sorry for the interruption, sir, but I wanted to repay the loan immediately." Julio handed the check to his boss. Mr. Baxter nodded, and returned to his phone conversation, letting Julio understand that he should close the door on his way out. "Thank you sir," Julio said. He wanted to ask for the IOU note, but was embarrassed to do so, for the boss was demonstrating obvious impatience. "Sir, could you please destroy the IOU?" Baxter nodded perfunctorily, and Julio left the office.

Baxter unwittingly put Julio's five hundred dollar check in an open file on his desk, marked, "Gerson vs. The State of Maryland". He was engrossed in a telephone face-off with the State's Attorney in Annapolis. "We both know that the State of Maryland is liable. Agree to a five hundred thousand dollar settlement, or I'll see you in court...that's fine with me, Mr. State's Attorney – do I agree to an initial hearing in twelve weeks? Mark it down on your calendar and send me immediate written confirmation." Baxter closed the file, placed it amid the foot-high mound of documents on his desk, grabbed his tennis racquet and gear bag from the coat closet, and left the office.

Six weeks later, Baxter pulled his strongbox out of desk drawer, and unlocked it. A signed IOU for five hundred dollars glared up at him. "Son of a..." fumed Baxter, "this note is more than a month overdue! How can I trust such a person on a million-dollar brief, when he can't keep his word to repay five hundred dollars on time?"

John Webster, founder of the firm, entered Baxter's office that very moment. "What's the matter, Paul? Looks like the secretary forgot to put sugar in your coffee."

"I wish that were the problem, John." Baxter told Webster about the "unpaid" loan.

"Paul, I don't like to pour salt on your open wound, but remember that Dick Jones and I had severe reservations about hiring a clerk with a barefoot, adobe background."

"C'mon, John, that's unfair. The boy was top of his class at Georgetown. A WASP clerk with his credentials would've cost us twice the money. Besides, this is the twenty-first century. We don't want our firm to have a Jim Crow image."

"Are you trying to convince yourself, Paul? If I were you, I'd cut my losses at the five hundred bucks. Send him packing."

Baxter didn't need much more of a push to stick a knife in Julio's back. "Okay, I concede the point, John. When it boils down to basics, you can take the boy out of the boon docks, but you can't take the boon docks out of the boy. You're right; he's not for us. I'll drop the ax on him today."

Julio received the news of his immediate dismissal like lightning on a clear day. "What did I do wrong, Mr. Baxter? This firm has become my life! I eat, drink, and sleep my work. Why are you doing this to me?"

Baxter flashed the IOU in Julio's face. "This is why. It's your signature here, isn't it?"

"Yes sir, but that's a mistake!" Julio happened to have his checkbook in the inside pocket of his blazer. "Look here – here's the stub of the check I wrote more than a month ago – five hundred dollars to Mr. Paul Baxter! I came right here in the office, and put it in your hand!"

"Gonzales, you are now reinforcing my decision to sack you. Not only are you untrustworthy, you're a liar, too. I don't want the five hundred dollars. I want you out of here in fifteen minutes."

Julio's world crumbled before his eyes. Here he was, out on the street with no recommendation, a blemished career, and a vicious blow to his reputation. What will happen when all of Washington discovers that Webster, Baxter, and Jones threw him away like a used rag?

"I'm going to be strong," Julio told himself. "I did nothing wrong. I repaid that loan. My beloved God is my witness. I love Washington. I'm not going to leave like a fugitive in the dark. Whatever will be, will be!"

Julio took a walk along the picturesque Potomac River, collecting his thoughts and communing with his Creator. "That's it! I don't spend much, anyway. I can live on bread and water if I have to. I'm going to be self-employed! I'll start at the bottom with my own little office."

Within a week, Julio had rented a shabby apartment on top of a grocery store in a slum neighborhood. Half of the apartment served as his office, and the other half became his living quarters, until he could afford something better. He began to represent the junkies and the petty thieves of the neighborhood, and more times than not, with no remuneration. Slowly but surely, he was earning the affection and admiration of the community. Within a matter of weeks, area merchants were turning to him for legal aid and advice. Julio tasted success in all of his endeavors.

Several months later, Paul Baxter drove to Annapolis for the Gerson vs. The State of Maryland hearing. Accompanied by a junior partner and a clerk, he took his seat by the plaintiff's desk and opened the thick folio file in front of him. A slip of light blue paper peeked out from among the laser-printed pages. Baxter examined the paper, and his cheeks turned a bright red. It was a check made out to his name for five hundred dollars, drawn on the Julio Gonzales account at the Georgetown Branch of the National Bank of Washington!

Baxter could barely breathe. His neck became so hot that – courtroom or not – he unbuttoned his collar button and loosened his tie. The combined feeling of embarrassment and guilt was suffocating. Gonzales *did* repay the loan. Now he remembered, just as he was arguing on the phone with the State's Attorney...

"Counselor!" The presiding judge was trying to get Baxter's attention, but the latter was daydreaming. Baxter's preoccupation with the Gonzales affair severely weakened his presentation at the hearing.

George Gerson was incensed with his attorney's miserable showing. "Baxter, I don't think you even read the daggone brief! My cleaning lady could have argued the case better than you did! If we lose, you can erase my name from your client roster! You'd better mend some fences, and fast!" Gerson stormed away.

Paul Baxter mistakenly thought that the Gonzales matter would somehow evaporate. He enjoyed no such luck. All three senior partners suffered an inexplicable series of setbacks that jolted the stability of the firm. After a number of sleepless nights, Baxter told Webster and Jones about the reappearance of the five hundred dollar check.

Dick Jones made no effort to hide his irritation. "I wasn't crazy about the idea of hiring him, but nobody consulted me about firing him, either. I'm not much of a believer, but it sure looks like we're paying tenfold for the damage we did to that young man. Find him, and rehire him right away, with three months of back pay!"

Webster nodded in agreement, and the task of locating Gonzales fell in Baxter's lap. He who spills the milk must grab the mop.

Baxter's secretary dialed the number she received from telephone information. Julio answered the phone. She identified herself, and passed the call to her boss. Julio wasn't surprised in the least.

"Mr. Gonzales, uh, th-this is Paul Baxter speaking." Baxter tried to sound composed, but a lump of embarrassment in his throat hindered his speech.

Julio replied as if he were to speaking to his favorite uncle: "Hello, Mr. Baxter! What a pleasant surprise! What can I do for you?"

"I don't know how to say this, but I must beg your forgiveness. I found your repayment check misplaced in one of my files. I wrongly accused you of shirking your obligations and of lying. I was terribly wrong."

"Mr. Baxter, I'm not slamming the door in your face, but your conciliatory phone call certainly isn't adequate compensation for the anguish and humiliation I suffered in public."

"We're prepared to reinstate you, with back pay and seniority…"

"No thank you, sir. I respectfully decline your offer. By the grace of God, my own modest practice is thriving. Although my clients don't travel in your social circles, they are for the most part genuine human beings."

Julio weighed his next words carefully. "Personally, all I ask from you is that you cash the five hundred dollar check. Getting the boot from Webster, Baxter, and Jones has proven to be the biggest blessing of my life. I know that you don't think you have anything to learn from a twenty-seven year-old muchacho like Julio Gonzales, but if you were a court judge, you would have convicted an innocent man. Think very hard if you would have acted like that if my last name were Marshall or Monroe. For your own good, promise yourself that you'll never again arrive at such a hasty misjudgment because of stereotypes and preconceptions – that's all the compensation I ask for."

Baxter was positive that Gonzales would exploit the opportunity to extort an enormous settlement, even a partnership in the firm. Again, he grossly misjudged the aspiring young lawyer from El Paso. Baxter replaced the phone and put his head between his hands. "That young man is an angel," he muttered. "I had better take stock of myself."

Moral of the story: Once Julio produced a check stub as proof of the written check, Baxter could have easily asked him to cancel the check and to write a new one as a replacement. After Julio's six months of impeccable performance on the job, Baxter should have discarded the preconceptions and prejudices that subsequently ruined his powers of discernment.

Much of the anger people harbor against others is unfounded, based on misconceptions rooted in stereotypes and preconceptions, all of which lead to faulty conclusions. When we dispose of our stereotypes and preconceptions, a significant portion of the anger in our lives disappears.

The above story teaches about faith, too. Julio was worried that his name and reputation were ruined at the outset of his career. He was surprised to discover the exact opposite, that his apparent misfortune was a blessing in disguise from God.

Julio never dreamed of opening his own practice. The Almighty didn't need a recommendation letter from Webster, Baxter, and Jones in order to establish Julio in an ultimately satisfying and more lucrative situation, for our beloved Father in heaven makes dreams come true. Not only was Julio's name and reputation unscathed, his prestige grew with each passing day.

Although they never fully acknowledged the hand of God, Webster, Baxter, and Jones sensed that their firm's turn for the worse was rooted in the injustice they did to another human being.

Point five: Projecting our own weaknesses, insecurity, and character flaws on others, and arriving at mistaken conclusions accordingly.

The Story of the Flat Tire. "Eric Carpenter" *(imaginary name)* felt a thud from the right rear side of his Jeep, stopped the vehicle, and stepped outside to see what was wrong. The Mojave Desert Sun was at its noontime crest, mercilessly baking the already-parched desert. Sure enough, Eric had a blown tire.

To his dismay, the spare was flat too. "Maybe it just needs some air," Eric mused. "Lucky I have my own pump." He tried pumping the spare, but to no avail. The spare tire was punctured long ago, and Eric forgot to have it fixed. Here he was, stuck in the desert, a good six miles from the nearest filling station.

With no other alternative, he took the better of the two tires, his hiking belt, two canteens, and began the arduous trek to the gas station.

The blazing sun pounded on his head. With two miles completed and another four to go, his back throbbed in pain from the constant bending, while rolling the tire. "The station owner will probably charge me fifty bucks to mend this tire," he pondered. With no competition for miles, he was sure that the gas station owner would take advantage of him.

Another hour's forced march in the heat of the desert transpired, and Eric still had almost two miles to go. He had consumed the contents of both canteens, and his throat was quickly drying again. "I'll bet the station owner will really stick the knife to me. He's bound to charge me eighty bucks for fixing the spare, and probably another fifty or sixty for driving me back to the Jeep."

Eric's brain felt like a baked potato; he no longer controlled the fantasies that flickered in his mind like a mirage on the horizon. With each step, he imagined paying a higher price for the tire repair and for the lift back to his car. By the time he caught sight of the filling station in the distance, his head had invented a price of three hundred dollars.

Exhausted, he reached the station. The owner ran to meet him with a cool bottle of water. "Hey mister, drink this! You look like you're about to..."

Eric yelled at the station owner, "You can forget about me paying three hundred backs for a lousy spare! What the heck do you think..."

"Hold on there, mister," protested the station owner. "I'll fix your tire for twenty five bucks, and if your car isn't more than eight miles away, I'll skip you back for free! Folks around here are happy to help a friend in need."

Moral of the flat tire story: The combination of a difficult predicament, the desert sun, and growing anxiety blew Eric's imagination out of proportion. Were Eric the station owner, he might have taken advantage of a person in a similar situation. He therefore projected his own character flaws on the station owner, convinced that he was about to be exploited. As in other cases of this type, reality proves that conclusions based on our own projected weaknesses are seldom accurate.

Summary of Chapter Seven

Let's take another look at the five points, which serve as the key to uprooting our anger against our fellow man:

1. Angry people and tyrants base their judgments on superficial or circumstantial evidence.

2. Angry people and tyrants violate the principle of innocence until proven guilty. They never grant the accused the benefit of the doubt, and therefore consider him guilty until proven innocent.

3. Angry people and tyrants make judgments on the basis of insignificant or incomplete evidence. Often, they fail to consider a key fact that could completely overturn their verdicts against the accused.

4. Angry people and tyrants base their judgments on stereotypes and preconceptions, and often reach conclusions before examining the evidence.

5. Angry people and tyrants frequently project their own weaknesses, insecurity, and character flaws on others, and then arrive at mistaken conclusions accordingly.

The above five points boil down to a single salient rule:

Always judge the other person fairly, with at least the same lenience that you would judge yourself. Give others the benefit of the doubt, and you'll walk away the winner, because you've uprooted your anger at your fellow human. When you judge another person fairly, you gain inner peace!

8

The Flakefoot Falcon

The previous three chapters taught us how to make peace with God and with our fellow man. This chapter presents us with a bigger challenge – making peace with ourselves.

The Flakefoot Falcon

Mount Patience, known also as Old Isaac's Mountain, is a haven for flora and fauna. Ornithologists and amateur bird-watchers love coming to this part of the mountain, the high cliffs overlooking Peace River Canyon. Here is the home of a unique and almost extinct bird of prey, the flakefoot falcon.

Flakefoot falcons get their name from a peculiar hereditary characteristic – they are born with a form of innate chronic psoriasis. The scales on their legs and feet flake their entire lives.

Falcons are the epitome of aviary splendor. They have proud faces, wings of aerodynamic perfection, and telescopic eyes with macro attachments that can hone in on a field mouse from a mile away. Their exquisite gold feathers literally sparkle in the sunlight. Yet, flakefoot feels very self-conscious and insecure whenever it looks at its own scaly feet; some falcons even lose their will to live…

As opposed to other species, the male flakefoot is a skilled hunter and sole provider, while the female devotes most of her time to the nest and to raising her youngsters. Flakefoot couples are fiercely loyal to one another, and religiously monogamous. If a flakefoot dies, the remaining mate won't live more than a week or two.

If you haven't seen a flakefoot falcon in flight, you can't imagine the meaning of poise, grace, and natural majesty.

On the ground, a flakefoot feels miserable. The falcon's emotions in flight though, switch from depression to exhilaration. Its inferior self-conscious image on the tarmac gives way to the royal bearing of an undisputed king up in the sky. In the clear blue, it forgets about its ugly, flaking feet; they're tucked away like landing gear.

The higher the bird flies, the stronger it feels.

Like all birds and animals, the flakefoot falcon is especially close to his Creator. At the apex of its flight, it chants a cry of victory, which is really a song of praise to God. Old Isaac says that the falcon repeatedly quotes a passage from the Book of Psalms (19:2), "The sky tells of the God's glory, and the horizon praises His handiwork."

Like a magnificent monarch surveying his domain, the bird banks along the wind current and completes an effortless three-mile circle of the canyon with ease, barely flapping his wings. The exuberance of high-altitude flight, the wind in its feathers, the royal-blue sky, and the bird's eye view of his kingdom give it a fresh new will to live.

Suddenly, the male flakefoot remembers the needs of his family. Thousands of feet above the canyon floor, he hovers like a satellite, scanning the ground below. There, he's spotted something! What a scary nosedive!

The falcon approaches ground level with remarkable speed, and at the very last instant, levels off in flight while nabbing a helpless little rodent in his beak. He now soars upward, and within seconds, arrives home to the niche in the cliff with luncheon for the family.

Spellbinding, isn't it? What a wonderful gift from heaven – the privilege of observing a flakefoot falcon.

By putting our powers of spiritual awareness to work, let's examine the many lessons we can learn from a flakefoot falcon.

Being at Peace with Yourself: The Ten Lessons of the Flakefoot Falcon

Lesson number one: Look for your good points; try to find your particularly special attributes, skills, or talents, and cultivate them to the best of your ability.

The Almighty creates each and every being with a unique trait of its own. You are no exception. The particular attribute, skill, or talent that God instills in you enables you to accomplish your own very special mission on earth. If you're unhappy with your lot in life, chances are that you haven't yet tapped your own rich resources, and therefore are not yet fulfilling your own distinctive mission. If you have the talent to develop a cure for cancer, you won't be happy as a cashier in a drugstore. If The Almighty gave you a brilliant mind, you're wasting your potential wallowing in front of a television screen.

Likewise, whenever a grounded flakefoot falcon looks at his scaly feet, he falls into a deep depressive state and loses all will to live. He thinks his life is worthless, and he's embarrassed for anyone to see him. Yet, the instant he spreads his dazzling golden wings and begins to fly – his own special talent, for no other bird can emulate the graceful and exquisite flight of a flakefoot – his entire outlook on life changes for the better. On the ground, a flakefoot is none other than a feathered sack of misery. In the air, he's the majestic avian king of the sky.

You and I are no different than a flakefoot falcon. When we identify and cultivate our own unique abilities, we not only survive, we unlock the doors to inner peace and success.

Can you imagine if Ray Charles or Stevie Wonder, both blind from birth, had dreamed of being fighter pilots? Their lives would have been a nightmare of frustration. Instead, they each developed their superb musical talents to bring joy to millions of people.

Likewise, if Franklin Delano Roosevelt had aspired to be an Olympic sprinter, his life would have been a complete waste.

FDR's crippled legs didn't prevent him from being the only American president in history that served three terms in office. Roosevelt circumvented his physical weaknesses to develop his strength of character and qualities of leadership, to successfully lead his nation through the trying years of World War II.

Wait and see how your life improves once you start cultivating your own special abilities. You'll be a lot happier with yourself, and at peace with the world around you. Others will like you much more as well. Your studies, your job, and your family life will soar upward, just like a flakefoot falcon spreading its wings in the wind.

Until you've found that one special quality or talent of yours that sets you above and apart from everyone else, you haven't yet started to live a truly satisfying life.

The Creator outfits every human with an outstanding quality in a raw state waiting to be developed, like a muddy unpolished diamond deep inside a South African diamond mine. Yet, unlike the South African mine, you don't have to travel to the far corners of the world to discover *you*. The more you gain spiritual awareness, the more you'll become aware of yourself and of your potential. SA helps you discover those unique abilities buried deep inside of you.

During one of my lectures, a person once asked me if the fires of purgatory are for real. I answered with the following allegorical dramatization:

The Heavenly Limelight

Imagine that your life in this world terminates, and you're carried up to a heavenly lecture hall. You are seated alone on center stage in the limelight, while thousands of eyes are watching you. Suddenly, the lights are switched off, and a projector illuminates a gigantic video screen behind you. Together with the thousands of observers, you turn around and see a movie about...you!

You recognize your parents, your house, your school, and your hometown. All of a sudden, the pictures become unfamiliar...

A narrator with a warm, rich, loving voice that makes your skin tingle begins to explain the scenes on the screen. You see yourself receiving a Presidential medal of honor for discovering a cure for cancer. Maybe you see yourself as the first special education teacher in the world to teach trigonometry to children with Downe's Syndrome. Or maybe you're leading your national gymnastics team to an Olympic gold medal. A different image might portray you as a benefactor signing a check to build an old-age home for penniless senior citizens.

The film is over. A bright spotlight shines on you. The voice returns, reverberating through loudspeakers in every corner of the lecture hall, and says, "That my son or daughter, is what you were destined to do with your life. Instead, you spent your time in idleness. You squandered your money on foolish short-term thrills. You wasted your razor-sharp mind sitting in front of a television and gossiping on the telephone. You never took stock in yourself. You neither discovered your outstanding qualities nor did you develop them..."

Thousands of eyes focus on you. You're devastated by the realization that you could have moved the universe. Instead, you wasted your potential on computer games, aimless surfing on the web, and soap operas. You misused your valuable energy. Rather than assuming your role as the king's prodigy, you acted like a simpleton. You're so embarrassed that you feel like a blowtorch is searing your face.

"That's the fire of purgatory," I answered.

* * *

Once you identify your good points, and begin to enhance them, you'll like yourself much more. I'll share a secret with you: The first thing I do in personal counseling is to try and make a quick and accurate identification of a client's strong points. So, get to work, dear friend; that diamond inside of you is waiting to be discovered.

Lesson number two: Divide your weak points into two categories: First, those you have control of; and second, those you don't have control of. Do what you can to improve the weaknesses you can control.

If you were a flakefoot falcon, your personal assessment inventory of talents and weaknesses would look like this:

Talents	Controllable faults	Uncontrollable faults
Flying ace	Periodic melancholy	Psoriasis on the legs
Master hunter	Shy in public	*
Superb Eyesight	*	*
Inspiring	*	*
Family-oriented	*	*
Highly spiritual	*	*

Look at the amazing results in the above table: The falcon has a list of qualities twice as long as his list of faults. Moreover, out of all his faults, only one is out of his control! If I were counseling a flakefoot falcon, the first thing I would do after our initial get-acquainted session would be to draw up the above table.

Now, imagine that *you* are the emotional counselor of a flakefoot falcon. The bird has been suffering from severe depression, and has come to you for help. After interviewing the falcon, you fill in the above table. Here's what you tell the bird:

Your Advice to the Flakefoot Falcon

Uncontrollable faults: Until veterinary science develops a cure for avian psoriasis, try not to think about your flaking legs. If you dream about being a peacock, a flamingo, or a fashion model for ladies' hosiery – forget it. Your good points vastly outweigh your sole uncontrollable weak point; focus on them, and you'll forget about the flaking feet. *(See the coming lesson for a continuation of this train of thought).*

Controllable faults: During our introductory meeting, Mr. Falcon, we concluded that the presence of other birds, animals, or humans causes you extreme self-consciousness and embarrassment. I would suggest that you limit contact with other beings to a minimum, and thereby spare yourself the unnecessary anguish. You're a wonderful husband and father, as Mrs. Falcon confirms, so your family unit can accord you all the social satisfaction you need. If that's not enough, establish relationships with other flakefoot falcons in the area. Birds of a feather can always flock together with no anguish or embarrassment.

As for the melancholy, notice that you become depressed whenever you spend too much time on the ground or in the nest. Therefore, I suggest that you increase your airborne time by at least 15%. Bring your flight logbook to our next session, so that we can keep track of your progress…

* * *

Dear reader, I'm so proud of you! Look what a fantastic counselor you are! What you just did for the flakefoot falcon, you can now do for your mate, your child, or your close friend. Better yet, you can draw up a table and assess yourself! You'll be amazed at the amount of anger, stress, and frustration that disappears from your life the minute you begin to honestly assess yourself.

Now, you can monitor your own progress periodically. List your own controllable and uncontrollable faults. Such an exercise helps you to get to know yourself better. Wait and see how wonderfully you begin to channel your energies in the right directions. I'm positive that you're a winner, and that you'll be a tremendous success.

For your convenience, here on the coming page is a blank table for you to fill in. *I know you have many more good qualities than what I've allotted space for, but I don't want my esteemed publisher to think that I'm wasting space.*

Your Personal Assessment Table

Talents	Controllable faults	Uncontrollable faults

Important! Be careful not to confuse uncontrollable faults with the controllable faults you can overcome with dedication and hard work.

As a little boy in elementary school in the late 1950's, my hero was Mickey Mantle, centerfielder of the world-champion New York Yankees. Mickey suffered from osteomyelitis, a bone disease. As a child, doctors predicted that he'd never walk properly; yet, he turned out to be a swift outfielder and the perennial home-run king of the American league. His success had a high price tag: Before each game, he went through a lengthy ritual of taping his legs, and endured excruciating pain his entire baseball career. His biggest victory in life was overcoming the bone disease.

At this point, we'll flash back up to our heavenly lecture hall with the giant video screen.

You now see yourself on center stage in the limelight as a self-pitying wreck in a wheel chair, full of anger at yourself, self-pity, and resentment. The lights go off, the projector lights up the screen, and you see a ball clearing the 420-foot centerfield fence in Yankee Stadium, while 60,000 delirious fans jump to their feet. Casey Stengel, Yogi Berra, Whitey Ford, Moose Skowron, Tony Kubek, Roger Maris, Clete Boyer, and Bobby Richardson meet you at home plate. The Yanks just captured another World Series title. You could have been Mickey Mantle...

The doctors told my parents that I wouldn't be able to live without periodic adrenalin shots. The rising pollen count in the humid late summer of suburban Washington, D.C. would aggravate my hay fever, which in turn would trigger my asthma. On numerous occasions, my father, of blessed memory, would rush me – his choking and gasping son – to the nearest doctor or emergency room for an adrenalin injection.

Mickey Mantle inspired me. Just as he ran on his bad legs, I started running on my contracted lung passages. By age eighteen, the asthma was gone. Who knows how many other children across the nation were inspired by Mickey Mantle? His positive influence on an entire generation of American youth outshines his homerun and World Series titles.

If I hadn't licked the asthma, I would have never been accepted in the army, much less Special Forces. Had I not experienced the ultimate high-stress situations of the army, I may have never developed the spiritual side of my life. Had I never developed the spiritual side of my life, I could never have written this book. Now, do you begin to understand the far-reaching influence that overcoming a seemingly uncontrollable handicap has on others?

Thanks, Mickey Mantle, wherever you are.

Sometimes differentiating between a controllable fault and an uncontrollable fault is difficult. When in doubt, ask a good Spiritual Awareness counselor for help; or, ask a Marine drill sergeant. Both of them can show you that you're capable of much more than you think you are.

> The strongest power on earth is human will. You can if you want. – Rabbi Shalom Arush

Lesson number three: The weaknesses that are out of your control are a blessing in disguise, to help you make spiritual growth and to channel you toward your real purpose in life. Resenting those weaknesses destroys your inner peace and keep you away from the truth.

For the sake of simplicity, we'll return to our example of the flakefoot falcon.

A No-nonsense Counseling Session with a Flakefoot Falcon

The bird comes to us for another counseling session. Whenever our falcon friend looks at his flaking legs and feet, his heart breaks in two. On the ground, he's prone to anger and frustration. The worst thing he can do is to mope around and constantly berate himself, "Why can't I have healthy legs and feet like all the other birds?"

Mr. Falcon, we tell him, you are not a run-of-the-mill bird; you are king of the sky. Rather than allow your anger and frustration to skyrocket, spread your wings and skyrocket yourself! When you're airborne, your problematic feet and legs are tucked away, and you don't even know they exist. In the air, your problem is neutralized, forgotten altogether!

The falcon looks me straight in the face with those piercing eyes of his, and says, "Lazer, it's easy for you to talk. You don't suffer from my problems!" Dejected, he sticks his head in the ground.

Sometimes, with certain clients, you have to employ a tough approach in counseling. "Listen up, flakefoot," I say in sergeant major's tone, "you're not an ostrich, so get your face out of the ground. The Almighty gave you a pair of sophisticated cameras in your eye sockets that any NASA spacecraft would be proud of. Your head should be way up in the air, because you're the king of the sky. Kings don't berate themselves."

The tough approach is working, so I continue: "Do you think you can run the world better than God can? OK, let's see: If tomorrow morning, you'd wake up with healthy and attractive feet and legs, you'd be clowning around in the treetops with all the pigeons and crows. Do you think The Almighty needs another crow or pigeon, and one less flakefoot falcon? Do you think you'd be better off prancing around the pond like a swan or a flamingo? Would you prefer to be a Canadian goose and free game during hunting season?"

Sometimes, a counselor can literally feel God putting the right words in his mouth. I drive the point home, and tell the falcon, "Your apparent handicap is really a blessing! Those flaky feet of yours keep you away from the chirpy little gossips around the pond and in the park. Your avian psoriasis forces you to cultivate your flying acumen. Thanks to your flaking feet, you're the undisputed king of the sky. You birds are nearly extinct as is. Do you know how many tourists and birdwatchers you've inspired? Have you ever heard of a crow inspiring somebody? Come on, man – I mean falcon – cut the self-pity. Here, you've got clearance on runway two-five-niner; get up in the sky and show us your stuff."

The falcon makes his grand exit out of the open window, soars upward, and salutes us with his golden wings.

Lesson number four: Judge yourself fairly.

Let's now focus our attention on you, dear reader. Do you remember the lessons we learned in the previous chapter, about judging other people fairly? You're just as important as the next person, so you deserve a fair trial in your own mental courtroom. Make sure that the attorney for the defense inside your head knows how to represent you. If he's incapable of presenting all your attributes, then I'll be happy to defend you. I can easily compose a long list of your superb qualities.

Now that you've learned to differentiate between those faults that are out of your control, and those faults that are within your control, you can begin to judge yourself fairly. Giving yourself a fair trial is the key to attaining inner peace, to overcoming guilt complexes, and to uprooting the anger you harbor at yourself.

Let's see how, with the following case study:

The Unlikely Inmate.

Dave Cummings, a successful investment broker, washed and dressed in eight minutes, while his wife prepared coffee and sandwiches for him. He grabbed his attaché case, the keys to the car, and the paper bag with the sandwiches. In another minute, he was out the front door. "Talk to you later, Patsy," he called over his shoulder. "I'm flying."

"Drive carefully, Dave," Patsy waved, "it's rush hour."

Dave zigzagged through the inner city streets on the way to his downtown office.

That same morning, on the way to school, two rival junior high school gangs challenged each other to a game of "chicken", to be played on Main Street in front of a bevy of squealing goggle-eyed female classmates. Each player had to dart across the street as close as possible to an oncoming car. A pair of thuggish referees crowns the more daring side as the winners, and condemns the losing side as "chickens".

Dave was contemplating his prospective fee from an eight-figure investment deal. Up ahead, the light was green. Time was running short. His foot pressed the accelerator a little harder. The odometer's needle reached the fifty mph mark; the inner city speed limit was twenty-five miles per hour.

* * *

J.T., the captain of the Sharks had just made a blood-chilling dash across the street, causing the driver of an approaching pickup truck to slam on his brakes. Four screeching tires filled the street with the stench of burning rubber. The kids on the curb whooped victory cries. The burly driver stuck his head out of the window, shook a fist at the gang, and roared, "You crazy kids are gonna get yourselves killed! If I weren't in a rush, I'd beat the daylights out of you!"

"Yeah, yeah, big shot!" chided the Sharks as the pickup drove away.

All eyes turned to Richie, captain of the rival Avengers. "Surrender, chicken!" yelled J.T., "no way you'll top me!"

The pickup missed J.T. by twelve inches, a tough act to follow. "Get outa my face", snarled Richie. "My grandma's got more guts than your yella butt."

A blue Buick was speeding down the street, faster than all the other previous cars. "Watch this, you chickenass Sharks!"

Like a rocket, Richie flew off the curb at the very last instant. He misjudged the speed of the oncoming Buick, and its startled driver – Dave Cummings – slammed on the brakes a split second too late. The car rammed into the boy's left hip, catapulting him a good thirty feet before crushing him under its skidding wheels. The Avenger gang captain became a lifeless nightmare of blood and broken bones in the middle of Main Street.

* * *

The prosecution was shooting for convictions on three offenses – speeding, reckless driving, and involuntary manslaughter. Dave Cummings, who never committed the slightest misdemeanor in his entire thirty-six years, faced the threat of a possible eight-year prison sentence!

Dave's attorney took advantage of the court's overcrowded docket to plea bargain with the prosecution. The speeding charge was indisputable. He could probably beat the reckless driving charge with a good defense. As for the third charge – manslaughter – the prosecution wanted Cummings' blood.

The defense counsel turned to the judge, and said, "Your Honor, that gang leader literally threw himself under the tires of my client's car. If the esteemed prosecution is concerned with public safety on our streets, why hasn't he sent the members of those two street gangs to juvenile court? They could have turned any one of us into a murderer!"

"What do you propose, counselor?" asked the judge.

"I won't deny the charge of fifty miles per hour in a 25 mph zone. The manslaughter charge is out of the question. As far as reckless driving…"

"Your honor, a fourteen year-old boy has been killed. Cummings was soaring down Main Street. He must go to prison," the prosecutor interjected.

"Slow down, the both of you!" said the judge. "I'll suggest a compromise, and we'll close the case. Mr. Prosecutor, I'll grant you a conviction and a prison sentence. Defense Counselor, I suggest that you consent to the speeding violation and a charge of fatal negligence. I realize your client's remorse, but the court can't ignore the speeding and the boy's death. A six month sentence is as lenient as I can be…"

* * *

A dark cloud of guilt weighed heavy on Dave's conscience; in prison, he fell into a deep melancholy. The horrid memory of the bloody accident played repeatedly in his head. His sleepless nights and untouched meals left him ashen-faced, with bloodshot eyes and deep wrinkles on his forehead. Almost overnight, he looked thirty years older. Worse still, his already slim frame was thirty pounds lighter.

* * *

Dave Cummings was one of the worst scarecrows of self-berating lethargy I'd ever seen, and a hard nut to crack. He had no sense of the Creator, nor did he want to hear about faith and spirituality. He only believed in what he could tangibly grasp – investments, stocks, bonds, money, and more money.

Thirty minutes into our first session, I had made zero progress. Cummings sat with his face in his hands, a stubborn bundle of guilt, misery, and self-pity. I had to throw a grenade-level comment to get his attention. "No wonder you don't eat and sleep," I said. "If I were in your shoes, I'd be dead already."

"What do you mean?"

Good! He responded to me for the first time. I decided to spin his head with a few questions that would take his brain out of the lethargy mode and stimulate some fresh thinking.

"What are you doing in this world, Dave? Why were you in such a hurry that particular morning? Why were you caught in a situation where you had to take the car to work on the *exact* morning that two gangs were playing chicken? How is it that you happened to drive down Main Street at the *exact* moment when that crazy kid decided to throw himself in front of a car?"

Dave asked for a glass of water.

"C'mon," I prodded, "investment brokers are aces in math. What's the statistical probability of you colliding with *that* boy, one in a trillion? One in a zillion?"

"I don't follow you, chaplain".

Terrific! He addressed me personally. Now we'll break through some ice. "My friends call me Lazer."

Dave's dreary bloodshot eyes widened. Is he opening up to me? Have I breeched the wall of his internal prison? This was the real issue: He was sentenced to six months in the penitentiary, but his soul was imprisoned for life. "Okay, L-Lazer," he said hesitantly, "Help me understand."

I convinced him that he was the furthest thing in the world from a murderer. We both know that the gang leader's recklessness was 99% suicide.

"You're miserable, Dave, because you hold yourself guilty for the boy's death. If that were true, you'd have been sentenced for a minimum of ten years on the charge of willful manslaughter. You're angry at yourself. Worse than that, you're tormenting your body and soul. Your personal penal system is much harsher than the prison. You are not guilty. The Creator used your free choices to put you in a situation where you overslept, took the car to work, and cut through inner city streets to arrive at that corner at the exact instant when some juvenile kamikaze decides to play chicken."

"You mean it wasn't fate, Lazer? Why would the Creator – if there is such a thing – set me up like that?"

"No such thing as fate, my friend. Who makes your heart beat? Who pumps your lungs? Why are you and I having this discussion? Fate? Certainly not!" I let the point sink in, and poured him another glass of water.

I managed one last sentence before one of the guards unlocked the door to our tiny meeting cubicle and informed us that our session time for the day had expired. "If the Creator hadn't concocted a scheme of throwing you in jail, you'd have gone through your entire life neglecting your soul." I left Cummings to ponder that thought overnight.

Cummings was much more receptive the second day. We talked about the Creator, about the human soul, and about spiritual awareness. Dave's eyes were beginning to light up. In our next few sessions, I taught Dave the following four guidelines:

The Four Guidelines of Judging Yourself Fairly

1. **Never look back.** Never say, "Why was I so stupid?" or "too bad I didn't act differently". Such expressions are the destructive advice of your evil inclination, which wants to keep you depressed, suppressed, and far away from God. At the time, you did the best you could under the circumstances. Fretting about the past is self-destructive, especially since you have no control over the past. Therefore:

2. **Stop torturing yourself.** You wouldn't agree to have your fellow man tortured in a kangaroo court, so why do it to yourself? Why remind yourself repeatedly of old mistakes? Correct them once and for all by asking forgiveness from God or from your fellow man, whichever the case applies, and then move forward!

3. **Be constructive.** Realize that you're human, and humans sometime err. A mistake is an opportunity for personal growth, when you learn from the past and subsequently

implement life's lessons. Constitutional law prohibits double jeopardy, so why destroy yourself with multiple trials for the same crime? Make your constructive conclusions, and move forward with your life.

4. **No Guilt!** No one has the right to remind you of old mistakes, or to lay a guilty conscience on you. Evidence from such people is inadmissible in your mental court. Once a person has apologized for hurting his fellow man, or asked forgiveness for transgressing against God – or as in Dave's case, once a person has served his time in prison – the case is closed. Don't ever reopen it!

When Dave was released on good behavior seven weeks before his six-month sentence was terminated, he took Patsy on a wonderful week-long second honeymoon. Happiness, spiritual awareness, and inner peace are phenomenal fertility agents; less than a year later, Patsy gave birth to their first child. A vast number of today's proud parents were childless before they began their own journeys up the trail to tranquility. Dave and Patsy were amongst them. Fortunately, the accident gave them a new start and they were able to become a family, not just a pair of young, upwardly mobile professionals sharing expenses at the same address.

Remember! Your life, well-being, and emotional stability depend on the ability of judging yourself fairly.

Lesson number five: Utilize your talents for the benefit of society.

Alfred Nobel, the brilliant 19th century Swedish chemist who invented dynamite, intended his innovation for the benefit of construction and industry. When he saw the death, pain, and suffering that the use of dynamite caused, he lost his sanity.

Our talents resemble nuclear power; we can use them to light up the world, or to destroy the world. God does not interfere with our free choice to do good or evil *(see lesson six)*. Yet, whenever we misuse our choices, we go against the grain of our souls – which are all a tiny, holy spark of the Almighty – and therefore create inner turmoil. Inner peace is dependent upon the utilization of our good points toward positive goals.

Let's return to our feathered friend the flakefoot falcon. Were he to use his strength and flying prowess to terrorize and to bully the little birds in the treetops, we wouldn't have much regard for him. Such a falcon would miss the boat of his life's mission as majestic king of the sky, and would simply become another tyrant – here today and gone tomorrow. When we are privileged to witness a flakefoot in flight, we are exhilarated. A noble flakefoot has the ability to elevate our thoughts, even beyond the wild blue yonder. If a bird has the ability of being either a terrorist or a lofty spiritual influence, can you imagine what a human's choices are? Think about it – it's mind-boggling.

Lesson number six: Don't be angry or disappointed when you fail. Never despair! Make a new start.

Don't be angry with yourself when you fail. Examine the following list of failure consolations:

The Five Consolations of Failure

1. **Only doers fail**. People who drive sometimes get traffic tickets. People who don't drive don't ever make wrong turns. Wouldn't it be ridiculous if a seventy year-old person bragged that he never committed a traffic violation, if he never drove a car? Failure's first consolation is the knowledge that you are a doer.

2. **Failure teaches, and usually triggers a stronger second effort**. Failure guards us against complacency and arrogance. When we fail, we realize that we need to improve. Oftentimes, a second effort is far superior to even a best first effort. Don't be angry with yourself; just try harder. Failure is like your soccer team losing a goal – the other team may have scored a point, but the game's not over! A setback helps us try harder and reach higher, thereby enabling us to fulfill a higher level of our potential.

3. **Failure brings us closer to God**. If we were constantly successful, we'd probably walk around with our noses in the air. Then, we'd be ugly, heaven forbid, because few things are uglier than arrogance. The Almighty wants His children close to him. After failure, we pray a lot harder and earnestly seek Divine assistance for our next effort. If our lives were a perfect string of successes, we'd almost certainly neglect our spiritual development.

4. **Experience is life's best teacher**. The experience of failure drives a lesson home immediately. Usually, we are slow in internalizing and implementing what we learn. When we fail, we have a golden opportunity to better ourselves immediately.

5. **Small-scale failure assures large-scale success**. Where would an actor prefer to forget a line, in rehearsal or on stage? A failure in rehearsal often assures a better performance on stage, since the actor makes a special effort to polish the rough edges of his or her performance. Sometimes, small failures are none other than preparations for large successes.

Important! Don't ever despair when you fail. Try harder, ask God for help, and then be positive that you'll do much better the next time. Depression stems from the dark, spiritually impure side, and prevents you from being happy. Despair perpetuates inner turmoil and creates a barrier between you and God's light. True inner happiness – the opposite of despair – is holiness, a sign that you're close to God.

Lesson number seven: Live your own life! Don't live according to society's expectations of you; in other words, don't play the world's game. Play your own game! Avoid competing with others and concentrate on competing with yourself.

Say Hello to Swindling Sam

Without our realizing, society, advertising, and the media are constantly bombarding our brains with absolute rubbish.

Swindling SAM (initials of **s**'ociety, **a**'dvertising, **m**'edia) constantly connives to convince us that we're deficient in many areas. He's a liar.

We all need to improve, and we all need to tap the wonderful resources that The Almighty has given us. Yet, we're not deficient the way Swindling Sam says we are. Actually, we can all blossom a lot faster without the garbage that Swindling Sam constantly tries to force down our throats.

I've seen Swindling Sam destroy many people's lives. The time has come that we expose this lowly swindler. What does he steal? Our inner peace; happiness depends on our being satisfied with what we have[31]. Swindling Sam tells us that we lack the "in" thing, or that we never have enough.

Let's examine a few classic Swindling Sam ploys, and examples of how you should answer him:

Swindling Sam: He flashes you a picture of a burly mustached cowboy on a shiny Palomino riding into the sunset. *Really, the cowboy is an agency model, who probably can't tell the difference between a horse and a mule.* He looks over his shoulder, and lights his favorite brand of cigarette, trying to convince you that you can't be a man if you don't smoke his brand.

You: No thanks, Sammy boy. You can be the macho of the lung cancer or the emphysema ward, not me. You can walk around with a yellow-stained mustache, stained fingers, horrendous breath, and a chronic whooping cough, but not me. Why don't we jog together for a few miles, and see who the real hero is?

Swindling Sam: He now flaunts a stunning young lady in evening attire; she's waiting for her suave Prince Dreamboat to open the door of that stylish $150,000 imported car. For only a

---

[31] Being satisfied with what you have doesn't mean complacency, or failing to strive for new heights. It means that once you've exerted your best effort, you're content with what God gives you.

dollar down and a dollar a week, you can be the Prince with the stunning young lady on your arm...

You: Get out of my face, Sam. I don't need an imported sports car, and I'm doing fine on public transportation. I don't owe anybody a cent, and I sleep wonderfully at nights. By the way, does that empty-headed model on your arm know how to make Lasagna? You bet she doesn't. Let's see if she knows how to spell her name...

Swindling Sam: London, Paris, and Rome have declared this year, the "Do Re Mi" year in fashion. **Do**natto of Italy has rejuvenated the ultra mini skirt. **Re**nee's of Paris has conquered Europe with their seductive silk see-through blouses. **Mi**chael's of London is featuring the skin-tight look in exquisite pants suits for today's foxy female. This summer, if you're not Do Re Mi, you're not a woman; you're probably wearing a linsey-woolsey hand-me-down from Little House on the Prairie.

You: Enough of your bull, Sam! "Do" stands for the dough you're trying to rip off of me. "Re" stands for my ray of hope of being an independent thinker, which you're trying to steal from me, too. "Mi" stands for *me*, my self-image as an intelligent, self-respecting, capable and solid young lady – not the cheap sex object that you're trying to make me into. By the way, I'm a few pounds overweight, I have a few varicose veins in my legs, and I suffer from chest colds in drafty weather, so I'm a lot happier and much more attractive in the longer and more loose-fitting garments I wear. So, do me a favor, Sam – close the door, but with you on the outside.

* * *

Does your father want you to go out for the wrestling team, while you prefer to play classic piano music? Does your family urge you to be an accountant, when you have a passion for art? Are your girlfriends trying to convince you that marriage is old-fashioned, when your heart's wish is to raise eight children? Politely tell everyone – including well-meaning loved ones – to please have the courtesy of allowing you live your own life, so you can cultivate the wonderful talents that God gave you.

Don't try to suppress your dreams and desires in life. Your aspirations are divine gifts that are designed to help you discover and implement your talents. Don't *ever* surrender your dreams to please other people – go for 'em![32]

Fighting or suppressing your own aspirations for the sake of pleasing others is a guaranteed formula for frustration, anger, inner turbulence, and failure. To paraphrase Henry David Thoreau, dance to the beat of your own drummer.

A good ploy in developing freedom and independence of thought is to get off the train of competition. Compete against yourself. Don't ever be angry about losing to another person. Is a beautiful young deer at fault if it loses to a wolf? A deer is a deer and a wolf is a wolf – nobody in the world expects them to compete. Why should you be expected to compete against others? Work with yourself, and develop your own qualities to the hilt.

Personal sports as jogging, hiking, or weight training give you the chance of competing against yourself. Personal activities – like the abovementioned sports, art, music, writing, or handicraft – are great for concentration and inner peace. You'll be amazed how you'll love the time you spend alone with yourself. Concentrate on playing your own game, and not Swindling Sam's game. Be yourself: If you succeed, you'll be right on the trail to tranquility.

Being yourself is the key to personal freedom. Don't let the Swindling Sams of the world lock you in a ball and chain of

---

[32] Keep in mind though, what we learned in Lesson number five: Utilize your talents for the good. Therefore, instead of fulfilling a dream to be a master bank robber, I'd suggest that you channel your talents into becoming a master locksmith. That way you can break open safes for the good of society, and get paid quite well while providing a service that you enjoy.

needless and detrimental conformity, dictated by people who are in no position to say what's best for *you*.

Lesson number eight: Don't blame yourself for your setbacks. Conversely, don't take the credit for your successes. Just do the best you can with the tools you have.

Lesson number six spoke about the consolations and hidden blessings of failure. Let's examine success and failure from a different viewpoint.

The Kabbalists say that a person's only option in life is the choice between good and evil; the rest is in God's hands.

How many times do you wake up in the morning with a long list of plans and good intentions, and then all of a sudden:

- ❑ The car breaks down, and you end up spending half the day in the garage.

- ❑ The school secretary calls to inform you that one of your children is sick, so you leave work, run to the school, chase to your family doctor, then to the pharmacy, and devote the remainder of your day to nursing a sick child.

- ❑ Your computer begins rattling, and then blanks out. Your PC technician arrives, and informs you that you need a new hard disk.

- ❑ The wall between the bathroom and your bedroom has a gigantic moisture stain. The plumber arrives, and discovers a cracked pipe. You have to stay home while the plumber breaks down half the wall to fix the pipe.

On the other hand...

- ❑ A caller from Japan received your name and phone number from the Web. Your product or service is exactly what he needs. Within four hours, a million-dollar advance is wired to your bank from Tokyo, and your business trebles overnight.

- ❑ You're worried about the economy and the rise in unemployment, especially in your field. Suddenly, with no initiative of your own, you receive a phone call from a leading firm, offering you a job that suits your talents perfectly, at a salary 50% higher than what you dreamed of earning.

- ❑ You're the quarterback: It's the fourth quarter, with less than one minute left in the game, and your team is trailing by three points. The ball's on your own twenty-yard line, at third down with eight yards to go. A second after the hike, all you can see is a thousand-pound wall of defensive linemen that's about to make a pancake out of you. You have no idea if you have a receiver down field or not. You make a blind throw with all your might, and then get pounced on. The wind's knocked out of you, but you hear sixty thousand delirious fans calling your name. Your tight end caught the ball, and carried it another ten yards into the other team's end zone. You win.

- ❑ Interest rates are on the rise, and it's a buyer's market. Three different realtors tell you that your house won't bring more than $230,000. Before you have a chance to place a private ad in the newspaper, someone knocks on your door and offers you $280,000 cash for your house.

The victim in each of the four setback examples had nothing to do with the day's misfortune. Conversely, the four "jackpot winners" in the success stories would be daftly arrogant to claim credit for their achievements.

My graduating class from rabbinical seminary in Jerusalem consisted of twelve newly ordained rabbis. One of the best young men in the group wrote thirty-two different job applications; two answered with a flimsy "maybe" that never materialized, eighteen sent rejections, and twelve didn't bother replying. One of the mediocre members of the class, with no effort on his own, received a superb position in Australia. How many times have you seen similar phenomena in your own life?

Here's another remarkable occurrence: "Gary Barrett" *(imaginary name)*, halfback on the varsity football team, Phi Beta Kappa, *and* the most handsome student on campus, had every other female at the University of North Carolina in Chapel Hill literally falling at his feet. Ultimately, he married a girl who suffered from Polio as a child, and was left with a crippled left leg. All the cheerleaders and the sorority beauty queens were both astounded and heartbroken, asking one another, "What does he see in *her*?" Gary's reaction: "She's all I've ever wanted". *Thirty years later, Gary's as happily married as ever, a father of three superb sons and an outstanding daughter, and a grandfather.*

Once we've earnestly done our best, the outcome of our efforts is beyond our control. God has a master plan for running the world, which includes every single detail in the universe, from the fate of major governments to the food of a flea. Each of us receives a unique set of skills that enables us to fulfill our role in society.

Although we can't determine success or failure, we certainly are free to choose between good and evil. God created the world with a perfect balance between good and evil, in order to assure a person's free will, since the notion of reward and punishment are senseless in a context of coercion.

The more we develop spiritual awareness, the more we see God's fingerprints on everything we do. The more we realize God's fatherly intervention in our daily lives, the less we worry. The less we worry, the more we can channel our energies into utilizing the tools that God grants to each of us. The more we utilize our tools for the best, the more we live at peace with ourselves. When we live at peace with ourselves, it's a lot easier to live at peace with everyone around us.

Lesson number nine: Understand your very special mission on earth. Try your best to understand why God created you the way He did.

Let's compare two airplanes: One is a Boeing 747 Jumbo and the other is an F-15 jet fighter. They have several things in common: First, they both fly. Second, they both have jet engines. Third, they both have the basic parts that all jet aircraft have – wings, elevators, fuselage, landing gear, etc. At this point, their similarity comes to a screeching halt.

Look at the differences between the two aircraft: First, the 747 is a commercial plane designed to transport hundreds of people, while the F-15 is a military plane which holds one person only – the pilot. Second, the 747 is equipped with complete service kitchens, including heating ovens and freezers, as well as other amenities designed to make passengers feel like they're sitting in their living room. The F-15 carries no amenities – only weapons, from air to air missiles and air to ground missiles to high caliber machine guns.

Clearly, a 747 can't perform the task of an F-15 and vice versa. We all understand that we need the services of a 747 to fly from London to New York, but we call on an F-15 to patrol our country's skies. A 747 is much too cumbersome to police the skies, but an F-15 is much too tiny to transport people. Yet, they each have their unique and essential missions.

Let's make one additional comparison, between a thoroughbred and a donkey. You'd probably prefer to own a thoroughbred, wouldn't you? The horse is faster and much more handsome than a donkey. Yet, a little donkey can carry a load that would break a thoroughbred's back. Donkeys are much more surefooted than horses, and can negotiate precarious rocky mountain trails that would break the legs of a thoroughbred. Like the 747 and the F-15, donkeys and thoroughbreds can't fulfill each other's duties. Each animal has its own special contribution to the world.

If machines and animals have their own unique functions, a person certainly does. In recent years, mankind is finally beginning to understand the unbelievable effort that God devotes in making each of us a special individual, via the discovery of DNA, RNA, chromosomal combinations, and genetic maps. Why all the bother? Why doesn't The Creator stamp us all out from an identical mold, and make life easier on Himself? The reason is simple: Each one of us has his or her own unique mission on earth, and God outfits us with the necessary talents and aptitudes in order to accomplish what we're supposed to, in a similar manner that the F-15 and the 747 are outfitted with the equipment needed to perform their tasks.

I see you nodding your head, dear friend. You want to tell me, "That's all well and good, but how do I know what my own special task on earth is?" I'm glad you asked.

Do you remember how well you counseled the flakefoot falcon, back at the beginning of this chapter? Do you remember the self-assessment table, where you listed your individual characteristics? By taking a good, hard look at yourself, you'll understand your ultimate mission in life. The self-assessment table, coupled with heightened spiritual awareness and talking to God (*which you'll learn how to do in the coming chapter*), are *the* tools in finding yourself. Sharing your thoughts with a spiritual counselor will also benefit you – the better the counselor, the better the advice.

Here's a brief example: "Pierre Plasse" *(imaginary name)* is a French toilet bowl manufacturer. Other companies manufacture toilet bowls, but for some inexplicable reason, Frenchmen prefer Plasse's product. Plasse is a simple man who possesses good common sense, but lacks a high school diploma. Yet, he's a multimillionaire.

Plasse once told me, "What shall my claim to fame be, that I devoted my life to helping people relieve themselves comfortably? I'm afraid not. When I realized that The Almighty was giving me fifty times the money that I need to live on, I concluded that philanthropy is my life's mission. Instead of wasting my time on squandering my wealth, I began shopping around for the best charities I could possibly find."

In the last ten years, Plasse has built an orphan's home, a halfway house for the homeless, a subsidized convalescent home for low-income mothers, and an outpatient clinic for battling drug addiction, just to name a few. "I guess that people insist on buying Plasse toilets so that I can have the funds to continue my work." Pierre Plasse combines his golden heart with his golden bank account to make this world a better place.

The minute you put your mind to the task, you too will understand your very special mission on earth, the reason God created you so special. The better you realize your mission on earth, the more fulfilled you'll be, and the more you'll be at peace with yourself.

Lesson number ten: Understand that your soul is timeless. Your actions will affect the world long after you've left this life.

This is our concluding lesson from the flakefoot falcon. Inherently, when our actions impart a positive influence on others, we are rewarded forever and ever. The body is limited, but the soul – like its Creator – is timeless. The soul continues to reap rewards for its good deeds long after the body has disintegrated. Likewise, an evil person – whose actions have caused pain and suffering to the world – condemns his own soul to a dismal future of eternal grief.

When we ponder the long-term effects that our deeds have on the world around us, we readjust priorities in life. The more we consider the long-term influences that our actions bear on our souls, the better we act. The better we act, the better we feel about ourselves, and the more we attain genuine inner peace.

9

The Mountain Serenade

We now begin the fourth and final stage of our journey up the trail to tranquility. Now that we've made peace with God, with our fellow man, and with ourselves, we feel an invigorating sensation of emotional and spiritual freedom. We're now ready to begin the final stage of our journey up the trail to tranquility and to pave our own personal road to lasting happiness.

This chapter introduces us to the art of personal prayer – how to develop an honest, loving, and no-middleman relationship with God.

Who doesn't love a mountain sky on a clear starry night? No honking cars, no flashing neon lights, and no police sirens – nothing interferes with creation's broadcast. Up in the hills or out in the woods, things are simple – your mind just doesn't seem to focus on material demands. A few whole-wheat crackers and a can of sardines with a fresh cup of coffee brewed over the coals of a bonfire are enough to make you feel like a multimillionaire. Under an open sky, you feel a unique sense of calm and inner peace – solid proof that happiness doesn't depend on material possessions. On the contrary – all the money and the frills of the material world won't buy tranquility.

The Mountain Serenade

Old Isaac and Jerry drink their coffee in silence. Their sipping seems to meld with the symphony around them.

They hear a coyote singing his soulful melody. A bullfrog joins in with a bass accompaniment. The crickets provide background music, and high up in a fir tree, an owl syncopates with an occasional hoot. In the distance, they hear the percussion of thunder, while the waters of a nearby spring harmonize the overture.

In the Marines, Jerry had spent plenty of time in the outdoors at night – in deserts, in mountains, and in the woods – but was always engaged in a mission or a maneuver. With Isaac, he's at liberty to enjoy the nocturnal concert.

Isaac says that the nightly mountain serenade is none other than each creation's song of praise to the Creator. He knows; for generations, wise men with fine tuned spiritual sensitivity have been able to understand the language of birds, animals, and even plants.

Old Isaac and Jerry are sitting by the glowing embers of their waning campfire, some 7000 feet above sea level in the vicinity of Purity Springs, and less than a mile from the top of Mount Patience. At midnight, both are still engrossed in the audible raptures of the night. Suddenly, Isaac asks, "Jerry, what do you hear?"

At midnight, humanity seems to relinquish control of the world to the plant and animal kingdom. Jerry feels an indescribable peacefulness – a rare type of simplicity – the extreme opposite from the hustle and bustle of the day. He concentrates on the sounds of the night, closes his eyes, and lets his ears predominate. He hears amazing sounds. "I hear applause – as if the trees are applauding."

"Good boy," Isaac says, "that's the wind blowing through the dry seed pods of the acacias on the ridge below. What else do you hear?"

Again, Jerry closes his eyes and concentrates on the night. He experiences a wonderful sensation, as if his entire being is in perfect fusion with the mountain environment. "I hear whispering, as if one person is whispering, and then a hundred others answer."

"Bravo!" Isaac applauded. "You are hearing the wind rustling the tallest reed by the spring, followed by the rustling of all the other reeds."

"Really?"

"Yes. Next time you see a clump of reeds, whether up here at high elevation or down in the valley, notice that the tallest reed is always in the center of the clump, surrounded by a few hundred congregant reeds. The tallest reed is the cantor – he leads the others in prayer. He sings a song of praise to The Almighty, and then congregant reeds follow suit in unison."

Isaac elaborates, "You know that the plants and the animals have spirituality on their own levels; you're hearing them. Concentrate now, and try to listen to something inanimate – minerals have spirituality, too."

Jerry is perplexed. What, rocks make noises? He puts his reservations aside, because when a person is fortunate enough to be with a spiritual master like Old Isaac, he shouldn't let his own limited thinking get in the way. So, Jerry does exactly as told, and concentrates on the inanimate. "Isaac! I hear giggling – from the north of us, about a quarter mile away!"

Isaac laughs his hearty laugh and congratulates Jerry. "Wonderful! I'm so proud of you! The giggling sounds are the waters from the underground spring that surface a quarter mile to the north of here – Purity Springs."

Old Isaac has phenomenal explanations for another dozen different sounds of the night. For each sound, he has three different legends from Talmud and Kabbala. They hear a bullfrog croaking nearby. "Are frogs mentioned in the Talmud, Isaac?" Jerry knows the obvious answer; he just wants Isaac to tell another tale.

"They certainly are," Isaac nods, and tells another one of his rich legends, that's just about as old as the foothills of Mount Patience:

King David and the Frog

When King David finished composing the one hundred fifty songs of praise that comprise the Book of Psalms, he looked up to the heavens and asked, "My Lord in heaven, do you have another being on earth who praises You as much as I do?"

Suddenly, a frog jumped onto King David's hand. "Excuse me, Your Majesty," said the frog respectfully, "but please don't boast. I praise The Lord much more than you do. You have written one hundred fifty songs of praise; I have authored three thousand – twenty times more than you. Not only that, but for *each* of my three thousand songs, I have three thousand proverbs that tell of the magnitude of God, and I'm only a frog..."

We ask ourselves, if the mineral, plant, and animal beings talk to God all day long, then why don't we? We're supposed to be higher beings, yet many of us don't even talk to God once a day!

Personal prayer – talking to God in your own language with your own words – has the power to cure one's emotional ills like no psychological or psychiatric therapy can. Those who make a daily practice of pouring their hearts to God *can* and *have* overcome alcohol, tobacco, drugs, and *all* forms of stress. They've saved tremendous amounts of money on analysts. Nothing is as conducive to one's physical welfare as the reduction of anxiety achieved by a daily conversational session with God.

* * *

The next portion of this chapter answers frequently asked questions about personal prayer, and gives advice how to make it work for you. The end of the chapter provides you with an emotional first-aid kit. Fear or aversions to organized religion, dogmatic doctrines, or self-serving clergyman no longer have to stand in your way to a genuine relationship with God.

Frequently Asked Questions about Personal Prayer

Not long ago, I had the privilege of taking a group of Australian exchange students on a nocturnal excursion to the desert in order to teach them the fine art of personal prayer. We sat around our campfire enjoying the starry night, before we separated – each person to his or her own lovely spot – for an hour of personal prayer. Most of the group had never experienced personal prayer, so I let them fire away with questions. Here's what they asked:

One: Who is really capable of talking to God?

You are! (*That's exactly what we've been talking about in the previous few pages.*) If all the members of the mineral, plant, and animal kingdoms speak continually with God – despite the fact that their spiritual profiles are lower than the divine soul of a human – you certainly can!

Two: What do I talk about?

Anything that's on your mind – your worries, your preoccupations, your deliberations, and your hesitations – get them off your chest. Anything you'd discuss with a loving parent or an understanding best friend is good subject material for personal prayer.

Three: Does God answer me?

Of course he does! There's not an atheist or agnostic in the world who has ever tried personal prayer, because if they did – sincerely – they wouldn't be atheists or agnostics any more! When you spill your heart out to The Almighty, telling Him your worries and your problems, oftentimes a sudden spark lights up your brain with an amazing solution or suggestion you hadn't thought of previously. If that little spark imparts glowing warmth on your heart, congratulations! You've just received a personal message from God.

Sometimes God answers immediately, like in the case of another two of Old Isaac's guests, Rodney and Judy:

Rodney and Judy

A few years ago, Rodney Hart, a computer programmer from San Francisco, came to Old Isaac's inn for the first time. Rodney seemed to have just about everything in life – a good career with a substantial income, his own condo in a desirable area, good health, a nice appearance, and a cordial personality. He was in his mid thirties at the time.

One evening at sundown, at the time when Isaac sits on the front porch drinking his herb tea and watching the sunset, Rodney sheepishly approached and asked, "D-do y-you mind if I join you, Isaac?"

"Please, Rodney, by all means! I'd be delighted to share your company."

Old Isaac is an unbelievable spiritual catalyst. People pour their hearts out to him, and Rodney was no exception. "Isaac, I've dated loads of girls in my time. I want to get married, but I can't seem to find the right person."

"Hmmm," Isaac nodded, looking out in the distance with his piercing hazel eyes, "what have you done about this problem, Rodney?"

"I've tried singles clubs, computer dating, and even professional matchmakers. One woman has a great personality, but she's too fat. Another one is attractive, but she doesn't stop talking. A third – who's both personable and good-looking – doesn't want to give up her career, which demands excessive traveling. Every girl I go out with is like a short blanket – if I cover my head, my feet protrude, and if I cover my feet, my head sticks out – there's always some deficiency. I know I'm not perfect, Isaac, but all I need is somebody who's right for *me*!"

"You know, Rodney, when an embryo is only forty days old within the mother's womb, a voice from heaven declares, 'the son of so-and-so shall marry the daughter of so-and-so'. The future Mrs. Rodney Hart is waiting for you to find her. Have you ever tried asking God to help you find your mate?"

"I'm not a churchgoer, Isaac."

"Who needs a church to talk to God? C'mon, let's go!" Old Isaac raised himself slowly from his straw rocker, and stretched his arms and back. The sun disappeared in the west, and a cool breeze began blowing from the north. "You and I are going for a walk before dinner."

"Where to?"

"To the apple orchard; it's not far from here, but you can yell at the top of your lungs, and no one will hear you."

Rodney was perplexed. Isaac was already down the stairs of the front porch and on his way to the orchard. Rodney, physically fit and thirty-five, was scurrying to catch up with Old Isaac's brisk walking pace. "W-What do I need to be yelling at the top of my lungs for?"

"You're thirty five and single! Some people your age have nine children already! You need to be pouring your heart and your eyes out to God, that He should have compassion for you and help you find your bride."

"Isaac, does this really work?"

"What have you got to lose, an hour of your time? Meanwhile, enjoy the surroundings. Feel how The Almighty is all around us. Can a painter paint such beauty? Try and make a connection with God. He's your Father, Rodney – He loves you and cares about you. Now, with that in mind, go up to that orchard," Isaac pointed to a hillock about two hundred yards ahead, surrounded on both sides by the forest. "Yell your heart out for an hour – not a minute less. I'll be waiting for you right here."

Later, Rodney reported that he felt like an idiot at first, standing alone among the apple trees. He mumbled a few words to himself, and then felt even more ridiculous. He looked up at the sky, and the first stars were assuming their respective positions in the heavenly honor guard. A whippoorwill sang its twilight melody from the adjacent forest, prancing up and down three octaves in one short lovely whistle. It seemed to Rodney that the bird was saying, "You can, too!"

"Yes, I can!" yelled Rodney, answering the whippoorwill. He decided to give Isaac's advice a try. "G-God, this is Rodney; Rodney Hart. I don't know anything about religion. Having met Isaac, I'd like to get to know You better. Isaac promised that You'd listen to whatever I have to say..."

Years of pent-up emotions flowed forth from the depth of Rodney's soul like a break in the Hoover Dam. He pleaded with God, requesting not only a wife, but many other answers to life's dilemmas as well. An hour later, exhausted, he returned to Isaac.

Isaac took one look at Rodney and said, "You've just discovered your soul, Rodney. Neither Microsoft nor IBM designed our spiritual anatomy. Therefore, to maintain your spiritual health, you have to plug in with God from time to time. You should see how your eyes are shining – after only one session in the orchard!"

While Rodney Hart was pouring his heart out in Isaac's apple orchard, back at San Francisco International Airport, Judy Sanders waited impatiently at the end of a long line. The queue to check in for the day's last scheduled flight to Denver was nearly as long as a football field. Judy was impatient; she longed for this vacation, eagerly anticipating a few days of hiking and relaxation in the mountains around the Boulder area. Finally, she reached the check-in counter.

"I'm really sorry, Miss Sanders, but this flight is overbooked. I'm afraid you won't be able to board."

"But I have a confirmed reservation!" protested Judy.

"I'll tell you what," said the ground stewardess, "the airline will pay for your hotel tonight, and we'll put you on the 6:30 a.m. flight tomorrow morning."

Judy sighed deeply, and then shrugged her shoulders. "I don't want to sleep in San Francisco tonight. I was looking forward to sleeping in the mountains. Do you have any other flights tonight in the vicinity of the Rockies?"

"As a matter of fact, we do! If you'd like, for the same price of your ticket, I can put you on a flight to Peaceville, not far from Mount Patience, which makes one stop in Riverton. Have you ever been to Mount Patience?"

"I'm sorry to say that I haven't," answered Judy.

"Then here's your chance," said the ground stewardess. "There are plenty of inns and hotels, and folks there are more than friendly. Mount Patience and its surroundings make Switzerland look like a rock pile. You'll love it. You don't even need to rent a car in Peaceville. All sorts of shuttle vehicles will take you wherever you need to go."

"That's great! I'm going to Peaceville."

The ground stewardess attached luggage tags to Judy's gear, and issued her a new ticket and boarding pass. "Run to gate 15 – they're boarding in ten minutes. Have a good flight!"

"Thanks so much," giggled Judy. She was never so happy to be bumped off a flight. She had a wonderful feeling that something very special was in store for her.

A few minutes before midnight, Judy reached Peaceville. Exhausted, she checked in for the night at a motel nearby the airport. Her room had a mountain view, and before going to sleep, she filled her lungs with the crisp mountain air. The sky was so clear that she thought she could have plucked stars with her eyebrow tweezers.

After breakfast the next morning, she described to the desk clerk more or less what she was looking for – hiking, relaxation, beautiful surroundings, and a quaint country-style atmosphere.

"We've got a lot of places in these parts that fill your bill, Ma'am. Is this your first time in this area?"

"Yes sir, it is."

"Would you like something off the beaten path?"

"I think I would," answered Judy.

"In an hour, there's a shuttle bus that goes up to Liberty Springs. On the way, about thirty minutes from here, you go by Mount Patience and Peace Valley. There's a small inn operated by an old European couple that's the most charming place you can imagine. Folks call it Old Isaac's Inn, and it's inexpensive but really nice. You'll love it."

"Sounds wonderful; can you call ahead and make a five-day reservation for me? I'll need a place on the Liberty Springs shuttle please, too."

"Consider it done, Ma'am!"

Two hours later, Judy Sanders arrived at the inn. Isaac greeted her at the front steps and grabbed her luggage. Rebecca sat her down at a lace-covered hewn oak table and served her fresh-baked oatmeal cookies and cinnamon apple tea. Judy was enchanted, as if in a wonderland.

While she sipped her tea, Rodney entered the dining room. "Judy – Judy Sanders – Is that really you?" Judy's older sister was in Rodney's class at high school, and their parents lived right around the block from each other.

"Yes it's me, Rodney Hart!"

"Where've you been all these years? What're you doing here? How did you…"

"Hold your horses, first things first! After nursing school, I spent a few years in the Peace Corps in Peru. Now, I'm a surgical nurse at Frisco General. I was supposed to be in Boulder, but I got bumped off my flight and I decided to come here."

"Of all places!"

Rebecca diplomatically tiptoed back to the kitchen, where Isaac was peeling potatoes. "Isaac," she smiled lovingly, "it's another match."

"I know, Rebecca; we'll probably be toasting them before the week's over…"

Rebecca and Isaac were correct. For the next five days, Judy and Rodney were inseparable. They loved each other's company, and their personalities complemented one another beautifully. The night before they checked out, they walked together into the kitchen, where Isaac and Rebecca were washing the dinner dishes. "Isaac, Rebecca, we want you two to be the first to know; Rodney and I are getting married!"

Rebecca caressed Judy and blessed her. Isaac embraced Rodney and wished him all the best. Isaac whispered in his ear, "Would you have ever believed how fast The Almighty juggled the entire world for you! Look at the succession of events that brought Judy here – a person would have to be deaf, dumb, and blind not to see the hand of The Almighty in this. That's the power of personal prayer; you spoke to God sincerely, and He moved mountains to bring Judy right here to you! Don't ever forget that, Rodney."

"I won't, Isaac. I promise."

Four: I haven't been on my very best behavior lately *(a few other people around the campfire giggle and blush)*, **so won't God be angry if somebody like me is cheeky enough to talk to him?**

Of course not! On the contrary, talk to God and tell him what you're ashamed of. Speak openly and honestly.

Five: Yeah, but won't I be punished?

On the contrary, I'll give you an example: Suppose you are a parent, and you have a ten year-old son who's playing baseball in the front yard. You are in the kitchen drinking your Sunday morning coffee and reading the newspaper. All of a sudden, you hear the crash of shattering glass. Your son has thrown a hard ball right through your six hundred dollar bay window in the living room. Since you are a wise parent, you don't react for the moment; you're waiting to see what your son's next move is.

Your son is a bright child. He runs in the house, tearfully throws himself at your feet, and cries, "Daddy/Mommy, I'm so sorry! I was careless and I broke the living room window! Please don't be angry *(he cries on your lap)* – I'll pay for the damage with my allowance and birthday money, and I'll do all the chores in the garden, too. Please forgive me!" You can't possibly be angry with such a child. On the other hand, if the boy runs away and hides, or denies breaking the window, you'd be furious.

By the same token, when you tell God where you've made a mistake, you invoke heavenly compassion. We are His kids and He is our loving father, simple as that!

The leader of the group, a forceful political science major by the name of Neville, looks like he's about to explode:

Six: Lazer, you make it all sound so idyllic, but the truth is that I'm sick of having religion stuffed down my throat and being forced to do things I don't believe in. I'm bored out of my skull sitting through services that don't say a word to me, and listening to clergymen who don't practice what they preach. How do you expect me to talk to God?"

Your question is superb; here's your answer:

Let me tell you about the "Cantonists", the little Jewish boys in 19th Century Russia who were ripped out of their mother's arms and drafted into the Czar's army for twenty-five years. Most of them never made it home again; of those who lived through their term of service, many became disheveled drunks in the slough of the gutter.

You ask yourself, how could that be? As soldiers of the Czar, they were impeccably orderly and disciplined. The answer is simple: When you're forced to do something against your own will and belief, you'll revolt at the first opportunity.

Your parents forced you to go to services, yet neglected – or didn't have the tools – to teach you *anything* about God. Neville, can you imagine how many millions of people attend religious services and *never* have never spoken one sincere word to God? They have a relation with God like you would have with your local bank teller – formal and polite, but without intimacy.

Personal prayer has nothing to do with religion, houses of worship, or clergymen. We're talking about your intimate relationship with the Divine power that not only created you, but sustains you every single second of your life. Do you know how vulnerable we all are? If we could see the trillions and zillions of viruses, bacteria, and life-threatening one-celled animals floating around in the air, we'd all die of fright! Can you imagine the havoc that a tiny ameba could wreak if it penetrated the human brain? We can't begin to imagine the mind-boggling numbers of favors the God performs for us each minute of our lives; God knows how many quadrillion favors He does for you, Neville. Don't you think it would be proper to begin with a small thank you? Religion has nothing to do with it.

You're not a goose; you can't be force-fed. On the other hand, you can't neglect the development of your spiritual self. No one can do that for you. Some people believe in secular spirituality; that's a negation of terms, like soundless music. If you want to grow spiritually, you have to develop a personal relation with God. Forget the coerced version – that's not spirituality at all. You wouldn't stop eating just because you ate at a bad restaurant several times, would you?

I'll give you an additional example. Elementary school children must learn arithmetic, whether they like it or not. Hopefully, teachers make the subject interesting. But, if you had the misfortune of having a fourth grade math teacher who didn't know how to deliver the subject in an appealing way, you wouldn't throw your hands up in the air and refuse to ever learn math again. Why? If you don't know basic math, your life will be miserable – you won't be able to balance a check book, you'll lose money right and left because you'll think that three soaps for a dollar are cheaper than a single soap for twenty-nine cents, and you'll never know if the filling station attendant or your employer is shortchanging you.

Don't be shortchanged in life, just because you don't like the so-called religious establishment. People squander billions of dollars searching for inner peace, and never find it. They never will, until they give their soul what *it* needs; you guessed right, a daily session of personal prayer.

Seven: But doesn't talking to God behoove me to be a goody-goody?

Do you believe in the Ten Commandments? *(The entire group nods in the affirmative.)* If refraining from idol worship, stealing, killing, and intimacy with another man's wife means being a goody-goody, yes – you have to be a goody-goody.

Eight: When's the best time to talk to God?

Any time is a *good* time to talk to God, but the *best* time is at night. Nights are more tranquil than days, and there's less spiritual static in the air to interfere with your speech and thought processes. Nevertheless, if it's difficult for you to find free time at night, take advantage of time during the day that you don't fully exploit, such as your train or bus ride to work. Many people spend close to an hour or more commuting every day. If you're not behind the wheel, close your eyes, blot the crowded subway out of your mind, and utilize the time talking to God. You'll be amazed how fresh you'll arrive at work, and how sharp your mind will be.

Nine: Where's the best place to talk to God?

Rebbe Nachman of Breslev teaches several important spiritual principles that answer this question.

First, try and find a place off the beaten path, where humans don't normally walk during the day. Here's why: Other people's worries, fears, and negative emotions spiritually litter an area. That litter interferes with our prayers, and prevents us from the crystal clarity of mind that is necessary for good soul searching and for spiritual awareness. We all understand how a good tracking dog can pick up a person's scent hours after that person has frequented a given area. Scent is the most refined of physical senses. Just because we humans can't smell other peoples' previous presence, that doesn't mean that the dog can't. The more you develop your spiritual senses, the more sensitive you'll be to the presence of others.

Second, try and find a place that hosts all four types of creation – mineral, plant, animal, and human. Since you're the representative of humanity and the ground you're walking on is a good representative of the mineral world, all you need is a place with some plant life, like grass or trees, and some wildlife, like birds or frogs. Once you begin to speak with God, the mineral, plant, and animal life will join in to your prayers. Spiritually, your prayers will assume the dimension of a symphony, which gives God unbelievable joy. Rebbe Nachman says that when one of God's children talks to Him, He drops whatever He's doing in order to listen to his beloved child's personal prayer.

Third, try to find a place where you're comfortable. If you're afraid to be alone in an isolated spot, then your soul won't be at ease. In that case, a park bench would be better for you than the backwoods.

Fourth, the more a place is naturally beautiful, the more the soul rejoices. We all love an exquisite sunset or a bubbling brook. A lovely view is always conducive to personal prayer.

If you can't fulfill all or part of the above four conditions, God will be happy to listen to you from wherever you call Him. I know many people who go to bed at night, pull the covers over their head, and talk to God until they fall asleep. People who talk to God literally *never* suffer from insomnia. I've had the privilege of helping quite a few people throw away their sleeping pills in this manner.

Ten: How often should I talk to God?

Daily, and at least sixty minutes per day will keep you at top spiritual health. People on high spiritual levels talk to God a lot more – the higher the level, the more they're "plugged in" to God. It resembles athletics – the better the athlete, the more time he or she spends on the track or in the gym.

Eleven: Can I ask for whatever I want?

Certainly! You're much better off asking something from God – who can give you *anything* – than asking from people, who can't deliver the goods.

We humans are ridiculous, the way we chase after others rather than asking our needs from God. Doctors can't cure cancer, but The Almighty can! Let me tell you a story about my father, may he rest in peace:

In October of 1991, I was in my final year at rabbinical seminary in Jerusalem. In seven months, I would be taking intensive written and oral exams on more than seven years of intensive study. The next few months would necessitate total immersion.

My father hadn't been feeling well, but I didn't know the extent of his ailments. One day, my sister Sheila called me long distance from the USA, and dropped a bomb on me: "Lazer, if you want to see Pop again, you had better catch the next flight out of Israel; the doctors have found four different diseases eating away at him. They can't give him blood transfusions any more, because his blood has developed antibodies. They're giving him between six weeks and three months to live."

I was strangely calm, despite the dismal tidings. I looked up from my open Talmudic tractate, and said into the phone, "Dear sister, doctors don't run the world. Anyway, I'll call you back in an hour to let you know what my next move is. Bye-bye."

Without a moment's hesitation, I went to see a righteous sage by the name of Rabbi Abraham Fish, of blessed memory. By Divine providence, he was home. "Rabbi," I blurted, "My sister called a few minutes ago, and told me that our father is dying. The doctors have identified four types of cancer – in his blood, bone marrow, joints, and in his left lung. The optimists give him three months, and the pessimists say six weeks. What do I do? The family demands that I get on the next plane to the States. I don't want to sound selfish, but if I take extended leave from seminary now, my studies go down the drain!"

"Lazer," answered Rabbi Fish calmly, "You're not going anywhere except to the northern hills overlooking Jerusalem. Cry your heart out to The Almighty, and beg for your father's life. Don't look at your watch, and don't stop praying until your clothes are soaked. I'll do the same at my end. Meanwhile, call your sister and tell her you're not visiting America until at least next year..."

I did exactly what the wise old sage told me. To make a long story short, my father made medical history; he lived for an additional eight and a half years, danced at two of his grandchildren's weddings and witnessed the birth of his first great grandson. He did undergo three operations – the removal of a bad lung and the replacement of a deteriorated knee and shoulder – but all four cancers disappeared!

(It was almost midnight, and the perfect time and place for personal prayer). Okay Aussies, one more question before we split up for personal prayer.

Neville shot his hand up in the air once more. "Lazer, my brain understands what you've been saying, but I don't yet feel it in my heart. Can you fire me up before we all go our separate ways?"

Okay, Neville.

Imagine this setting: Your pulse quickens as you reach your post office box. You're so excited, that your hand is shaking like a dish of Jell-O. When you finally succeed in inserting the key and turning the lock, the little door pops open, and...there it is! A legal-sized blue and gold embossed envelope with the Presidential Seal on the outside, addressed to your name! You want to rip open the letter this very instant, but reconsider – what a shame to ruin an envelope from the White House. Better to go home, to carefully slit the envelope with a sharp letter opener, and to savor the contents of your personal message from the President of the United States in the intimacy of your own home.

It's true! This time, your heart skips a beat and a quick shiver flashes down your spine to the soles of your feet. A second or two later, when you begin to breathe again, tiny beads of sweat emerge on your forehead. Your eyes deny what they see, so you read the letter carefully a second and a third time. No, there's no mistake. The President has granted your request for a twenty-minute audience. You can ask for whatever you want! Three weeks from now, you'll be an honored guest in the White House!

Nobody believed you'd ever reach the President. You waited a month to meet the mayor of your town, but came away empty handed. Several weeks later, you drove to the state capital. When you were fed up with the condescending state legislator who was willing to give you a seven-minute appointment in another three months, you decided to write the governor. Six weeks later, you received a form letter from the governor's office redirecting you to a series of bureaucrats, most of whom can't help themselves, much less you. This is ridiculous, you thought, so you sent a fax to your congressman. An aide answered you, with fifteen polite reasons why your congressman can't help you or meet with you at this point. You received a similar reaction from both senators. What happened to all the pre-election promises of the open-door policy?

Disappointed and disillusioned with the self-serving system that has long since forgotten the Gettysburg principle of "for the people", you pour your heart out in a letter to the President. Finally, after eight months of being tossed back and forth like a shuttlecock, you've made it to the top.

For the next three weeks, you eat, sleep, and drink your upcoming meeting with the President. Over and over, you rehearse your delivery. Every word has to count. Your appearance and manner must be impeccable. Nothing else concerns you. Suddenly, all the conversation around you is small talk, insignificant. "I'm going to be meeting the President," you tell yourself repeatedly. Who knows when you'll ever have another opportunity?

A nagging thought still upsets you. "Why did I waste all my precious time, nerves, and energy on chasing bureaucrats, state legislators, the mayor, and further up the ladder to my representatives in Congress, when I could have turned directly to the President in the first place. What a dunce I am!" *One who could have received an audience in the White House in the first place would be daft to approach lesser functionaries.*

Now, think how limited the President is. He can't grant you health, happiness, or length of days. He can't even control his own bodily functions. Presidential decisions can be appealed and overturned, so even if the President makes you a promise, you can't be sure it if he'll deliver the goods.

Dear friends, I'm now arranging a meeting for you that will be far more beneficial than anything you can accomplish in 1600 Pennsylvania Avenue, Washington, D.C. You'll be speaking to someone who isn't subject to reelection every four years, and not vulnerable to partisan pressure or political considerations. You'll be speaking to an entity than will let you talk as long as you please, and is patient enough to listen to all of your problems and pains. You don't have to be embarrassed to laugh, cry, dance, jump up and down, yell, or whisper as you please. You don't have to wait in line, and you don't have to grease the palms of any middlemen to get your audience. You can request whatever you want. How? Why? Impossible?

Nope. You're about to have a one-on-one session with God. Let's go.

Sure enough, Neville yelled louder than anybody else. He argued and shook his fist, aired his complaints, and ended up crying like a little baby. When we regrouped at the campfire site after our personal prayer session, he shook my hand warmly, and said, "Thanks, Lazer. I'll never forget you for this wonderful experience."

"Don't thank me," I answered. "I'm just passing on what I received from my spiritual guides, and what they received from theirs, all the way back to King David and to Moses."

Six Key Tips to Helping Personal Prayer Work for You

1. Be consistent; don't wait until you're "inspired" – your soul needs daily personal prayer just like your body needs food and drink. Without it, forget about *real* inner peace.

2. Don't be discouraged if you're suddenly tongue-tied. The fact that you set aside time to be alone with God is a

beautiful declaration of faith. To "untangle" your tongue, start thanking God for the simple, taken-for-granted blessings in life – your functioning heart and lungs, your eyesight, your hearing, etc. Once you begin thanking God, your soul will pour wide open with beautiful thoughts and words.

3. Give thanks for the past and submit your requests for the future. Nothing is too small or too big to ask from The Almighty. Leave no stone unturned.

4. Don't lose heart if your request isn't fulfilled immediately. In time, you'll see that God *always* provides whatever you need when you need it. When our request isn't fulfilled for the time being – that is, if we're not asking for something that's detrimental to our welfare – our faith is being tested.

5. Persevere! Sometimes, you may go for weeks without feeling any special inspiration or inner glow. If you don't give up, eventually, you'll make phenomenal spiritual growth.

6. Carry a little note pad in your pocket or purse. During the course of the day, all types of subjects will pop up in your mind that you'd like to discuss with God in your next personal prayer session. Write these subjects down, and refer to your note pad during your talk with God, in order to remind yourself of the topics on the day's agenda. When something troubles you or causes you excessive concern, write it down immediately. When you throw your problems in God's lap, you maintain a low anxiety level.

Remember! Nothing benefits your soul, brings you so close to God, and paves the way to genuine inner peace like personal prayer. Therefore, your evil inclination will go to extreme lengths to prevent you from personal prayer. Why? If you persevere, your divine soul will eventually subjugate your evil inclination. At that point, you'll have the spiritual status of a righteous person, and you'll enjoy an anger-free life with genuine tranquility of the soul. So, don't listen to that itty-bitty nagging committee in your head that's trying all kinds of tricks to keep you from talking to God. Your evil inclination wants you to continue to be nervous, anxious, angry, smoking cigarettes, drinking booze, spending your money on analysts, popping pills, worrying, biting your nails, and in debt. That way, your soul is stifled and the evil inclination remains the boss.

Personal Prayer as Your Emotional First Aid Kit

- Did you have a rough day at school or at work? Don't go home angry; it's unfair to vent your frustrations on your family. Call home, say that you'll be an hour late, and find the nearest place to collect your thoughts and to talk to God. You'll come home a new person. *(This ploy has saved dozens of marriages!)*

- Are you reaching for the tobacco, the drugs, or the alcohol again? You know that substances are destroying your health, but it's hard to kick the habit. Run out to the back yard or down to your basement and yell to the top of your lungs, "Please help me, God!" It works! Cry your heart out to God, and amazingly enough, the urge goes away *(tens of people have told me that this ploy played a crucial part in helping them overcome substance habits.)*

- Are you depressed for no apparent reason? Start talking to God as soon as possible, preferably in beautiful surroundings. Wait and see how you feel sixty minutes later.

- Insomnia? Start talking to God. You'll fall asleep in a few minutes.

- You've been humiliated or insulted? Something seemingly bad has happened to you? Talk to God, and He'll console you; He'll help you understand how things are actually for your own good, or what you need to change to improve your life.

- You're suddenly under extreme stress. Don't react! A winning football or basketball coach under extreme stress calls for a timeout; you can do the same. Politely ask for a timeout, excuse yourself from the room for a few minutes, take a deep breath, and ask God to help you think. Suddenly, the stress melts away and your mind gains clarity.

Dear reader, every single clause in this chapter has been clinically tested and proven under extreme high-stress settings, such as the military and prisons. If personal prayer can help a soldier under fire or a prisoner behind bars, it can help you too.

More than anything, not a single word you say to God goes to waste. You'll taste the rewards both in this world and in the world to come. Daily personal prayer will gold-plate your trail to tranquility.

We now move on to Chapter Ten, where we'll make our final ascent to our goal of lasting inner peace and a life free of anger.

10

Lasting Happiness

Just as falling rocks and precarious footholds threaten a mountain climber, recurrent anger threatens those fortunate people on the trail to tranquility. If a climber isn't careful, he or she is liable to suffer a dangerous fall. Likewise, if you're not careful, recurrent anger can catch you off guard, trip you, and destroy weeks of hard work and spiritual effort.

This chapter is designed to reinforce your emotional and spiritual resistance to recurrent anger. Section One is a review of the previous nine chapters, while Section Two demonstrates the life-saving tools for both overcoming failure and for successfully handling recurrent anger. These tools will enhance your confidence and self-image, and will open your door to lasting happiness, even in the environment of a turbulent world.

Section One – Looking Back at the Trail

We began our journey with the ten diagnostic levels of anger, beginning with the level of total anger and turbulence, and ending with the level of total tranquility. Peek back to chapter one; look at the progress you've made, and set your future sights on the goal you'd like to attain.

Then, we moved on to Deer Haven. There, we learned about the two main causes of anger – arrogance and lack of spiritual awareness. Knowledge and spiritual awareness enlighten our lives and bring us happiness. Arrogant people live in the dark; since they think they know everything, they have no access to knowledge, and therefore never learn. People who lack spiritual awareness consider the world a random planet of chaos with no rhyme or reason, whose unfortunate inhabitants lay at the mercy of the elements. No wonder that the arrogant and the spiritually unaware are always subject to inner turmoil.

At Bear Ridge and Lupine Valley, we saw the damages of anger. Immediately afterward, we learned that spiritual awareness is the key that releases us from the jail cell of anger. With our seven-day plan, we learned the basics of looking at the world from spiritual eyes, and set out sights on seeking true inner peace. The more we internalize the principles of the seven-day plan, the more we achieve spiritual awareness. The greater our spiritual awareness, the happier and more tranquil our lives become.

Do you remember that bluish green patch of forest with the wild raspberries and the mountain roses? There, we learned that everything The Almighty does is for our ultimate good, a principle that enables us to make peace with our Creator. Can you recall the quaint little cabin with the trapped pigeon? That's where we learned about the troubles we bring upon ourselves; correspondingly, we also learned the three stages in eliminating self-induced suffering – observation, self-evaluation, and implementation. Hopefully, these three stages, together with the principles of the seven-day plan, will soon be second nature to you. Don't forget to continue monitoring your progress with your own personal implementation of the Enhanced Spiritual Awareness (ESA) Workshop.

Having made peace with God, we continued to learn how to judge others fairly, thereby making peace with our fellow man. Remember irate Mr. Weatherbee? He was willing to execute a fellow human because of circumstantial evidence and a few lost eggs! Giving our neighbor the benefit of the doubt is a major key to our own inner peace.

We made peace with God and with our fellow man, and then came the tough part: From the lessons of the Flakefoot Falcon, we learned the principles of proper self-assessment in order to make peace with ourselves.

By the time we reached Purity Springs, we had learned how to rid our lives of anger and turbulence. By establishing our own personal relationship with God and speaking to Him daily in our own words – what we termed "personal prayer" – we add true inner peace to our lives. Thus, we fill the void of our eradicated anger with a new tranquility. Let's review the wonderful benefits of uprooting anger from our lives, which we discussed throughout this book:

The Benefits of Uprooting Anger

1. Prevention of damage to the soul.

2. Immediate relief from existing self-induced suffering.

3. Better interpersonal relationships, both with family and acquaintances.

4. Improved productivity and career satisfaction, more success and therefore an improved income (*in the long run, angry, overpowering, and aggressive people don't remain on the top of success's ladder - we'll soon discuss this point*).

5. Improved vitality, better mental and physical health.

6. Increased longevity.

7. Improved physical appearance.

8. Increased happiness and a major improvement in the quality of your life.

9. Less worry, more self-confidence.

10. Less sadness and fear.

11. Less stupidity and impulsive decisions, more rational behavior and decision-making.

12. A more truthful outlook on life.

13. Increased memory capacity.

14. Increased spiritual gain.

15. A closer relationship between your body and your soul, and therefore a closer relationship between you and The Almighty, Who's waiting for you with the open arms of a beloved father.

16. No more turbulence - a peaceful existence!

Fifteen of the above sixteen points, which we discussed in chapters three and six, are most likely clear to you by now. I'm sure that point four leaves you with a few nagging questions in your mind. Even though we showed in chapter three how anger is detrimental to our income, let's elaborate more on the relationship between anger, aggression, and success.

Ask your questions, and with God's help, I'll do my best to answer:

Anger, Aggression, and Success - Questions and Answers

1. **Lazer, you've taken me up the trail to tranquility. You've shown me of the benefits of an anger-free life. I admit - I do feel better out here on the imaginary trail with you. But, when I get home, I'll wake up to the stark reality of Monday morning in the affluent North American society of aggressive macho males and hard-hitting feminists stepping all over other people on their way to the top. And you know what, I see with my own eyes that the tyrants succeed! If I bring my goals of modesty, integrity, and spirituality to the cold, hard world of fast-lane competition and intrigue, won't I get trodden on?**

Superb question; at a superficial glance, you're correct - it does seem that the tyrants get ahead in the world. Let's examine your assumption on a deeper level, by viewing a few case studies of different tyrants *(in the case of those still alive, I can't reveal their full identity for obvious reasons, even though you may know who we're referring to).*

Case 1 - Idi Amin. Idi Amin was the President of Uganda. At first, he was an African freedom fighter trained and supported by the West. Following the overthrow of Milton Obote, Amin became President in 1971. Drunk with power, he declared himself President for life. Any Ugandan, who merely hinted that the Amin regime was distasteful, was put to death. Amin killed hundreds of thousands of citizens, throwing their bodies into Lake Victoria.

In 1976, he had the "distinction" of being the first head of state to grant official asylum to terrorists and hijackers, when he allowed four terrorists to land a hijacked Air France plane in Entebbe.

Amin's "closest" associates waited for the right opportunity to get rid of him. In 1979, he lost power and was exiled - first to Nigeria, and then to Saudi Arabia. In August, 2003, he died a lonely, miserable death as an exile, far away from home. Would you call this success?

Case 2 - "Mike". Mike is a former heavyweight boxing champion who punched his way to stardom. He's angry and aggressive, and has earned millions of dollars. In the ring, he once bit an opponent's ear off. Out of the ring, he was sent to prison for rape. He expressed no remorse for either misdeed. In August 2003, his attorneys declared bankruptcy for him in a federal court. Today, he's a loser, left with nothing but his anger, aggression, and base instincts. I don't think you'd call that success, either.

Case 3 - "Judy". Judy tenaciously worked her way up to the summit of a world-renown firm in Manhattan mass media. She terrorizes her employees, as well as the board members to whom she answers. Her rich vocabulary of epithets is more than colorful, and she has no qualms about pouring her unchecked wrath on anyone in her immediate vicinity. True, Judy is an extremely talented professional. She also doesn't have much to show from her seven-figure annual earnings, because of the massive amounts she's spent on the drawn-out court cases of four nasty divorces. After work, Judy goes home - alone - to the four walls of her penthouse, like an angry squawking parrot in a golden cage. Would you envy such a life?

Case 4 - "Ernie". Recently, Ernie was forcefully retired from his presidency of a major international banking firm. Like Judy, Ernie is also a brilliant professional. Yet, he alienated many associates by stepping all over them on his way to the top. Even Ernie's wife and children gave scoops to European journalists, telling them about their horrid life with their aggressive, angry, and egocentric husband and father.

The day Ernie became 65, the board of directors uncovered a finely printed clause in the bank's employee regulations manual: "Section 4, Clause 7: The bank reserves the right to retire *any* employee at *any* time, with no prior notice, commencing from the employee's sixty-fifth birthday." The board activated the clause immediately. Overnight, Ernie found himself on the outside - no more power, no more prestige, and no more position. Today, Ernie wastes much of his elaborate pension on analysts. He's brokenhearted, angry as ever, and frustrated. Not even his family wants anything to do with him. Is this the way you'd like your life to be?

Look at all the tyrants from time immemorial. None had happy endings. Their success was *always* short-lived. King David taught us that the meek shall inherit the earth (Psalms 37:11); Hollywood and Wall Street don't subscribe to King David's thoughts, but meanwhile, King David's principle has proved to be historically correct for thousands of years.

Maybe the role of a Spartan warrior, a Viking, or a Roman centurion is a lot more appealing than the humble role of a wise Talmudic scholar, yet the wise scholars are still with us today, while the Spartans, the Romans, and the Vikings have vanished from the face of the earth. I can go on and on with more case studies, but I think you get the point. Nevertheless, let's look at our album of "meek", handicapped anti-macho types, who really did inherit the earth:

❑ Franklin D. Roosevelt - paralyzed from the waist down, yet successfully led the United States through one of the most difficult times in its history.

❑ Helen Keller - blind, yet pioneered Braille and our entire system of special education for the blind.

❑ Thomas Edison - deaf; "I utilized my handicap to increase my powers of concentration, since I didn't have to listen to the small talk and nonsense of other people," he wrote in his memoirs, and rose to become the greatest of American inventors.

❑ Mahatma Gandhi - a frail weakling, but a giant of emotional strength. Gandhi was the father of "peaceful resistance," the mode of non-violent protest that led to the independence of India.

❑ Ray Charles - blind, but one of the giants of 20th Century American music.

Notice how history remembers all the above anti-macho types with love and admiration. Now, take a good look at the tyrants you know. Is there a single one who is happy? Has a single one been successful on the long run? Does history love and admire Hitler, Stalin, Idi Amin, or Saddam Hussein? I don't think so.

2. Okay, I get the point about the tyrants and the meek, but you skirted my question about getting trodden on if I don't play the aggressive game like everybody else does. How can I be tranquil, and yet succeed?

One of the basics of the traditional Far East schools of martial arts is a strong emphasis on character development, especially modesty. A real combatant must limit warfare to situations of impending threat only. The Japanese instill a severe code of moral behavior and modesty in their Suma champions. Braggers and macho types aren't accepted into the Special Forces units of the Israeli Defense Forces, and are considered bad security risks. Joon Rhee, who introduced Tae Kwon Do to America back in the early 1960's, was one of the gentlest, soft-spoken individuals I ever encountered. Yet, nobody dared trod on Joon Rhee.

Real strength comes from within. By implementing the lessons you've learned in this book, you've discarded a load of emotional garbage, developed spiritual awareness, and discovered an emotional strength under fire that you never dreamed you had. That's real power.

Machoism and superficial aggression is a bad façade for major-league insecurity. Millions of those go-getters, who are stepping on their colleagues to get ahead, are prime consumers of alcohol, tobacco, and drugs. I prefer to spend my money on a good book, a new garment for my wife, or on a hiking vacation in the mountains. Don't you?

3. I'm a little confused between anger and aggressiveness. Look how many want ads ask for an "aggressive" salesperson, etc. Is there a form of positive aggression? Could you clarify this point for me?

With pleasure; try these working definitions: *Anger* is the violent negative emotion - whether covert or overt - when things don't go according to our will. *Aggression* is the attempt to force things to go according to our will.

Who likes the door-to-door high-pressure vacuum cleaner salesman who tries to force his way into your house, even though you don't need another vacuum cleaner? To this day, I can't seem to get rid of the aggressive telephone marketing person who doesn't give up trying to sell me carpet shampoo service, despite the fact that I don't have carpets!

Who likes the aggressive person who elbows his way ahead of you in the line to the airline check-in counter? The answer is - nobody. Maybe aggressive people get ahead on the short term, but two things *always* happen to them: One, people dislike them. Two, someone comes along who's stronger and more aggressive than they are, and they end up with the bitter taste of their own medicine.

I don't believe in a positive form of aggression. I do believe in perseverance, willpower, and the inner strength (PWI). If you have **PWI**, you can accomplish anything in life. With physical strength and good looks alone, your success will be very limited. A tiny little one-celled bacteria, virus, or mold spore can destroy physical strength and good looks overnight. On the other hand, **nothing** in this world can destroy **PWI**. So, which path do *you* choose, cherished friend - the cosmetic corridor or the trail to tranquility? Sure, beauty and strength are nice assets, but the development of the soul must earn highest priority in order to achieve genuine, lasting happiness.

4. **Again, I understand your point. But, doesn't society prove you wrong? What about actors and flashy performers? Doesn't society reward beauty, strength, and ego?**

You're correct, but only on the short term. What good are five or six years of fame and success while you're young and beautiful? Would you like to know how many singers and actors in their fifties and sixties are divorced, penniless alcoholics, and chain smokers receiving unemployment checks? Ego, strength, or beauty-based success is only flash-in-the-pan achievement. Often, those very actors and singers whom you are referring to are emotional wrecks, with dismal, problematic lives. Don't confuse a moment's glory under the spotlights with a lifetime of fulfillment and tranquility.

Too many people play roles, and work on image building rather than on character development. This book has strived to help you develop your spiritual health and power, the foundation of strong character development.

5. **Don't be impatient with me, but I'm still concerned about going back to work on Monday morning. My boss is aggressive and angry, and my organization rewards a stab in the back. What do I do?**

If you're driving down the freeway while cruising at the legal 60 mph limit, and a flashy Mercedes darts by doing 120, don't get in its way. Pull over to the right lane, and allow the Mercedes to pass you by. If its driver doesn't cause a traffic accident, then the highway patrol will likely nab him. You don't have to emulate irresponsible or negative behavior, especially when it entails breaking the law.

People who stab others in the back in order to earn a dollar may be getting ahead on the short term, but like the driver speeding down the freeway at 120 mph, they're on a long-term collision course - sooner or later, they encounter tragedy.

Oftentimes, God lets nasty people succeed on the short term, as a test of our faith. If we all received monthly checks of a hundred thousand dollars for not lying, stealing, or killing, then there would be no basis for the notion of free choice, reward, and punishment. Long- term success depends on doing the right thing and treating others fairly. The Talmud teaches that the first question the Heavenly Court asks a deceased person's soul is, "Did you negotiate and transact honestly?" Aggression, anger, and a stab in the back can sometimes maneuver a promotion, but hold on - the game's not over! Such a success will be short-lived.

If you've got PWI, you're calm, confident, and pleasant, people will like you and trust you. Your superiors will seek to confide in you. Don't worry; in the long run, you'll be passing everybody both up the corporate ladder and up the spiritual ladder. Forget about the lessons of Hollywood and stick to the lessons of this book. The more you develop spiritual awareness, the less your boss - or anyone else for that matter - will be capable of intimidating you.

Section Two - Our Destination

While climbing mountains, we have to be careful of falling rocks or insecure footholds. In like manner, while striving for inner peace, we must beware of recurring anger. In order to reach our emotional and spiritual objectives, we must therefore learn how to cope with recurring anger.

Let's answer the frequently asked questions of inner-peace seekers and spiritual climbers.

Six Critical Questions of People Striving for Emotional and Spiritual Improvement

Question number one: How do I cope with recurring anger?

The answer to this vital question has two parts: First, the long-term method of dealing with recurring anger; and second, several emergency measures to utilize once anger sets in.

Long-term method of dealing with recurring anger:

a. Review this book until it becomes second nature.

b. Practice the "One-Week Plan": Review the seven points for opening the gates of spiritual awareness (see chapter four). In particular:

    i. Don't act according to instinct! Stop, compose yourself, and think before you act or speak.

    ii. Remember that everything that happens to you comes from God. Try and *understand* what angers you, instead of *reacting* with anger. By spiritual awareness, you'll defuse violent reactions and increase your understanding.

c. Always have a "pet parameter" from the twenty factors that affect Spiritual Awareness (*from the list that comprises the Enhanced Spiritual Awareness workshop, which appear in the second half of chapter four*) that you're working on. Monitor your progress in a diary. As time progresses, you'll be perfecting your character!

d. Work on the three-stage plan for the prevention of self-induced suffering (*see chapter six*), which includes observation, self-evaluation, and implementation.

Four emergency measures for dealing with recurring anger:

1. Delay tactics - the key to overcoming an anger spasm. Try to postpone anger for a few critical seconds. Anger is dangerous, because it creates a surge of extreme negative emotion from the left side of the heart that catches the brain off guard. As a result, the heart seizes control when the brain should be governing our lives. The surge from the heart doesn't last long in most cases; by delaying anger, the brain regroups its forces, overcomes the heart, and again takes control of decision making. Reacting from the heart is like shooting from the hip - impulsive, badly aimed, and a sure miss. A reasoned brain reaction is like a carefully aimed shot with the aid of a telescopic sight - almost a sure bull's eye.

Delaying the initial surge of anger that attacks us is like delaying the explosion of a bomb. Once the wave of anger passes, we can reactivate our thought processes and remember everything we've learned about anger control. Delaying tactics act like a bomb squad, which neutralizes the time clock of a bomb, until the munitions specialist defuses the bomb altogether. Anger of course, is the bomb. A delay tactic acts like a bomb squad, while our brains are the munitions experts that know how to dismantle the bomb.

The following are examples of how delay tactics work:

Case study: The "Bergman" *(imaginary name)* family came to me for marital counseling. Paul and Nancy Bergman - childhood sweethearts, by the way - were on the verge of divorce. They both suffered from short fuses; their relationship reminded me of nitric acid and glycerin - put them together, and you get nitroglycerin.

Paul and Nancy needed to strengthen their communication skills, especially their power of *listening* to each other. They had frequent misunderstandings, like the following:

Paul: Nance, what's for dinner tonight?

Nancy: I made a fantastic broccoli and cheese soufflé…

Paul (neither letting Nancy finish her sentence, nor concentrating on what she said): What, fish two nights in a row? I hate fish two nights in a row!

Nancy (now exploding): Since when does broccoli have fins and scales, dinglebrain!

Paul: Who the heck are you calling dinglebrain? Your mouth is even nastier than your father's!

Nancy: The nerve of you! I at least know who my father is, you sonofa…

I'm sure you get the point, dear reader.

I taught them how to treat their relationship like a basketball game; in a critical situation, a coach calls a time out. "Whenever you two feel the first drop of anger," I told them, "call a time out."

Now, here's how the delay tactic works: The two warring parties agree than an argument can't begin until a certain condition is met. In the case of the Bergmans, we decided that Paul must first wear his tuxedo and Nancy her best evening gown. I wrote a document that they both signed, that they may not argue until dressed in formal attire.

At the outbreak of their next argument two days later, they remembered the terms of their agreement, and called a time out. Nancy ran up to her bedroom walk-in closet, and began to get dressed. Paul flew down the stairs to his cedar closet, and went through his suit rack until he found his tuxedo. Thirty minutes later, they met in the living room. Of course, they forgot completely about the argument.

Paul looked at Nancy, "Hey, you're gorgeous, sweetheart!"

Nancy returned Paul's smile, "You're kind of suave yourself, handsome!"

They ended up in each other's arms. Gradually, they developed a pattern of listening to each other and mutual understanding. Today, they're simply a pair of turtledoves. Their own parents are astonished at the improvement in their relationship.

With another problematic couple, we wrote an agreement that they must dress up in their Halloween costumes before having an argument. The first time they utilized their delay tactics, they laughed so hard that their stomach muscles hurt, and like the Bergmans, ended up in each other's arms.

An anger-prone bank manager took my advice, and agreed not to get angry until he dons his old high school letterman's jacket, which he keeps locked up in a high security safe at the bank. By the time he gets through security and opens the vault, his anger has long subsided.

2. *Invoke your powers of compassion.* Imagine that you're walking down a busy shopping mall. From behind, someone whacks you over the head with a stick. You're so angry, that you plan to alter the angle of the attacker's nose - a lot faster than a plastic surgeon could. You whip around, fist cocked, and...

A blind man has slipped and fallen on the floor. His cane flew out of his hand, and that's what hit you on the head. You open your clenched fist, the muscles in your arms and legs relax, and your heart melts in compassion for the sightless person. Not only are you no longer angry, you bend down and lovingly, with extreme care, help the blind man to his feet.

If a mentally handicapped child were to stick his tongue out at you, would you be angry? Certainly not; on the contrary, you'd have pity on the child. Invoke your powers of compassion the next time someone angers you. Pretend that they're blind. Many people are blind to the feelings of others; we should feel sorry for them, because such "blind" people are far from happiness in life. Such compassion defuses anger.

3. *The Respect Tactic*. Imagine that you're in basic training in an elite military unit. During a training exercise, you make a critical mistake that would mean certain death in a combat situation. Your Drill Sergeant, a seasoned, decorated combat veteran, smashes you on the helmet, and gives you the scolding of your life. His voice thunders in your eardrums, "You idiot chunk of fresh meat - if I ever catch you pulling a stunt like that again, I'm gonna roast your carcass on a skewer..." Your face is a bright red, and your ears are ringing. Are you insulted? No. Are you angry? Certainly not. Why? You respect your Sergeant, you know he's right, and you know that he's concerned about your welfare.

The respect tactic works effectively in potential situations of anger against parents, teachers, athletic coaches, employers, and military commanders. When you become angry with people in one of these categories, think of your respect for them, and remember that they care about your welfare.

4. The Unconditional Love Tactic. Imagine that you're in Grand Central Station on a jam-packed Friday afternoon waiting impatiently for your train home for the weekend. Your nerves are frayed from a rough week at work. Suddenly, someone shoves you from behind and almost knocks you over. Your blood rushes to your eyeballs, and you feel like the bull in the Madrid arena that has just seen a red flag. You turn around with a clenched fist, like a bomb ticking in its final seconds before explosion, and...

Your favorite brother or sister, whom you haven't seen for ten whole years, is smiling at you with outstretched arms. You embrace each other. You forgot all about the shove. Your anger melts like dew on a sunny July morning. All you feel is love.

The unconditional love tactic works effectively in family relationships. The next time you *begin* to feel anger toward your partner in life, close your eyes; think of your lovely moments with your beloved partner. Is the sadistic pleasure of blowing your top worth jeopardizing a lifetime of future happiness together? Of course, not. Try to remember your unconditional love for your spouse and children. If you succeed, your anger will blow over like a wisp of a cloud in a strong wind.

Question number two: Why has my life has become even more difficult since I've started my quest for spiritual improvement?

The answer is simple: Where is the competition tougher, in the C-League Minors or in the Major Leagues? Naturally, the better the league, the more demanding the competition is. Minor league successes are normally below the level of major league setbacks. Everyone understands that the loser of the world boxing championship is a better boxer than the local college champion. Likewise, now that you've attained a higher spiritual level, your challenges are also more difficult than they used to be. Don't forget, though - a national league athlete earns ten times more money than a minor league athlete. Similarly, your spiritual rewards for succeeding on a higher level are also much greater.

By moving up the spiritual ladder, we encounter challenges that are more difficult, *for our own good and to stimulate even more gain.* Without these challenges, we wouldn't realize our own magnificent spiritual potential. If we don't realize our potential, then we never discover our *real* selves! Many people once thought of themselves as weaklings, and later discovered that they were capable of becoming emotional and spiritual giants. That brings us to question number three:

Question number three: How do I know if I'm making progress and moving up the spiritual ladder?

The latter portion of chapter four answers this question, so let's go back and review briefly. There, we learned the eight parameters of spiritual awareness, which are a superb self-check of our progress. Here they are again, in a nutshell:

- ✓ **Parameter one: Courage and inner security -** the higher our spiritual level, the less we fear anything other than The Almighty.

- ✓ **Parameter two: Happiness** - the higher our spiritual level, the happier we feel.

✓ **Parameter three: Peace, both internal and external, the opposite of anger** - progress up the trail to tranquility goes together with progress up the spiritual ladder.

✓ **Parameter four: Improved physical and mental health** - a fifty year-old Canadian woman visited a cardiologist after having suffered for several weeks from severe chest pains. She informed me that the doctor diagnosed a dangerously clogged artery, and wanted to perform heart surgery. I asked the woman if she suffered a trauma recently, and she answered in the affirmative - her son had recently been through a nasty divorce. At my suggestion, she agreed to try the seven-day plan for spiritual awareness. She implemented the plan in its entirety. The day after she completed the plan, she returned to her doctor. All traces of the arterial blockage simply disappeared.

✓ **Parameter five: Body - soul priorities** - The higher one moves up the spiritual ladder, the more one prefers the development of the soul to the appetites of the body. A spiritually aware soul won't let the body partake of potentially dangerous substances, such as alcohol, drugs, or the neighbor's spouse.

✓ **Parameter six: Giving - receiving priorities** - Takers are low on the spiritual ladder. Givers resemble God, and are therefore higher up the spiritual ladder.

✓ **Parameter seven: Efficiency** - Efficiency goes hand-in-hand with spiritual gain. For example, the spiritually aware spend less time on extraneous matters when performing a task.

✓ **Parameter eight: When I begin to realize that I know nothing** - Arrogant people think they know everything. Humble people think they know nothing, and therefore have tremendous learning capacity. The more one moves up the spiritual ladder, the more humble one becomes.

After we've reviewed the eight parameters, let's try the spiritual litmus test:

The Spiritual Litmus Test

Choose one of the following activities (whichever is *most* distasteful for you):

- Driving for an hour in bumper-to-bumper rush hour traffic.

- Listening to your mother-in-law's small talk for an hour.

- Folding laundry, pressing shirts, or cleaning bathroom fixtures for one hour.

If at the end of this test, you're smiling and a lot calmer than you ever were in the past under a similar situation, you've made outstanding spiritual progress! By making spiritual progress, you're accomplishing your *real* challenge in life and doing yourself an everlasting favor.

Question number four: What happens if I accidentally fall into an explosive anger tantrum? Have I lost everything I've worked so hard for?

Allow me to preface my answer with the following principle:

As we go higher up the spiritual ladder, our setbacks of today are actually *higher* than our successes of yesterday.

Let me explain: Think back to chapter one. Suppose you began this book as a level three, and now you've worked your way up to a level six. Something or someone irritates you, and your react like a level five. Even though you've had a temporary "fall" from level six down to level five, from an emotional and spiritual standpoint you're far beyond your incoming level of three.

Since we're human, and we *all* fall periodically, we must learn *how* to take a fall without getting hurt. The first thing a good gymnastics instructor teaches students is how to take a fall. A paratrooper spends days learning how to fall before he ever goes up in a plane. An experienced investments broker must know how to redirect investments when the stock, bond, or commodities markets fall. As we've pointed out several times previously, what holds true in the physical world holds true in the metaphysical world. If we must be prepared for a physical fall, we should certainly know how to handle an emotional or spiritual fall.

Basically, we're all spiritual babies, especially when compared to our potential. Babies can't possibly learn how to walk without falling occasionally. But, remembering the benefits of a fall is the best cushion for a fall.

This is an appropriate time to review the five good reasons why we sometimes fall or fail, which we learned previously in Chapter Eight:

The Reasons Why We Sometimes Fall

1. **Only doers fall**. If you don't climb mountains, you don't fall on the rocks, simple as that! People who drive sometimes get traffic tickets. People who don't drive don't ever make wrong turns. Wouldn't it be ridiculous if a seventy year-old person bragged that he never committed a traffic violation if he never drove a car? The first consolation of a fall is the knowledge that you are a doer.

2. **A fall teaches, and usually triggers a stronger second effort**. Periodic falls safeguard us against complacency and arrogance. When we fall, we realize that we need to try harder the next time. Frequently, a second effort is far superior to even a best first effort. So, if you fall, don't be disappointed; just "get back in the game". If you pick yourself up, then your fall is only a temporary setback - don't forget, as long as you're alive, the game's not over!

3. **Failure brings us closer to God**. If we were constantly successful, we'd probably walk around with our noses in the air. Then, we'd be ugly, heaven forbid, because few things are uglier than arrogance. The Almighty wants His

children close to him. After a setback, we pray a lot harder and earnestly seek Divine assistance for our next effort. If our lives were a perfect string of non-stop successes, we certainly wouldn't pray from the bottom of our hearts.

4. **Experience is life's best teacher**. The experience of a fall drives a lesson home immediately. Usually, we are slow in internalizing and implementing what we learn. When we fall, we have a golden opportunity to better ourselves immediately.

5. **Small-scale failure assures large-scale success**. Where would an actor prefer to forget a line, in rehearsal or on stage? A failure in rehearsal often assures a better performance on stage, since the actor makes a special effort to polish the rough edges of his or her performance. Sometimes, small failures are none other than preparations for large successes.

A New Beginning

Now, let's return to the heart of the question that utterly terrifies most people.[33] You ask yourself, "What happens if I fall?" If you were to fall off a horse, your riding instructor would tell you three things:

a. Pick yourself up.

b. Dust yourself off.

c. Get back on the horse, and make a new start.

Dear friend, I couldn't improve on the above advice. So, you've fallen into a relapse of anger? Big deal! How many times

---

[33] The fear of failure, like other fears, paralyzes people. Once we shed our fear of failure, we can "un-paralyze", and initiate a new and better effort. My old high school coach taught me a cardinal principle in wrestling that equally applies to any situation in life: "You don't lose the match by being thrown to the mat; the faster you're back on your feet, the better your chances of winning!"

have you succeeded in overcoming anger lately? No, you haven't lost everything. Make a new start, and apply everything you've learned. A new beginning is spiritually and physically beneficial to your life. Try making the following declaration:

So what, I didn't succeed? I lost my temper? From this moment on, I hereby declare a new beginning! Anger is no longer a boarder in my spiritual guesthouse. I'm now remodeling my life. The past does not concern me! I'm about to make a fresh start doing the best I can.

Declaring a new beginning is synonymous to spiritual rebirth. The spirit influences the body. So, when the spirit declares a fresh start, the body becomes rejuvenated! By removing the focus from your setbacks and disappointments, you avoid sadness and depression. By declaring a new start, you destroy sadness and depression. The cheerfulness of a fresh spiritual start will keep your face, body, and complexion looking younger than any spa or cosmetics will. A fresh start is *the* secret of staying young.

Let's take a day-to-day example. Suppose we're caught off guard, and we lose our temper with someone close to us. Spiritually, we've been knocked down, but the game's not over. If we suck in our pride *(remember Chapter Two - arrogance is the number one cause of anger)*, give our loved one a thoughtful little gift and a sincere apology, we turn our setback into a major victory. We rejuvenate ourselves, and our relationships with others. A fresh start keeps us happy, youthful, and optimistic.

Question number five: How do I deal with periodic melancholy or depression?

We've already answered this question in the previous question, but let's reiterate.

Periodically, most people succumb to temporary melancholy or depression, especially after a fall. A sad or depressed person is a spiritually neutralized individual, tantamount to a dead person. Dead people are ritually impure. Therefore, excessive contact with sad and depressed people can be very detrimental for our own emotional and spiritual health. Our evil inclination likes to keep us sad and depressed, because that way, our souls are enclosed in a spiritual darkness, far away from The Almighty's divine light.

Who isn't fond of a new car, a new dress, a new house, or new and exciting experiences? We all love nuances, because they rejuvenate our souls and add interest to our lives. Have you ever seen a camera enthusiast depressed while reading the owner's manual of his or her prized new high-performance digital camera? Of course, not! The moment we feel the taste of melancholy or depression, we should declare a new beginning in life. The following are a few examples of new beginnings:

- Decide to improve your stamina, exercising and/or walking for an hour a day, and talking to God while you walk.

- Decide to implement the one-week plan for more spiritual gain.

- Decide to learn a new hobby.

- Don't wait until New Year's Eve to make new resolutions - make them today!

As we mentioned earlier, new beginnings destroy sadness and depression, as well as the boredom of a gray routine. The cheerfulness of a fresh spiritual start will keep you young, healthy, and cheerful.

Once you declare a new beginning, don't ever delve in the past. Draw a line, and erase unpleasant memories from your cognizance as easily as you'd press the "delete" button on your computer. The more we live a vivacious present, the less we focus on an unhappy past. Remember, the past is out of our control; but, God gives us the power to make the best out of the present. Wasting precious time and emotional energy in doling about the past ruins the present and kills chances for a happy future.

Whatever you do when the gray cloud of depression appears before your eyes, don't reach for that bottle of pills that the drug company has been trying to sell you! Many of the licensed and authorized drug companies are none other than narcotics dealers in three-piece herringbone suits. If you stick to the lessons in this book, you won't be depressed and you won't need to be spending your money and your health on "uppers" with a fancy clinical name.

Question number six: How do I know if I've reached the top?

(Imagine that at this very moment, we reach the peak of Mount Patience, eight thousand feet above sea level. We're breathing hard, our lungs feel like they're burning, and every muscle in our arms and legs seems to scream in exertion. Yet, we're thrilled with our accomplishment and filled with a glow of joy that warms our insides. We've just completed an eighteen-mile hike up a challenging trail. Neither grizzly bears nor falling rocks have discouraged us. We have succeeded.

The magnificent view and the indescribable sense of being on top of the world completely neutralize our bodily pain. We feel the power of our spirit overcoming our bodies, and literally overwhelmed, we feel at unity with all of creation.)

When you feel your body becoming a servant to your soul, and your soul feels an awesome and loving oneness with God, then you've reached a new peak in life. Congratulations, partner. You've just entered the threshold of lasting happiness. Arriving at the right destination means that you've been hiking up the right trail, because the trail to tranquility leads to lasting happiness.

The more you continue to provide your soul with what *it* needs, the deeper you'll feel that lasting happiness. Genuine happiness is your lasting possession that no one can ever take from you.

Where do we go from here?

Spirituality, even more than mountain climbing, knows no limits. Since God is limitless, our spirits - the tiny spark of God within each and every one of us - knows no bounds. Our task in life is to strive for never-ending spiritual gain. Not even the sky limits us. Therefore, the peaks of tomorrow are loftier than our personal peaks of today.

You now possess the tools to achieve genuine inner peace. Soon, you'll be guiding your friends and family up the trail to tranquility. The 21st Century needs more people like you. Keep up the great work, and continue to cultivate that exquisite soul of yours. Don't ever forget that the body is temporary, but the soul is eternal. Don't discard eternal happiness for a few short-lived cheap thrills.

Now, put your personal flag atop the mountain. May The Almighty fulfill all your heart's wishes for the very best, cherished friend.

Epilogue

Back in the allegorical world, the crimson sun is dipping into the bluish hue of the western horizon. Isaac and Jerry, slowly bobbing in their straw rockers like two flickering candles, are sharing an intimate moment together. Jerry breaks the silence.

"Isaac, how long can you go on like this? You and Rebecca aren't getting any younger. The two of you are still baking the bread, milking the goats, and handling the inn all by yourselves."

"As long as The Almighty gives us strength…"

"But why don't you retire? Why don't you find a cozy little apartment with maid service in town? I'll help you sell the inn and the farmstead. Whenever you miss the mountain air, you both can come stay with me."

"That's kind of you Jerry, but what happens if tomorrow morning, somebody comes walking up my driveway, looking for the trail to tranquility? Maybe that person is a potential spiritual giant! Nope, I can't leave Mount Patience; I'm an old soldier in the Almighty's army, and the inn and this mountain are my post. Besides, old soldiers never die…"

* * *

The Old Isaac in my heart teaches me that each of our homes should be an "Old Isaac's Inn" - a haven of hospitality, tranquility, and brotherly love. Not only that, but each of our hearts should be a way station of good will, open to our fellow human, who like us, was created in God's image.

Once we reach the level of tranquility within, we emanate the light of peace and tranquility to the outside world. If enough of us follow the time-proven trail to tranquility - together - we can be the fulcrum that moves the world.

Real spirituality, as we've learned, is hard work. You, my dear friend, can no longer be fooled by fad spirituality and fancy parlor words that don't make a real change in your life for the better.

Would you like to help a friend?

If a person does a *material* favor for you - let's say, he or she loans you one hundred dollars - then you have to return the favor to the giver, and in the case at hand, repay the one hundred dollars. *Spiritual* favors don't work like that; rather than returning a spiritual favor, pass it on to a friend in need. You most certainly have friends or relatives in need of some happiness and peace of mind. Tell them about this book. Share your experiences with them, and offer a helping spiritual hand.

The next time we meet, *you* will probably be taking other people up the trail to tranquility. I wish you success and fulfillment from the bottom of my heart. Godspeed.

Thank you for the wonderful moments we shared with each other.

Your friend always,

Lazer Brody

More titles by Rabbi Lazer Brody

Chassidic Pearls

Rabbi Lazer Brody enriches the family Shabbat table with a unique and delightful new book based on the weekly Torah portions and festivals. **Chassidic Pearls** is a garden of relevant commentaries and original allegories that are ideal for anyone between the ages of 5 and 105. Rav Ovadiah Yosef shlit'a writes that Rabbi Brody is "an artist and master storyteller; honey and sweetness drip from his pen." The Melitzer Rebbe shlit'a of Ashdod adds that Chassidic Pearls is "a superb collection of commentaries, ethics, and original stories - all in simple, straightforward language - to help people enhance the spiritual dimension of their lives."

The Worry Worm

This delightful addition to the children's bookshelf is especially for growing kids with growing minds. Rabbi Lazer Brody's exquisite story of a philosophical debate between two sister-worms in an apple is now brought alive with the delightful illustrations of Rebecca Shapiro. **The Worry Worm** brings the lofty notion of faith to the eye level of preschoolers. Even so, it's a treat for the whole family, from toddlers to grandparents.

Lazer Beams

Rivka Levy has put together an exquisite collection of Rabbi Lazer Brody's most well-known and beautiful quotations, garnished from his award-winning "Lazer Beams" daily web journal, books, inspirational CDs and radio broadcasts. Together with her breath-taking illustrations, this exquisite book makes a perfect gift for someone you really care about.

Calming Waters CD

"Calming Waters" is a unique collection of Lazer Brody's inspiring original melodies, played on his Native-American flutes with musical accompaniment and arrangements by two of Jewish music's foremost musicians, Menachem Herman and Jeff Horvitch.

This CD is both gratifying and uplifting; its heavenly sounds not only relax the soul, but virtually heal it by helping the listener release his or her innermost emotions - the ones that defy verbal expression. While listening to this CD, you'll feel the gentle waves of the ocean washing away your negative emotions, you'll glide with an eagle, and you'll see from one end of the world to the other from the top of a great mountain, high above all your problems and stress in life. You'll also board the train that carries you to inner freedom and your personal redemption, and much more...

"Calming Waters" comes with a gorgeous full-color 28-page brochure that explains each melody as well as how to apply it to your own meditation, personal prayer, or simple listening pleasure.